A Handful of Emeralds

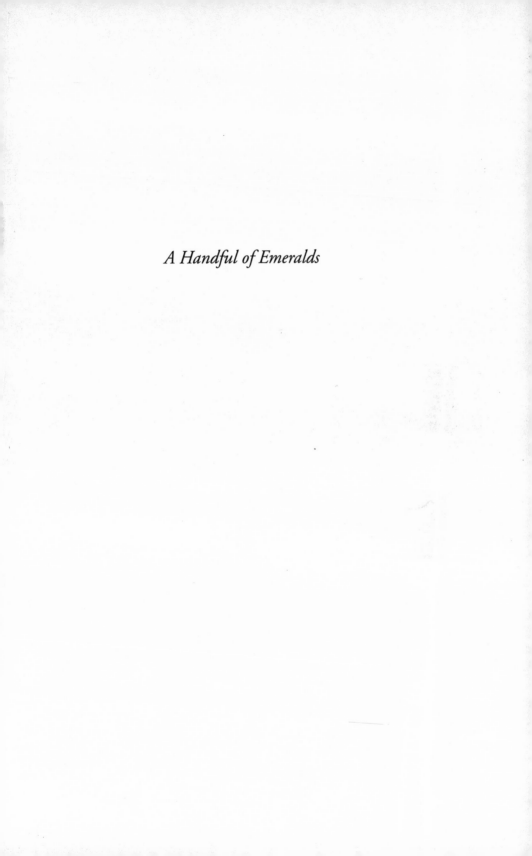

A Handful of Emeralds

*

On Patrol with the *Hanna* in the Postwar Pacific

Joseph C. Meredith

Naval Institute Press / Annapolis, Maryland

Library of Congress Cataloging-in-Publication Data
Meredith, Joseph C., 1914–
    A handful of emeralds: on patrol with the Hanna in the postwar
Pacific / Joseph C. Meredith.
       p.   cm.
    Includes bibliographical references and index.
    ISBN 1-55750-590-x
    1. Micronesia—Description and travel.   2. Meredith, Joseph C.,
1914– —Journeys—Micronesia.   3. Hanna (Destroyer escort)
I. Title.
DU500.M45   1997
919.6504—dc21   97-8510

Printed in the United States of America on acid-free paper ∞
04 03 02 01 00 99 98 97 9 8 7 6 5 4 3 2
First printing

Frontispiece: The USS *Hanna* (DE 449) riding at anchor in Ulithi lagoon.

To the men of the *Hanna*

A strange name wakes up memories; the printed words scent the smoky atmosphere of today faintly, with the subtle and penetrating perfume as of land breezes breathing through the starlight of bygone nights; a signal fire gleams like a jewel on the high brow of a somber cliff; great trees, the advanced sentries of immense forests, stand watchful and still over sleeping stretches of open water; a line of white surf thunders on an empty beach, the shallow water foams on the reefs; and green islets scattered through the calm of noonday lie upon the level of a polished sea, like a handful of emeralds on a buckler of steel.

Joseph Conrad, *Karain: A Memory*

Contents

Illustrations

Preface

Not long after retiring from active service in the United States Navy in 1962, I decided to learn more about islands in the far Pacific that I had visited during my tour of duty as commanding officer of the destroyer escort USS *Hanna* (DE 449) in 1952, 1953, and 1954. I had known some of these places earlier as a junior officer on the destroyer USS *Stephen Potter* (DD 538) in World War II, but I knew them simply as enemy positions that needed to be seized or neutralized. The current mission, instead, was to conduct patrol and surveillance throughout the Trust Territory of the Pacific Islands to provide assistance when needed and, in particular, to prevent alien fishing vessels from intruding in the islands' rich territorial waters. It was the most agreeable independent duty a young commander could imagine.

Later I became acquainted with a teeming literature of discovery, personal encounters similar to mine, the stories of men of all ranks and aspirations—explorers, soldiers of fortune, artists, poets, traders, privateers, drifters, missionaries, whalers, scientists—as they beheld the same distant shores and left records of their experiences, much as I also had been moved to do in a daily journal while at sea.

Looking back over those pages I have sensed a kinship with these voyagers that is worth celebrating—a thread of shared delight in new places, friendly strangers, bright days and soft nights, dangers met and overcome. And because it has all seemed to me something worth sharing with others even at this late date, I wrote this book.

Actually the *Hanna* spent some parts of those years in combat operations off Korea in antisubmarine patrol, convoy, shore bombardment, and the like. Some of this experience is also to be found in the pages of my journal, but it was not a happy time and I have chosen to let it remain there.

CONCERNING GEOGRAPHIC NAMES

The place-names used herein are the forms in general use at the time of our cruise among the islands and for several years afterward, as they appear in contemporary charts and in the *Guide to Place Names in the Trust Territory of the Pacific Islands (the Marshall, Caroline and Mariana Islands),* compiled by the late E. H. Bryan Jr. for the Trust Territory and published by the Pacific Scientific Information Center of the Bernice P. Bishop Museum, Honolulu, in 1971. The new versions that were subsequently adopted for a number of these names are listed in *Pacific Island Names: A Map and Name Guide to the New Pacific,* by Lee S. Motteler (Honolulu: Bishop Museum Press, 1986), and most recently in the U.S. Geological Survey's geographic names database.

Rather than needlessly distancing the narrative from the historic context, I have chosen to stay with the traditional forms. Most of them are unchanged anyway, but there are notable exceptions:

Traditional Name	*New Approved Form*
Ponape	Pohnpei
Mokil	Mwokil
Ngatik	Ngetik
Truk	Chuuk
Kusai	Kosrae
Palau	Belau
Angau	Ngeaur
Arakabesan	Ngerekebesang
Eil Malk	Mecherchar
Koror	Oreor
Malakal	Ngemelachel
Peliliu	Beliliou

Acknowledgments

To Robert H. Ferrell, distinguished professor emeritus of history, Indiana University, Bloomington, for his help, counsel, and encouragement in the shaping of this book, I am most grateful.

For making available the riches of the materials in their custody, I am also grateful to the staffs of the Library of Congress in Washington, the Lilly Library at Indiana University, the Houghton Library at Harvard University, and the libraries of the University of California, Chicago University, the University of Hawaii, and the Hawaiian Historical Society. I wish to thank documentalist Roderigue Lévesque, of Gatineau, Quebec, for his detailed critique of my sources, and Chief Journalist Philip M. Eggman, deputy public affairs officer of the staff of the commander, U.S. Naval Forces Marianas, for material bearing on present-day operations in the area.

The track charts of the *Hanna*'s patrols were prepared with the assistance of Michael S. Meredith and of John M. Hollingsworth, staff cartographer, Indiana University.

1

The *Romance* on the Rocks

Over forty years ago, in a large bound book of blank pages, I made my first journal entry of adventure in Micronesia:

> 8 December 1953—Took departure from Apra Harbor, Guam, at 0800 this evening on the first leg of a surveillance trip in the eastern Carolines. The crew is looking forward with some anticipation to this rare assignment, as am I. Everything lies ahead. Weather fair, with about 18κ wind from the east. Sea state 3 to 4.

When I think of South Sea islands I remember certain clusters in the western Pacific, half-known, half-forgotten, scattered like stars in the immensity of ocean: the Carolines, the Marianas, the Volcanoes, and the Bonins. Some are green caresses to the eye; others, forbidding piles of sulfurous rock. On some the eternal surf crashes unheard by human ear; on others dwell primitive people who carry in themselves a grace denied most mortals.

I remember a vastness of sky and water surrounding islands like Ngatik, Ngulu, Pulo Anna, Kapingamarangi, Iwo, and a thousand others.[1] The names of some are etched in our memory of the Second World War, out of which America's responsibility for these islands under United Nations trusteeship originated.

Because the USS *Hanna* came to these places, this book came to be written. The reader who chooses to accompany our ship on its solitary patrol should consider that latitude and longitude are purely relative and not very important. The islands we will visit make up a unique world where we may forget for a while the existence of any other.

The *Hanna* was a destroyer escort, a small naval vessel that fancied itself a destroyer—and indeed could be almost as lethal against any submarine, though nowhere near as sleek or fast. Its topside armament consisted of only two 5-inch guns and two 40-mm mounts. But it had excellent sea-keeping qualities, it could manage with a smaller crew than a destroyer, and it burned far less oil, making it well suited for the kind of long-range peace-time patrol duties to which we had been assigned.

We were glad to exchange the oven heat of Apra Harbor for the open sea, where the air was fresh, the water indigo, the horizon clean and straight all around. Except for three terns auditing our wake we were alone, and I relished the fact, as would the skipper of any small ship, because in company with others we usually had to rock along behind our seniors. For the next six months, as captain of the *Hanna*, I would be responsible only to the admiral in Guam for carrying out our mission.

Guam guarded an ocean area larger than the United States. To the south, the Caroline Archipelago stretched in magnificent disarray just above the equator, in a band three thousand miles from end to end. To the north were the Mariana Islands, a range of mountaintops emerging from the ocean, of which Guam itself is the southernmost. Beyond, still other islands—the black and yellow Volcanoes and the green and gray Bonins—traced a disjointed path toward Japan.

Assigned to patrol these lands and the waters between, the *Hanna* could cover only small segments at a time because our limited fuel capacity did not permit us to stay away from Guam more than two weeks; our itineraries always had to be planned with this fact in mind. My present orders read, "You will conduct surveillance and reconnaissance in the Eastern Carolines, visiting the following islands: Truk, East Fayu [Lutke], Nama, Losap, Namoluk, Mortlock, Nukuoro, Ngatik, Mokil, and Ponape." We should have been able to accomplish this mission with reasonable dispatch, following a spoon-shaped track southeasterly and back among the islands, at an economical speed of 18 knots.

Instead, late that same afternoon when we had barely settled down to normal routine at sea, came a message from Guam that caused us to change from this leisurely pace to full speed: "Civil administrator Truk reports schooner 'Romance' 45 feet 29 tons draft 6 and one half feet aground southeast and seaward side Truk Atoll, at Salat Pass, at 7–15 N. Long 152–2 E.; crew and passengers have been taken off to nearest island. Ship is leased to Catholic mission trust territories. Proceed at 20 knots to investigate and if feasible to tow clear. Keep me informed."

I had never heard of the *Romance,* which shows how little I knew of current Micronesian affairs. It was certainly an odd name for a missionary vessel, but it proved a suitable opener to the months ahead. As soon as we increased speed, each wave sent a shower of spray over the ship, and I called for the chart. Lt. Don Rayner, the executive officer, brought it to my room and showed me where he had plotted the position of the shipwreck, on the rim of Truk's great encircling reef, not far from the Salat Pass the message had mentioned. No doubt the schooner had tried to enter the lagoon at that point and had missed.

"How long will it take us to get there at this speed?" I asked.

"About thirty hours, which would make it about midnight tomorrow night."

"Not much point in arriving before daylight."

"No, sir." He paused. "Do you think we might still squeeze in East Fayu? It's not out of our way at all."

On a ship the size of the *Hanna,* the executive officer acts also as navigator. Lieutenant Rayner had joined the ship only a week before, and I was not sure just how good a navigator he might be, but felt I should make some show of trust. Big, square-jawed, nervous, and hard, he reminded me of a tightly coiled spring. I knew that such men needed continual challenges to work against, and that in them the release of latent power was not always smooth nor easy. Although I could only guess it at the time, the months ahead were to supply plenty of challenges for both of us.

"I suppose your landing party's all ready to go," I said.

"Yes, sir. I've organized two teams. The boys are all set for their first landing on a desert island."

"You too?"

"Yes, sir," he grinned.

"All right, as long as we can be off Salat Pass by dawn day after tomorrow. Meanwhile try to raise Radio Truk and find out the latest."

Rayner took himself and his chart back to the pilothouse, where I was sure he would double-check his calculations.

Our radioman raised Truk the next morning. Being accustomed to rigid radio procedure, he was somewhat flustered by the informality of his Trukese counterpart but managed to piece together word that the *Romance* was in no immediate danger of breaking up. I then informed Guam of my intentions, pointing out that it was best to approach the reef at Truk only under optimum light conditions. Guam gave tacit assent.

By noon we made radar contact with Namonuito Atoll and shortly thereafter sighted it as a smudge on the southern horizon. Passing by, we soon raised East Fayu Island dead ahead.

East Fayu has no fame, nor even a reputation. In 1828 an expedition of two Russian brigs commanded by Feodor Petrovich Lütke made a swing through the Carolines, discovering many new islands and rediscovering others that the Spaniards had either mislocated or deemed too insignificant to record. Lütke wrote:

> On the morning of November 12 was perceived an Island which we recognized as Fayu, the second of that name, which, in order to distinguish it from the other, we called East Fayu. [Lütke's footnote: "One often encounters the same names among the Carolines, which has done no little to contribute to the confusion concerning this archipelago."] At eight o'clock we were already close aboard this islet, the reconnaissance of which took only a short time, for it is only a mile long and three quarters of a mile wide. The Carolinians occasionally visit this isle to stock up on fresh water which the rains deposit in a small basin there.[2]

Although Lütke had little to say of his discovery, it is ironically the one island that bears his name—if only in parentheses!

To twentieth-century eyes, the place amply realizes the popular concept of a desert island: remote, serenely emerald, and small enough to be comprehended in the glance of an eye. There is a narrow protective reef against which the Pacific toils in vain, with a quiet lagoon inside. At the center of the lagoon, like a royal crown on a ceremonial cushion, sits a clump of jungle vegetation on an ivory-bright expanse of sand.

We came up under the lee of the island and launched a large black rubber life raft of the type once used in clandestine landings. It leaked. And its outboard motor refused to turn over, even though it had performed beautifully in a barrel of seawater the day before. (But then, all outboard motors are depraved contraptions.) Rayner and his party sloshed about in this raft for a while and finally transferred to a small yellow "ditching raft," strictly man-powered. As they left, paddles flashing in untidy disunison, deckhands on board the *Hanna* cheered them with a rousing version of the Hawaiian war chant.

I noted that where the *Hanna* lay to, only 250 yards from the reef, our fathometer showed 200 fathoms beneath the keel. This meant that the bottom slanted down at a clifflike 60-degree gradient. Small wonder no ship in history has ever anchored at East Fayu!

The landing party, having found a crack in the reef wide enough to admit them to the lagoon, made their way through without upsetting. On the ship, we started engines and began slowly circling the island, measuring contours by visual bearings and recording offshore depths. This was the kind of study I hoped to carry out on many of the lesser-known islands in our bailiwick to supplement our primary mission.

One member of the landing party carried a portable radio transmitter-receiver that allowed him to regale us from time to time with reports of progress ashore in the manner of "your roving reporter." We learned that the freshwater pond no longer existed, having become a cove of the lagoon. An "observation point" shown on the chart consisted of an eroded chunk of concrete, and the only other evidence that suggested the existence of the human race was a green glass fishing-float and a whitened drift log bearing the carved initials "JHB."

Later I learned from Rayner that the island would have been fascinating to a naturalist. Untroubled by man, nature on East Fayu should have been in perfect balance. But it wasn't. The birds that filled the sky over the island were triumphant, while the vegetation beneath them appeared to be doomed, raddled and seared by their excrement. Doubly doomed was a lone palm tree that hosted a family of coconut ("robber") crabs, who were ensuring their own extinction by consuming all its produce, unmindful that their host must soon die. A scrabble of hermit crabs enlivened the beach, and a colony of shrews lurked in the tall grass. This was the whole of life on East Fayu.

Rayner finished the survey in an hour and returned with his landing party to the ship, and we said good-bye to our first island. That night we steamed on down to Truk, through waters that I remembered from the days when they were infested with enemy planes and ships. Watching the radar scope, I thought how different it had been then and how my flesh had crawled the first time I saw the electronic "pip" of a Japanese plane closing in on our task group. It seemed strange for the *Hanna* to be blazing with lights instead of cloaked in darkness, with all hands at general quarters, stealing in for a strike.

The morning of 10 December we approached the southeast side of the huge complex of reefs and islands that make up Truk (there is no "Truk Island" as such) and found the *Romance* high on the barrier reef, canted disconsolately to port in such a way as to show an undignified expanse of russet bottom to the rising sun. The crowd of natives clustered in the knee-deep water around her had succeeded in rigging stays and "deadmen" to prevent her being bumped around on the coral.

A salvage party headed by Ens. Jerry Mathews, the *Hanna's* damage control officer, embarked in the motor whaleboat and made its way through nearby Salat Pass to the inner edge of the reef, from which it was possible to wade to the scene of the stranding. Meanwhile I reconnoitered the depths on the seaward side, nosing the ship to within a hundred yards of the coral rampart. If we were to pull the schooner off, we would need to run a hawser through the bullnose, reversing engines to back her away, for I had no intention of bringing the propellers any nearer the jagged rocks than necessary.

The salvage party had a portable radio transmitter with them, and now one of the loudspeakers on the bridge let out a squawk:

"Badger, this is Badger One. Captain, she's in pretty good shape. Only two or three holes. Largest is about a foot . . . [screech!]."

"Badger One, this is Badger. Say again all after 'largest.' Over."

"I say the largest is about a foot in diameter. We're patching them now. Over."

I dropped formalities. "OK, Jerry. How about pulling her off? Over."

"The Father in charge doesn't want to. I [eek!] . . . coral [awk!] . . . back to ship. Over."

"Roger, out."

So I brought the ship through the pass and anchored in the lagoon about a half mile from the wreck and an equal distance from an islet that looked so much like a cartoon we christened it "Corny Island."

The salvage party returned to the ship, bringing two strangers—both very wet and bedraggled. They introduced themselves as Brothers Whalen and Shea and explained why they opposed the kind of salvage measures I had in mind. "Although the sides of the ship are very tough," Brother Whalen said, "I think if we tried to pull it off the reef to seaward, the coral would rip it to pieces and the surf at the edge of the reef would make it impossible to control, and we might bang it up beyond repair before we could get in deep water." I agreed. It would be much safer and surer to work the schooner off on the lagoon side of the reef. This would take weeks of preparation, and meanwhile we could only hope that no storm would come up and finish her off. For the present at least, our services were ruled out.

While we were talking, a launch arrived from Moen Island, one of the high volcanic masses within Truk lagoon, bearing the district administrator together with the deputy high commissioner of the Trust Territories, who happened to be paying a visit in these parts. After they joined us, Brother Shea related his story: how the missionary craft came up from the Mortlock Islands to get supplies, how the native helmsman fell asleep at the tiller, how the schooner blindly struck the reef before anyone on board knew what was happening. Brother Whalen nodded from time to time but said nothing. They were both very young and seemed very much out of place in this part of the world. Brother Shea's glasses kept slipping down on his nose.

"Was there any panic after you hit?"

"No. We all prayed. And anyway, the natives are at home on any reef: they spend so much of their lives fishing. In the morning after we struck, the people from the little island over there came and helped."

"Which of you is actually captain of the *Romance?*"

"Well, neither of us, exactly. We act as sort of managers. The captain is a Lukunorian, who is probably a good navigator but not used to anything larger than a canoe. As for me, I'd never even been on a sailboat until I came out here last fall. And Brother Whalen, like me, is more at home in city streets than in the South Seas. However, here we are." He sighed. "I think maybe we'll try Trukese crewmen next time. That is, if we can get the *Romance* afloat again."

The *Romance* was not, of course, the first missionary vessel to ply these waters, nor in fact was her present predicament anything new. The most famous of her predecessors was the Protestant schooner *Morning Star*, actually a succession of seven vessels of that name sponsored by the American Board of Commissioners of Foreign Missions in Boston. Almost every *Morning Star* in turn came to grief on one or another of the coral reefs of Micronesia. And although one can question the missionary concept, the story of these ships is bright with adventure. One cannot help admiring the bravery of the men and women who sailed in them, pioneers responsible for the world's first detailed knowledge of Micronesia.

The first *Morning Star* was a packet of about 150 tons, built at Chelsea, Massachusetts. Its $13,000 purchase price was raised by Rev. Hiram Bingham, by way of ten-cent "subscriptions" bought by Sunday school children, for which they each received a steel-engraved certificate representing a "share of stock in the Children's Missionary Vessel." Bingham plied the children with compelling images of the dangers on the faraway islands:

The immense Pacific smiles,
Round ten thousand little isles
Haunts of violence and wiles.[3]

The ship sailed from India Wharf, Boston, on 2 December 1856 with great flag-waving and singing of hymns. On board were a captain, first and second mates, a steward, a crew of six seamen, and several missionaries with their wives. From way-points during their long journey Reverend Bingham sent stately progress reports, duly published back home in the New England *Missionary Herald*.

The packet's first stop in the Carolines was almost its last: "While attempting to get out to sea," Bingham wrote, "she struck on one of the thousand reefs with which these waters abound, where she thumped about for ten or fifteen minutes; but the Keeper of Israel cared for us; and before night we were safely under way."[4]

For various reasons the first *Morning Star* proved inadequate and was sold. Another was then built and after several voyages was wrecked on the reef at Kusaie Island in the eastern Carolines. A third *Morning Star* provided by the children's inexhaustible store of dimes was driven ashore at exactly the same spot. The fourth *Morning Star*, a barkentine of 430 tons, fared better than the others and was joined eventually by the schooner *Robert Logan* and a gasoline-powered craft named after Parson Bingham himself.

No one doubted that the "savages" should be saved at whatever cost, even though the missionaries' flowing prose sometimes revealed glimmers of broader understanding, as in this letter from the Rev. Benjamin Galen Snow to a group of Sunday school children:

The garments you sent were very acceptable. Besides these there were several pleasant little notes from the misses who made them, in which many questions were asked:

Q: Were the people as wicked and cruel as they are in many heathen lands, when you went there?

A: They did not seem so. They certainly did not eat one another. Nor did they kill one another, as they used to do years ago. I have never seen men fighting among themselves, and very seldom have seen children get into a quarrel with their playmates. But they think it no great crime to lie and steal, if they don't get caught; and they are guilty of many other wicked things.

Q: Did mothers murder their children?

A: I have never heard that they did, and from their exceeding fondness for children, I judge that they were never so cruel as to murder them.

Q: Did they worship gods of wood and stone?

A: I think they never had such gods here. By some process they deify the spirits of their departed people, and worship them. Some of them have sacred places on this island; some live on other islands, and some live in the sky.[5]

The idea that the clothing and much else sent out from Boston violated an innocent culture probably never crossed the writer's mind.

✳

After the salvage party had patched and shored the unfortunate schooner, we got under way and threaded northward past coral heads and sunken hulks to an anchorage off Dublon Island, one of the sizable islands within the reef enclosing Truk—each of which has its own coral barrier, with countless off-lying shoals. I was intent on visiting this place, partly because it had been a citadel of Japanese power and partly because my predecessor on similar patrols never stopped there. This latter consideration, as at East Fayu and many islands to come, was to be an important factor in planning our itineraries, for I saw no point in going back to the same places time after time just because they were readily accessible.

It was late afternoon when we reached our second anchorage, and to make the most of remaining daylight I left the ship immediately with a landing party of twenty men and two officers, Lts. Richard Bland and Gordon Lee, respectively the operations officer and the gunnery officer of the ship. Our coxswain was a stolid youngster, Sn. William V. Baker, who I knew could take us anywhere a motor whaleboat could possibly go.

We needed to find an opening in Dublon's reef, and the chart was of little help. Landmarks—streets, buildings, beacons—had vanished. All we could see was green jungle edged with mangrove. We passed over sunken relics of the Imperial Japanese Fleet, whose broken spars still pierced the surface to mark their graves. Here lay the cruisers *Naka, Agano,* and *Katori;* the destroyers *Yoburi, Oikaze,* and *Nagatsuki;* the submarine tender *Heian Maru;* and the seaplane tender *Akitsushima*—all sunk during the American air attacks of 17–18 February 1944.[6] Close inshore on the west side of the island, we spotted the 2,500-ton floating dry dock that the Japanese brought here in 1941, and we headed for it on the theory that some sort of channel must exist in the vicinity. We found, indeed, a clear passage to shore and the remains of an elaborate amphibious base.

Baker brought the boat alongside a fine quay wall, and we jumped out. I told him to go back for another load so that as many men as possible could say they had been ashore on Truk, and I further instructed him to find a landing place nearer the ship, if possible. He was to send up a white flare to show us where he landed a second time.

After picking our way along the quay, through a deserted pigpen, we started down an old road skirting the island—twenty footloose sailors in white hats and dungarees and three rubbernecking officers. This onetime thoroughfare with its twin rows of decorative palms amounted now to nothing more than a footpath through high grasses, chunks of asphalt, and tumbled curbstones. On the right were occasional huts contrived out of corrugated roofing and old boards, among heaps of rubble and rusty iron festooned with vegetation. Naked foundations showed where shops, barracks, and warehouses once stood. On the left a green-clad hillside shot upward to catch at its summit a final ray of sunshine. All sounds were hushed in the darkening corridor below. Like a blotter the jungle soaked up even the shouts and horseplay of the men.

The few natives we met along the path hardly looked at us, either through shyness or politeness—or probably a combination of the two. But when we reached a break in the road where a stretch of swamp seemed to bar the way, one of them laid a row of coconuts for us to use as stepping stones. A hummock that looked like solid earth proved to be a concealed gun position, and I ventured inside, taking precaution against the possibility of a booby trap by stepping carefully over the strands of wire that crisscrossed the floor. Through an embrasure the *Hanna,* cheerfully lit, was visible. I wondered how the Americans would have fared had we attempted to seize Truk in 1944.

As a matter of fact there were few such beach defenses at Truk earlier in the war, and had we only known it at the time, "Fortress Truk" could have been taken cheaply. Earlier still, in the 1920s and 1930s, Truk was just a sleepy colonial outpost, its sole defense consisting of six guns left over from the Sino-Japanese War of 1894–95. The secrecy that the Japanese spun around Truk served to conceal an embarrassing weakness. Even after the Imperial Japanese Fourth Fleet was organized in November of 1939 to defend the mandated islands, and after some base facilities were built on Eten, Moen, and Dublon, rumor far outstripped reality.

As it turned out, the Japanese never managed to turn the place into a major base. They waited too long, then made a hasty and poorly planned investment of men and materials. Major construction was begun in late 1939, when four thousand workers were brought in. The number was later increased to ten thousand. They installed six fuel storage tanks on Dublon, built airstrips on Eten and Moen, mounted additional artillery—four double-purpose 12.7-cm guns on Dublon and Eten and eleven 8-cm rifles on the reef near the passes. Two 8-cm antiaircraft guns were mounted on Fefan and Eten. About a hundred additional antiaircraft guns were installed in 1943, and beach defenses and pillboxes the following January.

But these preparations proved worthless a month later, in February 1944, when the Fifth Fleet struck. Aside from gun positions, the target consisted of about seventy repair shops, two marine railways, a thousand-watt generator, four torpedo-boat nests, and a seaplane base. The civilian population were a mixed lot: at the surrender there were 1,338 Japanese, 252 Koreans, 6 Chinese, 8 German missionaries, 7 Spanish missionaries, 793 slave laborers from Nauru and heaven knows where else in Micronesia, and 9,082 native Trukese. The military consisted of 24,000 navy and 14,000 army personnel.

The huge garrison never paid its way. Lt. Gen. Shunzaburo Mugikura, IJA, was beset with fear of invasion and never used his troops for forward staging nor trained them while they waited for the expected invasion. For early warning against air attack the defenders depended on crude air-search radars, supplemented by six "Jake" scout planes patrolling irregularly out to 150 miles. It was thought that the ships in harbor could provide their own defense without too much difficulty. As it turned out, the first air strike against Truk sank eight naval vessels and thirty-one merchant ships. Defending aircraft were completely ineffective: 128 were destroyed at a cost of only four of our planes. The garrison went underground in a hurry after that one raid.

Truk was attacked again on 29 and 30 April, when 423 buildings were destroyed. From that time on, it ceased to exist as a major target. But this did not deter the British a year later when they bombed and strafed what the Japanese reported as insignificant targets. The affair did result in the destruction of many records, however, and the embattled garrison destroyed the remainder in the belief that the day of invasion had finally come. Two months later came v-j Day, and General Mugikura surrendered Truk and its satellites to Vice Adm. George D. Murray, usn, on board the heavy cruiser uss *Portland*.[7]

The tumult and shouting have long since died, and the ruins of Truk belong to the dark people who were here long before the Spanish, the Germans, the Japanese—or the Americans.

✳

Our road brought us along the shore, where naked children played on a stone embankment and hibiscus blooms gleamed in the dusk. Here we came to a concrete blockhouse, once headquarters of the Fourth Communication Center, and a paved parade ground, in the middle of which stood a flagpole flanked by two ancient fieldpieces. In this place where falsetto orders once rang out, there was nothing to break the magic of tropic night descending. Close inshore a Japanese floatplane loomed, its red disk barely discernible, as if waiting to take off on a last, ghostly sortie.

But what now? We had found an excellent boat landing, perfect for our return to the ship, if we could only get word to Baker. Thus far none of us had seen a flare, and I regretted not having brought along a portable radio (an omission never repeated on subsequent landings). While we were discussing the situation, the boat came in view—too far away to see or hear us—and traversed beyond the point of land in the direction from which we had come. I saw no purpose in marching the men all the way back to the original landing place, for there were too many pitfalls, and in the darkness someone might have been hurt.

So Lee and I returned alone, leaving Bland in charge, much to his chagrin since he was eager to make the dash through the jungle. We found the boat at the original landing, for Baker had been unable to find anything better and had grounded once or twice in looking for one. The second landing party was waiting, and Lee and I returned to the ship with them. Back on board I studied the chart again and laid out a route to the new landing, a rather tortuous one, to be sure. To help us navigate it I had the radar manned, and I instructed the radar officer to coach us along the way.

Meanwhile the party at the parade ground built a large bonfire, an excellent beacon. This together with radioed instructions from the ship—"You're too far right; steer two degrees to the left," for example, and "Head for the fire; reefs are on both sides of you now," and even "Slow down!"—enabled us to reach the new landing without mishap. The men had overcome the natives' reticence while I was gone, and all joined in singing "Bless Us All," led by Bland. The light of the fire danced on polished torsoes that gleamed like mahogany. They really were an extraordinarily handsome people.

We started loading the boat. A sleeping native blocked the steps and so furnished the ultimate South Seas touch as twenty men stepped over him. We backed away from the landing while our new friends on shore called and waved as long as we could see them. I resolved to call on Bland again in difficult situations, for his cheerful genius had turned this one into an episode to be fondly remembered. All the way back to the ship, little silver fish leaped in the beam of our searchlight.

2

Coconut Kingdoms

TRUK LAGOON

We remained at anchor through the night, and when morning light of 11 December 1953 became strong enough to show the sunken hulks and coral heads in the crystal water, we returned southward through the quiet lagoon to Salat Pass. A rain squall with an attendant double rainbow drifted over Udot Island, and all the other islands stood green and gold in the new sunshine.

NAMA

Our schedule provided that we next visit a number of low islands, the kind much more abundant in the Carolines than the so-called high islands like Truk, Ponape, Yap, Palau.[1] First was Nama, an islet once known as San Rafael, a speck of land about thirty miles southeast of Truk that is mentioned only briefly in chronicles of exploration and discovery and in annals of missionary societies. Like East Fayu it is the capital of a gigantic pillar of coral rising from the ocean floor. And like East Fayu it has no anchorage—a fact that has allowed it to escape the ministrations of conquistadors, whalers, blackbirders, and other agents of supposed civilization.

In 1806 a Spaniard named Monteverde discovered Nama and named it

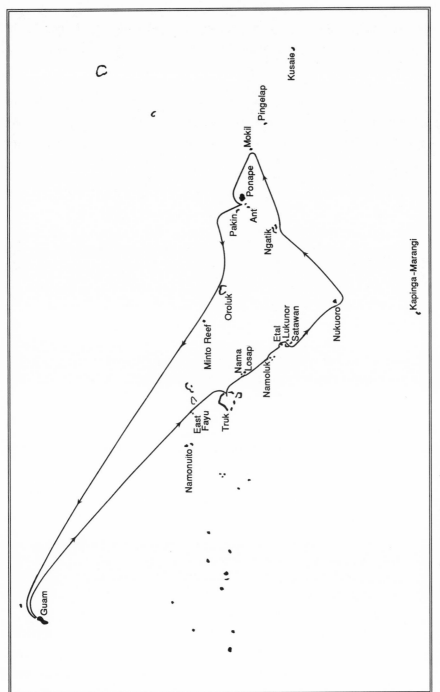

Itinerary in eastern Carolines 8–17 December 1953.

after his ship, the *San Rafael*. A Frenchman named Louis Isadore Duperrey discovered it again in 1824 and called it D'Urville Island, after one of his contemporaries. An admirer of Duperrey came along later and called it Duperrey Island, adding to the confusion of mapmakers. Its native name all along has been, and remains, *Nama*.

We arrived about midmorning and found a mile-long patch of beautifully wooded land surrounded by a narrow shelf of coral with a neat village edging the shore, from which several brightly painted canoes soon headed out to the ship. Since there was not enough water over the reef for our own boat, I was glad to accept the offer of a lift. Micronesian canoes are not hollowed out of a single log but are built up of individual pieces of wood butted together and sewn with cords of sennit to form a smoothly contoured hull. Any boatbuilder in the world would be impressed. After pausing for a moment at the coral barrier, our hosts gave a shout, dug in with their paddles, and flashed through a crack in the reef at just the right moment to use a surge of water that carried us all the way to the beach.

People streamed out from under the shade of the palm trees—old men whose earlobes had been distended into loops for carrying small objects, cotton-frocked women hovering at a respectful distance, scores of children dressed for the occasion in odds and ends of Western raiment, in some cases only an old army undershirt concealing nothing. Our party was met by what seemed the entire population, save for the chief of the island, who waited to receive us at his hut.

Wherever we looked were smiling faces. Four young men in white cotton shirts and trousers came forward. "We are schoolteachers, and speak a little English. The others cannot understand. You come meet chief?" They led us to the chief's house, where a bench had been set for us in the middle of the street. Freshly tapped coconuts were handed round. (In the months ahead I was to become quite partial to this delicate drink of welcome.)

Chief Elias carried himself with a grace and dignity that the mayor of any American city might envy. We started with an exchange of presents, namely a container of ice cream and a carton of cigarettes for some beautiful seashells and a purple garland. I asked, "Is everything all right on your island?"

"Yes."

"Is anybody sick?"

"Yes, a little."

"Doctor has medicine," I said as I indicated the ship's chief hospitalman standing nearby.

"Thank you." The "doctor" withdrew, followed by most of the women, who appeared to be more curious than infirm, and we started on a conducted tour of the island. It was as neat, in a tropical way, as a city park. Rock-bordered paths crisscrossed it, opening onto vistas of palm and breadfruit trees, papayas, bananas, and the like. Most spectacular of all were the trees with yellow, perfumed flowers resembling those of the dogwood at home. A little boy skipping at our heels tore off a flower and handed it to me, indicating that I should put it behind my ear. I couldn't resist patting him on the head and was surprised to see a look of alarm cross his face like a sudden shadow.

"Not good," said my guide in a low voice. "Some people believe soul lives in head."

I never made that mistake again. It seems that children are considered to have a special *manna,* or magic power, all their own, especially if they are good children. They are pampered and petted, for the happiness of a child makes everyone happy, and their laughter drives bad spirits away. The manna lives in the head and may be offended by a careless touch, or even be frightened away if one were to speak the child's name too loudly. I asked my companion about some of the other beliefs, but he said uneasily that they were all dead and that Nama was now a Christian island. Eventually I was to learn far more.

Before the missionaries came, the sea around Nama and the sky above it were invested with spirits: the north, where the wind lived, was called *efang i lang.* In the northwest, many days' sailing, was *lang en inemak,* the heaven of the god of love. Another heaven, reserved for Trukese only, was *muteress uduress,* while Nama's own departed souls ascended to *sabada* which lay directly overhead. The spirit of the rainbow, *Anu ne maresi,* arched over all heavens and all places. Permeating this universe were countless spirits good and evil, such as *Thauuor,* the breadfruit god, and *Anusor,* "who is big and strong and can do what he likes; whomsoever he wishes dead, dies, and all the people of Nama fear him, for he can make the soul sick or dead."[2]

At the end of our tour of the new, enlightened Nama, we were taken to see the schoolhouse, a concrete structure open on all sides, that probably dated back to German colonial days. It was cool and clean, without a stick of furniture or a book to mar its simplicity. Over the door was a single, printed sign that established a quick kinship with many a school and office back home: "Think!" So I thought—and decided I'd best get back to the ship and be about Uncle Sam's business.

That afternoon we continued south to Losap Atoll, which consists of a handful of sandy islets scattered along a narrow ribbon of reef. I would have liked to enter the lagoon within but could not be sure if the channel were deep enough. The statement in *Sailing Directions* that a small cargo ship had entered in 1946 was no help at all, and I did not want to spend two or three hours waiting for the whaleboat to take soundings. So I put the landing party ashore on the ocean side of one of the leeward islands. Again while they were engaged, the ship slowly circled the atoll. By now our "hydro-survey" team had learned to function smoothly, observing and recording combined visual and electronic data. Antisubmarine instruments provided a continuous picture of underwater shapes, so we were able to parallel the reef more closely than would otherwise be prudent and to obtain soundings that would ultimately find their way into U.S. Navy charts and sailing directions.

The age of striking discoveries has long since passed, but there are many gaps to be filled and inaccuracies to be corrected. At Losap we established the *non*existence of an islet shown on the chart at the northeast corner. A pity, because it had the wonderful name of Alanmwassel. Probably washed away in a typhoon.[3]

At one time Losap figured into Germany's plans for a coconut empire in the Carolines. After the Spanish-American War the Germans snapped up the Caroline Archipelago, plus all the Marianas except Guam, for the sum of twenty-five million pesetas (about four million dollars), paid to Spain. The Japanese gladly would have paid the same, but Spain refused to sell to them. Ironically the Japanese later acquired the islands for nothing under a League of Nations mandate.

At any rate, Germany then launched a program of commercial development, financed in part by the state and in part by merchants of Hamburg. The German overlords had no particular antipathy—or, indeed, any feeling one way or another—toward the natives, regarding them simply as a labor pool. Germany shifted whole island populations here and there to suit its needs. Later the Japanese operated the much same way, so that by the time of our visit, on almost every island in Micronesia were living one or two old men who had worked in the phosphate mines of Nauru or of Angaur in the Palau Group, or in the cane fields of Tinian or Saipan. In contrast, the American trusteeship constituted the first island administration dedicated to the idea that Micronesia belonged to the Micronesians, and the underlying purpose of the *Hanna*'s patrol was to ensure that no one, not even a fishing boat, should violate this principle.

The Losap landing party found little of interest ashore. The island where they landed appeared less clean and prosperous than Nama. There was no doctor, no schoolteacher. The German Lutheran mission was in ruins. The orderly rows of palms and the crumbling wharf emphasized that the "master races" had departed, leaving things no better than when they had come.

THE ISLES OF KU

On 12 December we again headed south. Namoluk Atoll appeared on the radar screen about midnight, and not long afterward we discerned it as a band of black somewhat more intense than the rest of the moonless night. Namoluk's lagoon is so tightly circumscribed that not even a fishing boat can enter, so we were able to determine by radar alone that no intruders were about. As the ship circled the atoll, occasional flashes of light shone through the trees with such staccato brilliance that the quartermaster on watch insisted that someone on the beach must be trying to signal us. But the message was in a code never seen on land or sea, and he finally conceded that the flashes came from firelight, interrupted by tree trunks moving across our line of vision.

We had only forty miles to go to reach our next landfall, the Mortlock Islands, and over four hours to spend getting there. I tried 8.5 knots, but at that speed the *Hanna* behaved like a drunken camel, so we increased speed, adopted a dogleg course, and enjoyed a good night's sleep.

The Mortlock Group consists of three atolls disposed in a triangle: Lukunor, Satawan, and Etal, supposedly discovered in 1793 by a Captain Mortlock in the *Young William*. The natives have no separate name for the group but combine them with Namoluk under the regional name of Ku, which I like better. "The isles of Ku" sounds far-off and mysterious, like the whispering roar one hears in *charonis tritonis,* the giant orange and gold conch shell found here.

The isles of Ku are well known to ethnologists, thanks to a group of German scientists who came here in 1909–10 as members of what is sometimes called the Thilenius expedition—named after the editor of the resulting report covering the life, language, beliefs, and customs of the inhabitants. From this report we learn that in the Mortlocks, for example, the natives consider the world to be arranged in a long row of scattered islands. The stars circulate across the sky from one end of this world to the other end, where they sink in the ocean. During the day they circle back underneath.

We are further told that the natives' universe, called *pallauu,* is divided by two cross-verticals, the one forming a longitudinal axis east and west, the other being a meridian running north and south. Each extremity of these planes has a name: *etuu* for east, *lotou* for west, *effen* for north, and *yer* for south. Between these four cardinal points are many intercardinal points, each named after a certain star when that star is near the horizon. At all times *effen* can be found in the Little Dipper and *yer* in the Southern Cross. These people were accomplished celestial navigators long before Columbus set forth on his first voyage![4]

American missionaries of former times made an quite an impression here. It was on Lukunor that the first *Morning Star* was most favorably received—in contrast to Ponape, where the pride and self-assurance of the natives made preaching the gospel a rather hazardous occupation. The Rev. Hiram Bingham Jr. reported that a royal princess of Ponape, Opatinia, relinquished her opportunity to become queen and offered herself as a missionary to the "dark islands of the west"; accordingly she was conveyed to Lukunor in 1873 along with her husband and two other teachers.

When the little schooner arrived, the natives were asked if they would welcome and provide for the missionaries, and they agreed to do so. Soon afterward a typhoon swept over the island and destroyed most of the breadfruit trees, and many islanders starved. But still the natives fed the missionaries: "After a year the *Morning Star* again arrived, a multitude of natives gathered on the beach singing songs to welcome her, and the missionary delegate was conducted to an elegant house of worship that had been built, and a large number of natives were organized into a church."[5] The generosity and forbearance of the natives in this case is amazing in view of the fact that only three years prior to the coming of the *Morning Star* some Germans descended on the atoll and carried off eighty men to work on the Godeffroy plantation in Samoa, none of whom lived to return.

Lukunor marks the southern extremity of a diamond-shaped area notorious as a birthplace of typhoons. The storms rotate to the left and as a rule proceed northwesterly, so they seldom strike these isles with much force, but an occasional maverick strays directly over the coral shelves, whose highest elevation is only about five feet, and at such times the shrieking winds and stupendous waves obliterate all vegetation and human life.

As we approached Lukunor on this particular day, 14 December 1953, the weather was far from reassuring, and the wind began to blow suspiciously like a gale. A band of black clouds ringed the horizon, and I wondered if I should abandon the idea of entering the lagoon. My uncertainty contended with my desire to carry out our mission—plus, I must admit, my curiosity and pride. "If I take her in and anything happens," I thought, "I'll be damned for a fool. If I don't, I'll gain probity as a cautious skipper. But. . . ."

So I went up to the entrance, looked it over, and took the ship in. Just inside, there is a sharp turn that a ship must negotiate in order to avoid a patch of coral. But after that, one is able to proceed directly to Chamisso Harbor. This haven, lying within the crook of arm-shaped Lukunor Island, is fittingly named after a poet.[6] On this day its waters shone luminous green in the pearly light around us, as whitecaps hustled across its surface and piled themselves on its sandy shore.

Our boat landed at a stone jetty, where in the forefront of a crowd of natives stood a tall, bearded American in a flowing white robe, Father William J. Rively, S.J., missionary to Lukunor, who welcomed us to the island and took us to meet the chief, following which, Rayner and I accompanied the missionary to a rectory made of coconut logs and matting—modest but well stocked with groceries, books, and papers, and presided over by a lordly cat. We shared cigarettes and news of the world with our host, and of course the account of the *Romance*'s calamity dismayed him.

"I instigated the purchase of that boat. In fact I sailed it out here from Sausalito, California, three years ago. But it hasn't been too practical for us, as you can see for yourselves. Maybe it's too much of a ship for the natives to handle."

"How did you happen to buy it?"

"Well, when I first came out here, the only means I had of getting around my parish was by native canoe, and it made things very difficult. Once I was caught in a typhoon and cast up on a little island north of Truk—you've probably never heard of it—called East Fayu."

"We were there just three days ago."

"Well, well. You know, then, that being marooned there wasn't much of a lark. Anyway, I really did need some dependable form of transportation, not only for myself but to get supplies and building materials for a new church, also to carry students to the seminary at Truk, and so on. Since we've had the *Romance* the natives don't go by canoe to Truk any more,

The missionary vessel *Romance* on arrival off Truk from Sausalito, Calif., September 1951. *Photo courtesy of Fr. William J. Rively, S.J.*

which is probably just as well, for they've had some pretty rough experiences that way. They're great gadabouts, you know, and think nothing of taking off for a place hundreds of miles away on the slightest pretext. Back in 1938 six men left here by canoe, nominally to trade for cigarettes at Truk. A typhoon caught them, their canoe was banged up, they got lost and drifted in the open sea for three months!

"Sounds impossible, doesn't it? Well, they wound up in Puluwat, in the central Carolines, by which time four of them had died. One of the remaining two died in the act of crawling ashore. The other is living on Satawan now and not at all interested in travel."

"What was the history of the *Romance* before you acquired her?"

Father Rively riffled through a stack of papers and photographs on his desk. "An Englishman named Green built it in Hong Kong in 1934," he said, pulling out pictures of the schooner in happier days.[7] "He and his son and a Chinaman crewed it until his wife's death, when I understand he sold it to the Seattle people from whom the church bought it.[8] The *Romance* is an amazing ship from a construction standpoint, stout enough to have withstood two reefings before this one. But—enough of our troubles. The people would like to welcome you to Lukunor with a song or two at the community house. That is, if you don't mind."

We were delighted. Accordingly the priest took us to a palm-thatched pavilion where a hundred or more men, women, and children sat facing a row of chairs arranged for us. As we took our places, each of us was handed a freshly opened coconut, and the singing began. Without director or accompaniment the song rose, in harmony that sounded like organ tones from long ago—flawless. When they finished the first song, I was hesitant about applauding (maybe it had been a hymn?), but Father Rively said, "Go ahead. I'm not sure they'll know what it means, though." We spent an hour bathed in this lovely sound. "Let me know when you've had enough," the priest whispered. "They can keep it up all day and never repeat themselves."

The wind was becoming more insistent, and at length I said we must go. Boating would be too hazardous to defer longer, and so the word was passed for all hands to assemble on the dock. By noon we were back on board, and quickly weighing anchor, we left Lukunor.

TYPHOON

In the next two and a half hours we circumnavigated Satawan Atoll, which sprawls ten miles west of Lukunor and about the same distance southwest of Etal Atoll. This time prudence triumphed, and I did not try to enter the lagoon. We paralleled the reef at 15 knots, greeting with arm-waving and whistle-blasts the fishermen busy with their spears. They responded enthusiastically, and one little fellow kept it up until he could no longer be seen in the distance except by long-glass.

Soon after our taking departure from Ta Island at the south end of Satawan and again heading south, I received an emergency message from Guam: the storm was being promoted to a typhoon of indeterminate location; its name was to be "Doris." My immediate concern was how to avoid this young lady.

Fortunately we were at sea, for there is nothing worse than being caught by a typhoon in an unprotected harbor. In *A Footnote to History* Robert Louis Stevenson gives a graphic example of what can happen in such a case, telling about how the great typhoon of 1889 struck Apia Harbor. Germany, Britain, and the United States each had dispatched a warship to Samoa to bolster their respective claims for control of that island group. Despite a rising storm none of the ships' captains was willing to leave port lest one of the others seize the prize. Stevenson describes the storm, violent beyond imagining, and the ships clawing to hold on, dragging their anchors and then trying to escape:

A reef is not only an instrument of destruction, but a place of sepulture: the submarine reef is profoundly undercut, and presents the mouth of a huge antre, in which the bodies of men and the hulls of ships are alike hauled down and buried. . . . Conceive a table: the *Eber* in the darkness has been smashed against the rim and flung below; the *Adler*, cast free in the nick of opportunity, has been thrown upon the top, the hugest structure of man's hand within a circuit of a thousand miles, tossed up there like a schoolboy's cap upon a shelf; broken like an egg; a thing to dream of.[9]

With memories of my own of typhoons in the Second World War, I set myself the task of estimating Doris's movement. Based on local observation supplemented with information from Guam, my guess was that the center lay about two hundred miles northeast of us, tending slowly westward. Thanks to the counterclockwise rotation of cyclonic weather in the Northern Hemisphere we were in the least dangerous sector, the speed of the wind being partly offset by the opposite drift of the "eye." On the other side of Doris's track the two factors would have joined against us. Our best escape lay to the southeast, in the direction of Nukuoro. The fact that this island was to have been next on our tour was of no consequence; the storm, not the island, dictated our course.

Movies that evening were shown in the mess hall instead of on the fantail, where we usually had them. It was a scene of bedlam. The projector had to be lashed to a bench. With each roll of the ship someone would wind up on the deck or in someone else's lap. Before the last outlaw bit the dust, I headed for the bridge and my long vigil.

Soon the wind began to haul around to the east-northeast, the seas became longer and more regular, and the ship rode quite well. At midnight we obtained radar contact with Nukuoro, and as we approached the island, the ship came under the influence of a powerful current setting toward the reef, so strong that we had to steer twenty-five degrees to the right of base course to make good our desired track.

Here as at Namoluk we saw the light of occasional fires. Why should they be blazing so long after midnight? Were the natives sacrificing to the god of storms? Were they in trouble, clinging to tree trunks in order to keep from being swept away? A large white bird flew distractedly in the aura of our running lights while the wind howled in the rigging. An eerie night.

To pause here would be out of the question. We rounded the island and set off in a northeasterly direction at 12 knots, riding well—so well, in fact, that I issued night orders and put my tired and somewhat bruised body to bed.

During the night Doris fulfilled predictions and whirled off to the northwest, making it safe to proceed to our next atoll, Ngatik. We had performed a gigantic pas de deux with the storm and could only hope that it wouldn't capriciously reverse its direction.

At Ngatik the surf was too high for us to send a boat ashore, but we were able to come close enough to see that the island was little damaged. Natives clustered on shore did not seem to be in distress.

Next, on 14 December, came Mokil—easternmost of all the islands in the bailiwick of Commander, Naval Forces Marianas (ComNavMar)—and we raised it at first light on the following day. During our approach we picked up a radar contact about five miles off the reef. It turned out to be a Japanese fishing boat, but since it was outside territorial waters, I was limited to coming just close enough alongside to be able to identify the craft. I suspected it had been loitering much closer to the island, and subsequently my hunch was confirmed.

3

A Place of Violence

On 14 December 1953 we came to Ponape, island of legend. I had seen its rain-swept slopes from the deck of a destroyer during the war, when all one morning our ships shelled Japanese installations.

I still remember the fragrance of tropic flowers mingled with powder smoke, and the excitement of wondering if the defenders would answer our challenge. Intelligence had indicated the presence of two 18-inch guns brought in from fallen Singapore—which, if they existed, could have chased us clear over the horizon. But either they did not exist or were not prepared to fire, for there was no response.[1]

Ponape is shaped round, like a coolie's hat, with mountains crowding into a lofty center. Thick mangroves line its shore, and in its deep interior stand silent rain-drenched forests. Extending outward from the island for a distance ranging from one to ten miles is a classic barrier reef laced with shallow lagoons and low islets. Four small openings in the reef give access to Matalanim, Kiti, and Lot Harbor on the south side, and to Ponape Harbor on the north. This last is sometimes called Jokaj Harbor, after the Great Cliff of Jokaj, which can be seen from miles at sea. Most of the civilized life of Ponape huddles in the shadow of this rock, in the town of Kolonia. Here the colonial efforts of Spain, Germany, and Japan in turn were centered, and here the Japanese fortified themselves most strongly.

I was glad for the chance to visit Kolonia to learn what I could of Ponape in the war years. The harbor is infested with coral reefs and "foul ground," but the markers placed there long ago by the Germans were still reliable, and we found good anchorage without difficulty.

Once ashore, I reported to district administration headquarters, only to find that the "Distad" himself was away. However, he had arranged jeep transportation for us, and so I started out with some *Hanna* officers to tour the island. However, one couldn't go very far on wheels on the island at the time of our visit. When the Germans were here, they had built a road all the way to the south coast. The Japanese had extended it clear around the island, through the districts of Kiti and U. But while the "Road to U" might sound romantic, as a road it no longer existed. War and torrential rains had wiped it out long ago.

We chose another destination—one called "Mpomp," the plantation of Carlos Etscheit. The Etscheits are Belgians who by the time of our visit had lived on Ponape for almost fifty years, under three flags. As I sat in a comfortable rush chair on their veranda, drinking good German beer, Mrs. Etscheit told me of wartime experiences under the Japanese.

"They had very little defense here," she said. "In a way it was rather pitiful. For example when the time for surrender came, and they were ordered by radio to stockpile all their weapons in a certain open area, you Americans flew over and looked, and accused the Japs of holding back. But they weren't. It was all they had."

"Did they lock up the whites when the war started?"

"No, they left us alone, except that we had to report twice a day. Here at Mpomp we have our own garden, and some cattle that run wild in the hills back of the plantation, so we didn't go hungry. Our greatest danger came when the Americans bombarded the island, for the Japanese were sure an invasion was imminent, and they told us that in that case we must be killed. Fortunately the invasion never came—for us." She sighed. "On the other islands many whites were killed—our friends on Woleai—Satawan—Truk—Kusaie."

I changed the subject. "In 1944 we were told there were some 18-inch guns here. Was that true?"

"Yes, I believe so. In fact my daughter has told me of some very large guns at Jokaj. It is very difficult to get up there, but she found some steps cut by the Japanese."[2]

We left Mpomp and the hospitality of the Etscheits and continued our bumpy ride. Along the road we picked up two *Hanna* sailors (there is always room for more in a jeep), starry-eyed over having seen a maiden bathing in a mountain pool. As nearly as I can tell, this was the pool in the Pillapenchakola River, where half a century ago a German anthropologist named Kubary is said to have loosed a pair of crocodiles, for reasons not entirely clear. The creatures must have long since departed, however, or there would have been no idyll of a nude maiden for my two lads to remember.

Nevertheless the crocodiles would not have been the most disagreeable denizens of the island. There is a lake somewhere in the interior that is said to be full of poisonous snakes. A species of green sea snake inhabits the mangroves at Nan Matal, waiting to drop on the unwary canoeist. And most revolting of all, Ponape has a large black and orange lizard reputed to feed on corpses.

In cheerful contrast with such dank inhabitants, the people of the island seemed carefree—even exuberant, as if cherishing some private joke that only they could know or understand. The streets of Kolonia were lined with hibiscus and flame trees and imposing gateways every few yards that framed empty, sun-drenched vistas. There was so little of the town left that it was hard to imagine it as a bright jewel in any colonial empire. Yet so it was—briefly for Spain, Germany, and Japan in turn. From documents held in the national archives, I was many months later to learn the story of the last of these regimes.

As with other islands that were seized by Japan in World War I and subsequently confirmed to its custody by a League of Nations mandate, Ponape was first administered by the Imperial Navy. Later a civilian "South Sea Company" took over, under the supervision of the Japanese Imperial Ministry of Colonial Affairs Overseas. A large and complex bureaucracy staffed with civil-service career personnel was installed in the early 1920s. Although the natives were not completely ignored, their rights counted for very little, and as more and more Japanese poured ashore, native affairs were assimilated into the tinkling life of a Japanese community, complete with brothels and bathhouses.

Ponape became center of a large fishing industry, with a fleet of sixty boats. An agricultural station founded by the Germans before the war was enlarged to become the finest in the Japanese empire. Out of eleven thousand persons on the island, over half were Japanese or Okinawan. Micronesians were permitted to choose between competing in the new order or dying out.

The story of the fortification of Ponape parallels that of Truk: too little and too late. Apparently the main buildup did not take place until the autumn of 1943. When our Fifth Fleet succeeded in isolating Ponape a few months later, it trapped a garrison of 5,993 army and 2,291 navy personnel. Of these, 281 either were killed or made their escape. On 11 September 1945, Commo. Ben H. Wyatt, USN, accepted the surrender of Gen. Masao Watanabe, IJA. The war was over.

The principal installations found by Commodore Wyatt consisted of two airfields, one of which was located on a plateau that seriously limited the length of its runways. The other, built hastily by hand in February and March 1944, was hemmed in by hills, ravines, and rivers; only one takeoff and one landing were made there before landslides rendered it unusable.

The Japanese might have fared better had their supply lines withstood the depredations of U.S. submarines. One day in January 1944, a construction corps, having finished grading an airstrip at Satawan, loaded its machinery in the 6,600-ton *Okitsu Maru* and set off for Ponape to accomplish a another such task. It was accompanied by the subchaser SC-32, a water-supply ship called the *Nippo Maru,* and the destroyer *Suzukase.* When only sixty miles from their destination, the destroyer was torpedoed and sunk. Five hours later the *Okitsu Maru* went down, with 144 lives and all the heavy equipment. The situation on Ponape was now hopeless because fighter aircraft could not be brought in. For the island's people, there remained only the prospect of fighting with spears instead of guns and then dying for the emperor.

After the surrender, Commodore Wyatt's task of repatriating the motley population was well executed. For transport he used two Japanese destroyers and two of their cargo ships, together with an assortment of American landing ships such as the LST (landing ship, tank). Between 14 October and 23 December 1945, he returned all of the Japanese to their home islands. In addition, 76 Saipanese, 585 Koreans, and 406 natives of Mokil, Pingelap, and Eniwetok were taken back to the places from which they had come. The operation meant tragedy for many mixed Japanese-Ponapean families, but war is an affair of tragedies, and these were minor compared with those inflicted by the Japanese in their days of power.

The U.S. Navy administered the islands initially; then in 1950 the U.S. Department of the Interior assumed responsibility. It was hoped that the Ponapeans might recover a measure of pride of their ancestors, a people who had once held their own against whalers, missionaries, Spanish garrisons, and German empire builders. That hope has now been largely realized.

A CONFEDERATE RAIDER

One returns to the story of Ponape again and again, for it is as colorful as any in the Pacific and reflects a hundred and eighty years of Pacific history, as in a small, cracked mirror.

Ninety years before the guns of our seven battleships thundered over the island, another warship created havoc here. It was a mighty ship for its time: the Confederate raider *Shenandoah,* Capt. James I. Waddell commanding. Waddell knew that Ponape was a favorite resort of Yankee whalers, and he decided to pay it a visit. On arriving off the southern harbor of Lot, he was delighted to see, lying peaceably at anchor within, three Union whaling ships and a Hawaiian bark. The *Shenandoah* flew no colors, and a local pilot named Thomas Harrocke unsuspectingly brought her into the narrow cove, where she dropped anchor in fifteen fathoms.[3]

Although the growth of coral during the last ninety years may have narrowed it somewhat, even in those days Lot Harbor was a tight little place—at most, only four hundred yards wide.[4] In order to keep the *Shenandoah* from swinging against the coral heads, two hawsers were run out from her stern and secured to palm trees on a nearby islet, effectively blocking escape. The raider was like the cork in a bottle.

Still no alarm sounded on board the ships in harbor. All four skippers, it seems, were away on a visit to the Reverend Doane on the north side of the island, several hours' trip by boat through the encircling lagoon. Waddell ordered the starboard guns manned, while four prize crews of six men each stood by in the ship's jolly boat and cutters.[5] When he gave the word, a gunner touched his match to the signal gun and the Confederate flag was run up.

The prize crews met little resistance, for the black muzzles of the *Shenandoah*'s guns were sufficiently compelling, and by the time the boat bearing the missing skippers rounded into sight, the scene was as peaceful as when they had left. There was a difference, however, in that the whalers *Edward Carey,* out of San Francisco, the *Hector* of New Bedford, the *Pearl* of New London, and the *Harvest* of Oahu were spoils of war. A cutter dashed out to intercept the ships' masters, who were brought to the *Shenandoah* and clapped in irons.

The Yankee ships yielded gold, guns, delicacies, and tons of supplies. The *Harvest* proved to be the plumpest hen in the little roost and was hauled alongside and relieved of her entire food supply along with five tons of valuable sperm oil. The other three were beached and the natives told to help themselves, which they did with enthusiasm, even stripping the copper sheathing from the hulls.

Finally the order was given to burn the whalers, and first the *Pearl,* then the *Hector* and the *Edward Carey* were put to the torch. The *Harvest* was spared to the last, but finally she too was destroyed. A tower of oily smoke and flame stood over Lot Harbor for three days while the natives danced and feasted. It is not recorded whether the Reverend Doane witnessed the pyres, but if he did so, it was probably from a discreet distance.

The captains of the Yankee ships were given a choice between being transported to Guam or left with their crews in Ponape. They elected to stay, and on Thursday, 13 April, the *Shenandoah* stood out to sea and pointed her sharp bow north to the Arctic whaling grounds, where she was destined to wreak more destruction than any other timbered ship in history, anywhere.

WHALERS VERSUS MISSIONARIES

Had the rebel cruiser reached Ponape a month earlier, it might have made a far greater haul, for in those days dozens of ships would have been wintering there. Local reaction to this annual influx varied. Generally the natives welcomed the whalers, and eagerly traded breadfruit, yams, pigs, and chickens[6] for the Yankees' iron tools, firearms, ammunition, clothing, trinkets, liquor, and tobacco. Many natives also found they could enjoy a handsome income by making their female relatives available to the whalers for a fee. The women enthusiastically cooperated and gained prestige by having intercourse with white men.

Sometimes the natives would become too exuberant, someone would be killed, and the miscreants would disappear into the bush for a while. One time a drink-sodden captain and crew of a ship in Matalanim Harbor were killed in the night and their ship burned to the water's edge. But then, the Matalanim tribe was always a thorny lot.

Of course the missionaries viewed the doings at Ronkiti, Lot, and Matalanim with utmost revulsion, even though the whalers brought New England to their doorstep. It was particularly galling to the missionaries to be obliged to traffic in tobacco in order to obtain funds for items available only from the whale ships—medicine, clothing, implements, and the like. The whalers, for their part, regarded the missionaries with distaste but were reluctant to confront them directly because the men of the cloth were quick to name names back home.

Of the missionary effort in the South Seas it has been said, "They played a great part there; or at any rate have had the good fortune of telling it themselves." Their accounts are indeed impressive. Our admiration is diminished, however, by their exaggerations and their blindness to any religion or culture other than their own. As the same writer remarked, "We are often ready to assume that a work must be good because those who do it are men of noble spirit and unselfish practice."[7] Of these men, and their work, good or bad, Ponape certainly had its share.

The first missionary to land on Ponape was Louis Maigret, a priest of the Order of Sacré Coeur who sailed from Honolulu with another priest named Alexis Bachelot in a small schooner they had bought and renamed the *Notre Dame de la Paix*. Father Bachelot died at sea, and his body was brought ashore and buried at Matalanim on 6 December 1837. His companion remained, set up a small chapel, and labored without much success for the next few months until he was removed by the same vessel that had brought him there. The Protestant missionaries who came much later never mentioned him, except for a single paragraph headed "A Protestant Missionary at the Grave of a Catholic" published in *The Friend* (Honolulu) for February 1860.

The author of the item was Dr. Luther Halsey Gulick, who came to Ponape in 1852 with his wife and another missionary couple, Albert and Susan Sturges, along with a Hawaiian assistant, in the chartered brig *Caroline*. They were here under sponsorship of the "Boston Mission," whose overwhelming success in the Hawaiian Islands gave rise to hope of similar conquests throughout the Pacific. Dr. Gulick settled at Matalanim, the Sturgeses and their assistant at Ronkiti. Though the white traders and whalers opposed them, the natives responded warmly and the chiefs ordered the common people to embrace the new cult. The Sturgises commandeered the finest feast house on the island and turned it into a church.

A tract writer of the 1860s rhapsodized: "The island is a veritable paradise in its natural features. . . . From the mangrove trees which line its shore to the pinnacles of the mountains it is a succession of natural terraces. These are covered with a vegetable growth as beautiful as can be conceived, and of almost endless variety, from the humble taro (a kind of potato) to the mighty breadfruit. The climate is one of the most delightful in the torrid zone."[8]

Every prospect pleased, and only man was vile. The missionaries proceeded to attack the main hobbies of Micronesia: sex, dancing, tattooing, and the drinking of kava (*jagow*). Even painting the face and body with turmeric was forbidden, in spite of the fact that it is a good insect repellent. Kava, a liquor brewed from the sakao root, has been found to have mild beneficial properties, but this benefit would have made little difference even had it been known at the time. These deprivations were minor, however, compared with the ban against premarital sex. Such a prohibition was wildly preposterous to a Ponapean and of course had little effect even though the missionaries dressed as many native women as possible in shapeless clothing from neck to ankle.

The missionaries' attack on tobacco was a blow against traders and whalers alike, and they longed for revenge. An opportunity came sooner than expected, produced by a calamity no one could have wished. In 1854 the American whaler *Delta* put a man infected with smallpox ashore on a small reef island off the south coast of Panope in order to isolate him from the rest of the crew. During the night some natives stole his clothing, and in a short time the whole island was infected. In the next year over three thousand natives died, and at the height of the epidemic some traders started a rumor to the effect that Dr. Gulick had caused the disease with his incantations. Under deep suspicion and in mortal peril, he continued to go about inoculating natives who would consent, and eventually the success of these inoculations worked his deliverance.

Undaunted by this episode the missionaries on Ponape continued to flourish. The Rev. Edward T. Doane and his wife arrived in 1855 and settled in the Jokaj district on the north side of the island. Two years later they gave up and left on the newly commissioned *Morning Star*, together with Dr. Gulick's wife and three children; Gulick himself followed four years later. But new missionaries arrived to fill the gaps, and even Doane returned in 1865, with a new wife, to renew his tussle with the devil for possession of the natives' souls.

THE COLONIALS

The year was 1885. There were thirteen churches on Ponape, a missionary institute for the training of native preachers, and a school for girls. Yet "When at length all Micronesia seemed about to be illuminated by Christian light kindled from island to island," as James M. Alexander later wrote, "dark clouds rose."[9]

For several years Spain had considered taking formal possession of the Carolines and finally sent a warship from the Philippines to accomplish this aim. The Germans, who had ideas of their own concerning the area, received intelligence of the plan and quickly moved to seize the Marshalls, Yap, Kusaie, Truk, Ponape, and lesser islands, using the gunboat *Iltis* for the purpose. There was violent reaction in Madrid that could have led to war, but the matter was resolved when Germany oddly agreed to adjudication by Pope Leo XIII.

The pope confirmed Spain as legal owner of the Carolines, and the Germans withdrew. So in 1886 Spain sent two ships to Ponape to take possession. Alexander continued: "The commander, consulting as little the natives as he did the crabs that scrambled over the sands and the birds that flew over the island, required the Ponapeans to cede their property and sovereignty to Spain, and under duress, with heavy hearts, they 'made their marks' to the document of cession."[10]

The appearance of the Spanish brought an end to the plans of the American missionaries. The dream of another Hawaii collapsed overnight. When the Spaniards condemned part of the mission grounds to create an administrative center, Doane protested so vigorously that he was packed off to Manila. "And so, while the Spaniards have done nothing for the welfare of the Ponapeans since they discovered them," asserted Alexander, "they claim authority by 'right of discovery' to expel the American missionaries, who have spent forty years [actually thirty-three] in costly, arduous, and perilous labors for the Ponapeans, and have lifted them out of pagan barbarism into a considerable degree of Christian civilization."[11] The American missionaries were not to be easily displaced, however, and not without a good deal of kicking and scratching. They secured the release of the Reverend Doane by exerting pressure through the State Department and then stood by to watch the blunders of the island's new masters.

First the Spaniards put the natives of Jokaj to work constructing a settlement. But when, in accordance with the time-honored practice in other Spanish colonies, the overseers embezzled their wages, the workers decamped. A party of soldiers marched into the jungle to bring them back and, in trying to coerce them, opened fire, killing two and wounding three. But instead of fleeing, the rest of the natives rushed the Spaniards and with their spears killed every one.

After this unexpected turn of affairs the governor and remaining members of the colony shut themselves in the fort. In the next few days, natives gathered to attack, but before they were ready, the Spaniards tried a midnight dash to the shore, hoping to reach one of their ships riding at anchor in the harbor. That was a mistake. Floundering through the shallow lagoon, they were easily run down by native canoes, and only a handful managed to reach their goal.

Eventually a relief expedition arrived from Manila, by which time the natives' rebellious ardor had cooled to a point where they were willing to accept a general amnesty. The Reverend Doane took all the credit for this, though other sources indicate that the intercession of the Capuchin priests was more to the point. At any rate two whole districts, Jokaj and Not, accepted conversion to Catholicism forthwith.

The Spaniards set to work with renewed zeal, not omitting this time to erect a stronger fortress for their headquarters. Roads were pushed through to Matalanim, Kiti, and U, and Capuchin priests established missions alongside the Protestant stations, a move leading to more violence and bloodshed. The whites found themselves hopelessly outclassed in jungle warfare and in one affray lost 369 men and some 100 weapons before giving up in despair. Of the 110 natives who opposed them, only six lost their lives.

The colonials now had a tiger by the tail, and they tried everything to make it disappear. They partitioned Matalanim, giving half to Catholic Not district and half to the chief of U district. The chief, who had embraced Catholicism for this purpose, was thereupon deposed by his people. At length, in 1890, the American missionaries were formally expelled, being given a $17,500 indemnity for their property.

Spain's war with the United States in 1898 doomed Spanish sovereignty over the Carolines. Our own failure to assume control of these islands at this point is a classic example of shortsightedness. Germany, on the other hand, saw a chance to accomplish its earlier ambition and acquired dominion over the entire Caroline Archipelago together with the Marianas (except Guam) and their vast potential for copra, sugar, and fishing industries. Angaur alone held reserves of over two and a half million tons of the highest grade phosphate in the world.

The new owners of Ponape duly arrived to assume control. They established headquarters for the entire eastern Carolines on the site of the old Spanish fortification, which they demolished. Natives were freely admitted to the settlement for the first time, and a period of relative peace ensued. The Spanish Capuchins were replaced with Rhenish-Westphalian

Capuchins without undue friction, and in 1907 the Lutheran Liebenzeller Mission of Würtemburg set up a station to represent the Protestant sect.

There was, however, a growing source of discontent with certain changes the Germans sought to impose. The governor abolished the feudal system of landholding, which was the only kind understood by the Ponapeans, and substituted one whereby the natives would perform fifteen days of work per annum for the whites for the sum of fifteen marks. Half of this was to go to the natives and half to the chiefs in recompense for their loss of feudal rents and services.

The plan looked good on paper, and it might have succeeded but for a certain Carl Boeder, who came to the island in 1910 to assume the governorship. He refused to honor the agreement made by his predecessors because apparently the natives were behind with their part of the bargain. He ordered the natives of Jokaj to perform thirty days' labor forthwith. When they assembled in order to protest, the governor had one man seized and flogged. Instantly the Ponapean courage and pride that had so dismayed the Spaniards twenty-three years earlier flared anew. They set upon Boeder and three of his men, cutting them to pieces that they then dumped into the lagoon.

The German response was devastating. Warships appeared in Jokaj Harbor and sent ashore a force of Melanesian warriors brought up from south of the equator to quell the revolt. These men, as well-versed in jungle fighting as the Ponapeans, routed the rebels, pursued them into the mountains, and rounded up the entire population of the Jokaj district. The 416 men, women, and children of the Jokaj tribe were put aboard ship and carried off to Palau, where they were put to work in the phosphate mines. As a tribe they were extirpated forever. To fill the empty villages, the Germans brought in a shipload of equally helpless natives from Lukunor. Ponape was finally subdued.

BACK TO THE TIME OF OUR VISIT

On my way back to district administration headquarters, I noticed a small Gothic chapel, centered in a deep, rolling carpet of moss. It was a vestige of the old Liebenzeller mission—more beautiful, with its dove-gray walls and the branches of a flame tree wreathed over its door, than any church I have ever seen. Further along, a rusty water tank lay on its side, encased in brambles; a Quonset hut stood with camouflage paint peeling; and a roofless, windowless concrete shell of a building looked forth gauntly from the green tangle.

Completely cheerful amid the residue of a hundred years, the people wandered along the narrow paths, waving to us as we passed. Some of the elderly ones even bowed from the waist. Everyone wore Western clothing, but I heard that on a little island in the harbor the people wore next to nothing, and the same was probably true everywhere except in Kolonia itself. (The Japanese did one sensible thing: they outlawed Western clothes except for Sunday wear.)

I found the district administrator in his office, seated before a huge chart of the islands and smoking a mighty cigar. This was Mr. Henry Hedges, owner of a handsome black sloop I had admired earlier that day in the harbor. "Had it built in Holland in 1940," he told me. "Sailed it from New York up the Hudson, to the Great Lakes and Chicago, down the Chicago and Illinois Rivers to the Mississippi, Caribbean, Panama, Galapagos, and from there across the Pacific by southern routes. Got out here just in time for the start of the war. In those days I was supposed to be retired." He laughed heartily at the recollection.

"Well, sir," he went on, "I got caught down in Fiji and the navy heard that I knew something about civil engineering, so I spent the next few years building airfields. After the war I took a job at Saipan as the civilian assistant to the military governor, and when Interior took over the Trust Territory I came on down here."

"No more retirement for you?"

"No indeed. Not while I'm getting as much kick out of a job as I do from this one," he declared. "I think we can do a lot for these people . . . with a little time and money. For example I want to encourage the native fishing industry and I think I know how to do it. Got the idea over at Mokil. They have a fishpond there staked out in the lagoon where they keep their fish alive and kicking until they're ready to eat them. Now if I could get a boat to go around and pick up the fish from this pond and similar ones on other islands, we could accumulate a very respectable cargo. As it is, the natives get no income from their fishing because they can't keep 'em fresh. By the way, how about snagging a Jap boat for me, not too large?"

I told him of missing one early that morning.

"Oh, I wish you'd nailed him! That bastard has been hovering around Mokil for weeks, and I *know* he's landed there too. We did catch one, you know. Had him right here in the harbor, with a guard on board, and I myself went and pulled the distributor out of his motor. But do you know, that rascal had a spare!" He jumped up and pointed out the window. "He fixed his motor and putt-putted out of the harbor right under my nose. Put the guard on the reef on the way out!" He laughed. "Anyway, Captain Meredith, do what you can, and I'll see you next time. By the way, I hope you've cautioned your men on behavior with the natives. Last time a DE was here, some of the sailors chased the wrong woman: it was the chief's wife."[12]

The sun was setting by the time the motor whaleboat returned us to the ship, and fortunately Rayner had already set the special sea details in anticipation of a fast getaway. He greeted me at the quarterdeck with "The ship is ready for getting under way, sir."

"Heave right up!" I called to the bridge. The anchor windlass began grinding away. The chain came slowly through the hawsepipe with a loud chuck! chuck! as each link passed. I sprinted to my conning station atop the pilothouse, and soon we were on our way, hoisting the motor whaleboat as we threaded the channel. So brief is tropic twilight that it was almost dark before we escaped the coral-studded harbor and headed our small ship for Guam.

4

Something about a Ship

At sea, 15 December 1953, we skirted the north side of Oroluk Atoll at sunrise, and although the entrance looked easy, we didn't go in. At the northwest corner was a small island, also named Oroluk, surrounded by a broad band of coral sand. A mysterious object on the beach tempted me, but I would have had to go five miles out of my way to reach the nearest entrance, then enter against the sun—a risky business for little purpose.

While we were passing Minto reef a few hours later, the radarman on duty reported an object on or near the reef. It proved to be the hulk of a Japanese cargo ship and would have made a fine gunnery target, but our schedule would not permit us to take advantage of the fact this time. Reluctantly I turned away and headed the ship toward Guam. We had seen the last of the eastern Carolines for the present.

That afternoon we held swimming call, an event all too rare in today's navy because of chronically tight schedules. And the weather has to be just right, the water calm and clean, far from any land. Whenever we were able to indulge in the practice, I would pass the word about 1600 in the afternoon and stop the ship wherever we happened to be. After the ship lost all headway, we would check her drift. The side of a ship presents a huge sail area, so that even a light breeze can move the vessel sideways at a fair clip—

The destroyer escort USS *Hanna* (DE 449), launched 4 July 1944, at Newark, N.J. Christened the *Hanna* in memory of Pvt. William T. Hanna, USMC, who was killed in action at Guadalcanal 9 October 1942.

Displacement 1,350 tons; length overall 306'; beam 36'8"; draft 9'6"; propulsion 2-shaft Westinghouse geared turbines, 12,000 shaft horsepower, 24 knots; complement 186; armament two 5"/38, four 40-mm, ten 20-mm; depth charges.

From 9 June until 28 September 1945, the *Hanna* served with the Marshall-Gilberts Surface Patrol and Escort Group. After the Japanese surrender she and the U.S. prize *Tachibana Maru* evacuated Japanese military from Wake Island, reaching Tokyo 12 October with 700 passengers. Thereafter she was assigned to rescue and weather reporting duties off Guam until May 1946, when she was decommissioned at San Diego.

With the outbreak of Korean hostilities the *Hanna* was recommissioned and in April 1951 sailed for escort duties in the far Pacific. She operated mainly with the blockading forces of Task Group 95 until returning to the U.S. in November. In 1952 the ship returned to Korean waters for more blockading, escort, and shore bombardment duties, supplemented by patrol duties in the Trust Territory of the Pacific Islands in 1953–54. The latter assignments were continued in subsequent deployments until November 1957, when she was designated a reserve training ship home-ported at San Pedro, California. She served as such until 27 August 1959, was decommissioned a second time on 11 December 1959, and joined the Pacific Reserve Fleet. The *Hanna* was stricken from the navy list 1 December 1971 and was sold two years later to Levin Metals Corp., San Jose, California, for scrap. *U.S. Navy photo* something that can be quite disconcerting and even dangerous to swimmers. Once satisfied on this score, we would rig a cargo net over the side, lower the motor whaleboat, and put out a rubber raft tethered to a stanchion. Gunner's mates stationed at high points in the superstructure would grip their M1 rifles purposefully and scan the water for sharks.[1]

The first tentative swimmers would emerge from below, buck naked and all tawny color by now, lifting their feet gingerly over the hot deck. A whoop and a splash and suddenly they would all crowd over the side. Some hit the water any old way; others would make fair dives even though the level of the water constantly rose and fell. And one man named Renner, as trim and poised as a ballet dancer, would sail off from the top of the bridge, away and down like a kingfisher.

Few of the men lingered in the water but scrambled up the cargo net to dive again and again. There is a strangeness about swimming in the middle of the ocean, even in the sunniest of climes—a ghostly unease in knowledge that the bottom lies thousands of fathoms below. Peering down, one can see only a few feet into the silky cone of light that penetrates this dusky world. One thinks of leviathans loitering beyond, against whose coming the high-powered rifles are poised. The ship's hull, rounded off not far from the surface, is a gourd suspended over oblivion—a preposterous home.

For me, the *Hanna* was more than a home. I had commanded her for twenty-one months before coming to Guam, and the crew were mostly old-timers. We had gone through a bleak and fiery winter in Korea together. The officers were young and alert; the men were proud of their ship. As one said, "There just ain't *nothin'* we can't do!" Yet I must concede that the person least qualified to write about a ship is its commanding officer, for in him the currents of hope, pride, and loyalty run so swift that he cannot avoid sometimes being swept off course, and knowing the springs of his own actions so well, he is prone to ascribe the same to others who in truth only follow where he leads.

Physically the *Hanna* was an unlikely subject for eulogy. She was one of the hundreds of escort vessels stamped out in the 1940s. Her design provided no refinements, nor much regard for the dimensions of the human frame. She was cluttered and dumpy, certainly no "greyhound of the sea." The only thing she shared with her sleek cousins was the ability to hunt down and kill a submarine. Against surface targets she was not much to brag of, but against a submarine the *Hanna* could be as lethal as any ship afloat. And for the present task she had advantages of seaworthiness, versatility, and economy in man power and fuel.

Before dinner that evening, as we were speculating on the number of bags of mail waiting for us on the dock, an "Operational Immediate" message came in from Guam. I was ordered to increase speed so as to return to port as soon as possible; no reason given. We cranked her up to top speed. The forced-draft burners began pouring nine hundred gallons of oil per hour into the fireboxes—oil all the more precious because we had so little of it left. The ship shuddered and vibrated as it passed through its critical speed—about nineteen knots—and smoothed out as it "put on legs" and gained more speed. The wind and spray of our going stung the faces of the men on the open bridge that night, and for all of us it was like riding in a boxcar. But dawn found us waiting at Orote Point, requesting permission to enter port.

THE LONG SEARCH

On Guam, 17 December, at the headquarters of ComNavMar, I learned the reason we had been hurried into port. It seemed that typhoon Doris, whose existence I had almost forgotten in the peaceful waters around Ponape, had hit the Marianas with full fury—damage to the northern islands still unknown. Worse, much worse, a four-motored weather reconnaissance plane was down somewhere near Pagan Island, two hundred miles north of Saipan, and my orders were to stand by on one-hour notice to join the search. Our sister ship, the *Whitehurst,* was already on the scene.

Any thought of liberty on Guam was swallowed up in preparations now afoot. Conduct of a search and rescue mission (SAR) is a highly refined operation requiring coordination between all services in the area—army, air force, navy, marine corps, and coast guard. The SAR organization at Guam was centered in a typhoon-proof shelter at the Naval Air Station, where Lt. Comdr. Ray Tufts presided over a battery of teletypes, radio receivers and transmitters, telephones, charts, and plotting boards.

The atmosphere was tense when I arrived, for the men and officers called to duty at the Rescue Coordination Center (RCC) were daily intimates of the missing plane's five-man crew. The plan at first was to send the *Hanna* out right away, but it was then decided that we should wait until morning.

The pages of my journal tell the story of the next few days better than I can, the sharp edges of emotion and the fatigue having been long since dulled.

At sea, 18 December
I write this at 2330K,[2] with the ship making 20 knots on course 008° True, which should bring us by about 0800K to Agrihan Island, where I believe we will be directed to send a landing party ashore. So far, my orders are only to get there. Agrihan is about 300 miles north of Guam, and is the top of a gigantic volcano rising 15,000 feet from the ocean floor to the surface, with another 3,160 feet on top of that. It may be necessary for the landing party to go all the way to the crater's edge for a look inside.

The typhoon is still in the general area, at the moment 240 miles WNW of Agrihan. Hope she moseys off to the west.

Bespoke the merchant ship *Graigaur* bound for Fiji, meeting on opposite courses off Saipan. He told me weather was very rough, with swells from Doris, where he had been.

19 December
The search plan for today arrived by radio at 1 AM, and is quite a complicated affair. My own job consists primarily of scrutinizing the three islands of Agrihan, Pagan and Alamagan. Secondarily I am responsible for maintaining contact with five Air Force search planes. They are supposed to check in every thirty minutes with an "operations normal" message, and on the whole the system has been working very smoothly. RCC sets up the various search sectors.

Arrived off Agrihan about 0900K. Decided against sending a landing party ashore because of the surf. . . . The island has been thoroughly worked over by the typhoon: two or three buildings on the SW side have been demolished, and whole forests of coconut trees have been (to borrow Holmes's expression) *shredded.*

The famed ability of palm trees to withstand the blast by yielding to it hasn't saved them this time. Thousands of trees have lost all but a frond or two, and hundreds lie about like dumped handfuls of matches. I wonder what the top wind velocity here must have been.

Several people from the village came down to the shore, but we couldn't reach them, and they didn't give any sign of distress or dismay . . . or perhaps I should assess their attitude more along the lines of inborn resignation to fate.

Circled the island at a range of 500 yards, failing to see any trace of the lost plane. About noon we left for Pagan Island.

Pagan is blessed with a tiny spit of land curving out arm-wise to form a cove three hundred feet wide off the slender waist of the island. It was calm enough there to land a boat-load of men and two officers (Rayner and Lee). These went ashore at an old Japanese wharf. Meanwhile I held the ship about four hundred yards off the murderous black rocks against which the surf crashed and exploded. One could only guess the power of the geysers shooting over a hundred feet in the air.

Rayner learned that although the storm had given the natives some 50 hours of acute danger, they had fared well and needed no medical assistance. Crops were destroyed, also about 8 dwellings, but the coconut plantation was not as hard hit as at Agrihan.

In recovering the boat I had much fear for the men in it because of the roughness of the water. One man did get a 2" gash in his forehead from a swinging block.

Circled the island, a jumble of volcanoes old and new. Volcanoes upon volcanoes, cones, and lava flows tumbled down each other's sides, wreathed in vapor.

Here, as elsewhere, no indication of wreckage.

20 *December*

I am on-the-scene controller, with two ships and six planes. Busy day.

(Later) Had fair communications all day and dashed here and there at the instance of RCC. All searches negative. Investigated debris at L 20° 20' N., 145° 34' E., but it turned out to be only coconut driftwood: bits of logs freshly stripped of bark, nuts, fronds twigs . . . all within a 1000-yard circle. The bright yellow would certainly look like a partially deflated life-raft from the air.

(Later) Am now writing this with the greatest of difficulty owing to the vibration of the ship. Another plane may be down—"Playmate 19" as he is known on the voice circuits. He hasn't reported "operations normal" since midmorning. We notified RCC a long time ago, and now a new emergency has been declared. We are steaming now at 21 knots for Pagan Island, where he was last heard from. *Whitehurst*, who is north of us, is going to Agrihan. All of our planes have been put on the search, but it will soon be dark, and they are running low on gas.

The missing plane may have flown too close to a volcano and have been caught in one of the tremendous downdrafts which sweep down their flanks, or, for all I know, into their craters. If it is a crater, the wreckage would be obscured by clouds indefinitely.

Very tired and depressed. . . .

Now passing Maug Island . . . we go past Asuncion next, then Agrihan. Expect to reach Pagan about 2200K.

(Later) Passing Agrihan. A plane has sighted some debris, at Alamagan, I believe. Anyway I've been told to keep going down to that island. Earlier, a plane reported seeing a flashing light on the southwest corner of the island. This of course may have been an ordinary light in the village there.

Asuncion, my first view of it, is an awesome sight . . . so simple and majestic a cone, and so very evil . . . heaving its black shoulders out of the sea, curving disdainfully into its private cloud . . . no one can see its face. Streaming away in the evening sky from its dark summit, a line of sooty clouds. . . . I can get two hours' sleep now, before midnight and Alamagan.

21 *December*
Sent landing party ashore at Alamagan's southwest village. Have had two planes, one of which dropped flares to show location of debris. One flare landed in the water offshore, the other one on the island. Now it turns out that the debris was nothing more nor less than the southwest village.

Landing party reported by flashing light that natives know nothing about plane crash. One woman had been badly hurt in the typhoon, and the hospital corpsman treated her. The landing party is now back on board.

(22 hours later) I set a course for Pagan Island about 0300 (yesterday morning, actually, though it doesn't seem so). My reported intention reached RCC about the same time as their daily search plan reached me. I was supposed to spend the day checking the area around Alamagan and Guguan, to the south. However, I saw no reason to change my initial plan, which was first to revisit Pagan and question the natives there about the new crash.

Reached the now-familiar cove at sunrise, put a landing party ashore, and had them back on board within the hour. Circled the island again, then left for Alamagan and Guguan to carry out orders. At Pagan my people learned only that a blue 4-engine plane had flown over on the day before and dropped a flare.

Made a third landing at Alamagan, this time on the northwest corner, and probably the most difficult landing so far, for the surf was really high and the beach composed of football-size rocks. No information here, either, except that the inhabitants have run out of supplies. I passed this along to the District Administrator to act on. The people will at least have plenty of coconuts to eat.

Inevitably a plane saw a patch of debris many miles away from our position, and I had to steam 84 miles at top speed to look at a few shredded branches. It also wasted the time of a 4-engine plane for five or six hours. Very discouraging.

Now I'm night-steaming near Saipan, and tomorrow shall be straight man (guide) for one of their "checkerboard" air searches.

22 December

Started out with ten planes today, all navy and coast guard. The Air Force is running its own show, staging planes from Japan through Iwo Jima. They will use an airborne RCC, but we'll monitor their circuits anyway, as a safety measure.

Shortly after starting the checkerboard search referred to above, one of our planes reported definite aircraft wreckage inside the crater at Agrihan, strewn along the southeast wall.

Now I am making 21 knots for that island, and expect to arrive about 1715K, when it will already be dusk. Landing party will have to climb the mountain in the dark.

Whitehurst yesterday evacuated all the inhabitants, so I'm asking him to obtain trail information from the native chief.

Also asked RCC for an airdrop of batteries for my portable radios. Rayner and Bland are to lead the rescue party.

Passing Pagan, making good speed. We should be lying off Agrihan by 1632K. So far no reply to my request for batteries. I will not like sending those men on a dangerous task without radio. They will be out of visual signalling distance if the island wears its customary halo of cloud . . . which the latest weather report indicates will be the case.

Diversions come at odd times: someone has found a large fruit-bat clinging to the anchor windlass. Body is about 8 inches long, covered with brown fur. Wings black and leathery furled like a wet umbrella . . . probably a 3-foot span. The wind and spray of our going rattle his framework and he turns sleepy brown eyes on his tormentors. Helpless, and yet so feral!

The crater at Agrihan is erupting mildly.

Shortly after writing the above I received the following message from RCC Guam: "Organized search party consisting of marine land rescue party, medical personnel, native guides, departing Guam on Whitehurst. Estimate time of arrival Agrihan 1300K 23 December. Pilot reports indicate crash scene will be very difficult to reach. Do not desire Hanna attempt groundsearch. Batteries requested by you are on Whitehurst."

It was with combined relief and disappointment that I read this message: disappointment because a job I knew the *Hanna* to be capable of had been taken out of my hands, relief that I need not risk any of my men in a dark climb up an unknown mountainside. The pilot's description of the crash scene virtually ruled out any chance of there being anyone alive, and I had to realize (time being no longer of the essence) that this was a job for professionals, with full equipment.

That night I stayed in the vicinity of Agrihan as directed. The *Whitehurst* arrived on schedule in the morning and landed its party of marines on the northwest corner:

[36 hours later] Things have not gone well for the landing party; the route they picked was not the best, and they have been taken off the island and relanded at another spot.

After transfer of the batteries, I went back to Asuncion for another look. This time the late afternoon sun had dissolved practically all of the cloud-cap. We still had hopes of locating the wreckage of the first plane. Nothing.

This morning we were stationed 25 miles west of Asuncion, controlling ten planes, a duke's mixture of navy, army, and air force. Bludworth did a magnificent job in handling many radio circuits at once. About 1300 an air force plane reported wreckage 80 miles west of us. Subsequent reports built it up into a life-raft with one survivor, and I thought "Here at last is the end of the search, and a beautiful Christmas for some family!"

After running four hours at 21 knots, we reached the scene and found the usual . . . a few bits of storm driftwood. . . .

Tonight we have only one thing to be glad of . . . that we're headed for Guam. I have just written the shortest night orders in my career (5 lines) and I made them so in order to write this before I collapse.

It's Christmas Eve, and I'm beginning to know what Christmas really means. The gift from Deity of part of Himself to live with us and be part of the world is the greatest and fairest gift . . . its essence being the impossibility of return. Reciprocation thins. The gift should be sole.

Thus our (attempted) gift will have some value, and I can find peace, perhaps, in knowledge of the attempt, even though we failed. The people who loved those ill-starred flyers can never know, nor can they ever reciprocate, the effort of our brains and bodies these seven days past . . . but it is a joyful gift to give.

As for death, I think of it as only a comma in a long narrative.

5
North to Chichi Jima

The *Hanna* remained at Guam until 22 January 1954, and the place became very tiresome to me and to most of the crew. Strange to say, our inactivity was an operational requirement in that we were assigned to "Search and Rescue Ready-Duty" as a result of the plane crashes in December and the fact that the coast guard cutter previously assigned this duty had been withdrawn due to lack of funds. Under the new rule, one of the two destroyer escorts assigned to ComNavMar had to be kept at Apra Harbor with steam up, ready to sail on two hours' notice. Since the *Whitehurst* was on an extended stay in Japan, the *Hanna* had to be the one to stay idly in port.

I grumbled at this because our mission called for reconnaissance and patrol, with search and rescue purely secondary. Also, since emergencies have a way of occurring at unpredictable times and places, I felt there was no advantage in standing still and waiting for one to happen. Wherever she might be, the ship would have ample fuel to reach the scene of an emergency in the crucial first phase. From the standpoint of the crew, morale was bound to suffer from the combined effects of heat, boredom, cheap drinks, and lack of females ashore. Day by day I could see that my dockbound sailors were losing their edge. As Joseph Conrad wrote long ago, both ships and men rot in port.

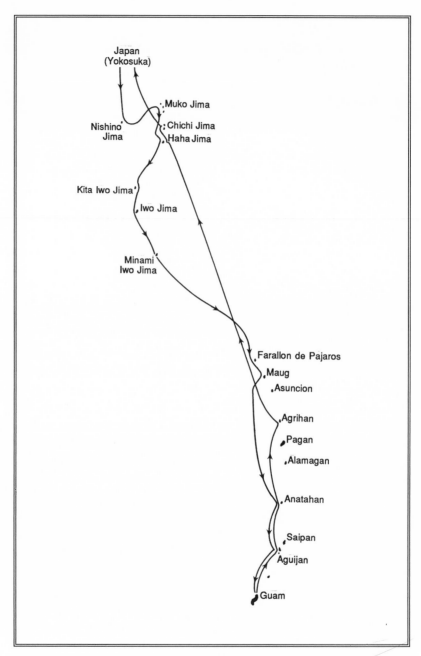

Itinerary in Northern Marianas, Bonins, and Volcanoes—22 January–11 February 1954.

So I was glad when the *Whitehurst* finally returned and we were ordered to sea once again. Our instructions were to patrol in the Mariana, Volcano, and Bonin Island chains, then proceed to Japan for a five-day holiday and return. In addition to the usual routine, a special diversion had been planned for 24 January, when we would rendezvous with an itinerant submarine, the USS *Pickerel* (SS 524), and conduct eight hours' training in undersea warfare.

The Bonin and Volcano Islands were unfamiliar to me and thus offered interesting possibilities for amateur exploration. Even the Marianas shouldn't be too bad under conditions other than those we had known in December.

The list of islands we were to visit ran as follows: Rota, Aguijan, Anatahan, Asuncion, and Maug in the Marianas; Minami Iwo Jima and Kita Iwo Jima in the Volcanoes; and Haha Jima, Chichi Jima, Muko Jima, and Nishino Jima in the Bonins. In the Marianas, we were responsible only for the uninhabited islands, which explains the omission of Rota, Tinian, Saipan, Guguan, Sarigan, Agrihan, and Alamagan.

And so once again we were off and away, and early the first day came to Aguijan, a tantalizing spot for anyone with a flair for exploration. An island without beaches, it has only steep cliffs all around its six-mile circumference. A second and third series of cliffs are stepped back from this formidable base, giving the island somewhat the aspect of a wedding cake.

Because of its closeness to Tinian, which lies across a six-mile strip of water, Aguijan is well situated to dominate the larger island with long-range artillery, and it would no doubt have been armed for the purpose had not the difficulty of landing guns been almost insurmountable. Of course these same conditions made the place nearly assault-proof. At about the same time as Tinian was captured in 1944, an amphibious assault on Aguijan was planned and a party of marines reconnoitered the coast, but when it became apparent that the enemy had no long-range guns on the island, the idea of storming it was given up as not worth the cost.

On 4 September a year later, three weeks after V-J Day, the coast guard cutter 83525 appeared off the island and lay to. On its small deck Rear Adm. M. R. Greer, USN, received the sword of 2d Lt. Kinichi Yamada, IJA, senior officer of the sixty-seven-man garrison.[1] (The sword Admiral Greer wore was actually a borrowed one, located by his staff after a frantic canvas of Tinian.)

During the palmy days of sugar culture on Saipan and Tinian, the Japanese operated a large plantation on Aguijan. They solved the problem of access by rigging an aerial trolley attached to a derrick on the edge of the cliff and run out to the kingpost of a ship anchored a few yards off the rocks. But how did such a derrick get built in the first place? There must be a way of getting ashore by small boat, and if it could be done, we would do it. However, this project had to be deferred if we were to pay our respects to Anatahan and Maug on schedule and meet our tame submarine according to plan.

Later in the day, some miles north of Saipan, a sonarman reported that the fathometer showed rapidly decreasing depth of water under the keel, revealing an undersea mountain—a mighty cone shooting up from a depth of seven thousand feet to within 660 feet of the surface. Nothing of the sort showed on the chart, and I called it "Mount Keim," after William S. Keim, sonarman striker, who detected it.[2] Crossing and recrossing the spot to establish the peak's highest point cost us an hour, so we didn't reach Anatahan until late in the afternoon and could make only a token landing there.

Anatahan, the first large island north of Saipan, was uninhabited at the time of our visit. We could see the vestiges of a coconut plantation clinging to the flanks of a large plateau within a mile-wide crater. My predecessors on patrol had always made their landings at the site of an abandoned village on the southwest side. But I decided to try another spot—one with a beach somewhat vulnerable to amphibious attack and probably defended at one time by several well-concealed guns. Certain holes in the cliff looked suspiciously man-made.

The beach proved to be very rocky, so we had to strip and swim ashore from the boat. With me were Ensign Whitesides and two enlisted men: EM2 Don E. Tarvin and a salty old chief boatswain's mate named Theiss. Near the beach we found the remains of a fairly large encampment: a cistern and an open well that would have been a real hazard at night, a cement floor for some sort of shop or warehouse, and a row of three large kettles that could have sufficed for a whole garrison. Actually there were only thirty souls on the island at the time of surrender, so this had probably been their main base.

We split into parties of two each for further exploration. Neither party got far. Tarvin and I were soon turned back by a swarm of hornets—one of which wounded me in the seat, and four of which got Tarvin, I asked not where. Whitesides and Theiss frittered away their time climbing for coconuts, and I later scolded them for missing an obvious machine-gun nest. Landings like these were valueless unless some intelligence could be gleaned from them.

We waded back into the water, delightfully cool and clear over the smooth rocks, through the surf and back to the waiting motor whaleboat. The chief had spent himself climbing trees and had to be helped.

We were lucky weatherwise. All traces of Doris were gone, and the sea lay flatly inviting the ship to cleave its blue-black surface. We were proceeding thus serenely at 0430 in the morning, when the chief hospitalman woke me to say that Ensign Bludworth had suddenly developed acute appendicitis.

I ran to the bridge and headed the ship south at top speed. Soon radio central was flashing a request to Guam that we be met by a flying boat to which we could transfer the patient. But Operations was reluctant to trust a water landing, even in such good weather, and we were directed to make for Saipan instead.

Bludworth was the one, during those grueling days and nights of the search and rescue mission, who talked to the planes on voice radio, and his strong, cheerful voice had been a great source of reassurance to the pilots. Now this lad, a clean, rock-hard "all-American boy," was really sick. Thanks to penicillin the chief hospitalman was able to keep the infection under control until we arrived at Tanapag Harbor the following afternoon and lowered the patient, stretcher and all, into a waiting boat.

Climbing again the glassy ladder of latitude, past Alamagan, Pagan, Agrihan, Asuncion, and Maug during the night, I could only hope that the submarine would wait for us, for we couldn't help being three hours late at the rendezvous. Meanwhile I sat down to write in my journal before turning in, and ended the day's entry with: "Bludworth [as he was being lowered over the side] felt my look, and opened his pained eyes to see me far above him on the bridge, and smiled halfly and moved one hand. A radioman just brought me a cup of coffee and thanked me clumsily for some Christmas candy I passed around yesterday. Of such are my pleasures constructed."

The *Pickerel* did wait for us, and together we spent an exhausting day of simulated depth-charge attacks. Finally we parted, and the submarine headed for Pearl Harbor, the *Hanna* for Haha Jima 360 miles to the northwest. The next day we ran into a cold front, with gale winds and high waves that mocked our softness from all that time dockside in Guam. We pitched so violently that I slowed down to make life a little less tragic for the chief petty officers quartered in the forecastle.

The Bonin Islands were called "Japanese islands of mystery" almost from the time of their seizure in 1875 by the sons of the Mikado. Only by luck and the persistence of men such as Willard Price, who visited them in 1935, do we know anything at all about them. After the war, mystery still cloaked the Bonins, even though the United States continued to control them, because of their strategic importance and the avidity with which the Japanese began to demand their return.

Haha Jima, the southernmost group of the island chain, was to be our first objective.[3] Arriving about noon on 25 January 1954, we inspected it as closely as possible from seaward without making any landings. Haha Jima has steep mountains and lush green fields slanting down to the sea. Along its craggy shore the rocks in many places are cut through with huge arches and caverns. During the war the Japanese kept a garrison of 2,989 army, 3,270 navy, and 244 civilian laborers on Haha Jima, and supposedly all were removed after the surrender. From February 1946 to the time of our visit, the land had known no human habitants. If our binoculars had revealed otherwise, it would have been a spine-chilling discovery.

At one point along the coast, a two-hundred-foot half-dome hill named Kofuji-ya confronted us with three large caves that must at one time have contained major guns. I remembered the scream and "crump" of shells from a North Korean shore battery trying to hit the *Hanna* at Song-J'in only a year before, at almost the same point-blank range, and I shuddered involuntarily. "Let's keep moving," I said to Rayner; "this makes me very uncomfortable." The sight of such a fortification is enough to make anyone nervous, even knowing that the last enemy is now either dead or far away.

We hurried on to Chichi Jima and arrived late in the afternoon. Because its appearance from seaward is quite confusing, I took the conn when we reached Port Lloyd, alias Futami Ko. It would have been helpful for me to have had in hand the following from the log of a young master's mate, one John R. C. Lewis, who sailed these waters with Commo. Matthew Calbraith Perry in 1854:

> The island has a somewhat rugged appearance from the sea, but when you get nearer, it presents a somewhat different appearance. Port Lloyd is a pretty Situation being only open to the Sea in the SW quarter where it has its narrow entrance. The way to enter is to keep about two ship lengths off from a large rock on the Starb hand steering then for Castle

Rock (a small rock near the other side) until about a quarter of a mile. Vessels coming in will avoid the reef on the Port Side by keeping near the large rock on the Starb side. Then Starb your helm a little by little until she points North, ship going ahead all the Time, and when she gets nearly abreast of the peaks on the Starb side, then let go anchor.[4]

These directions are completely reliable and indeed would suffice for any ship entering Port Lloyd. In addition to the usual hazards, the place had been considered dangerous for a ship of any size until quite recently because of sunken hulks still littering the bottom. In fact, when Adm. Arthur W. Radford, commander in chief of the Pacific Fleet, paid an inspection visit in 1951, the destroyer that brought him remained outside while he and Rear Admiral Hardison came ashore in the captain's gig, followed by staff in a one-lunger dubbed the "white boat," manned by locals.

If Lewis could have been on board the *Hanna* on 25 January 1954 he would not have been any more impressed than was I with the fortifications that ringed the harbor. From the face of the large rock that he mentions, two neatly cut embrasures stared out at us. Within the harbor, similar windows of death revealed themselves wherever we looked.

Little was to be seen above ground: a neat cluster of buildings used by the naval colony, a few scattered dwellings of the Bonin Islanders, a large radio tower toppled from the crest of a ridge, and assorted rusty skeletons of shops and machinery. For the rest, greenery of every description covered the island from the blue waters of the bay to the tops of the hills.

A road laboriously cut and tunneled, virtually invisible from the water, circled the harbor. Every fifty feet or so along its route were cave openings, some of which we explored later in the day in company with the naval administrator of the Bonins, Lt. Comdr. Paul ("Jack") Frost. Many were only a few feet deep; others were giant caverns once used for shops, storehouses, and barracks; still others led to integrated gun positions carved out of the living rock. Deep inside one of the larger caves our host pointed out a wall of gasoline drums extending to the overhead. "It goes back about two hundred feet," he said, "and there are more caves like this one, all filled with aviation gas, lubricating oil, diesel oil, and alcohol. The gasoline is getting to be quite a liability, for the drums are beginning to leak and I can't get rid of the stuff."

At one place where the road burrowed through a cliff, near the *Hanna*'s anchorage, I noticed a steeply ascending shaft and stopped to explore it.

There was a pair of vertical timbers that had once supported steps, and we managed by bracing ourselves against these to ascend to a room filled with weak daylight from a gun port in the face of the cliff, perfectly framing the ship. At one side lay a shattered 8-inch gun. A gallery off to the left led to a similar emplacement two hundred feet away. Between them, and slightly higher, a rangefinder position had been carved out. A gallery led to ammunition magazines, a kitchen, and sleeping quarters. Nothing usable remained.

"When the marines occupied Chichi," our host explained, "they were told to flatten the place, and they certainly did a good job. I sometimes wish they hadn't been so thorough, for they destroyed lots of equipment and supplies I could use now to eke out my budget. However, it's still a wonderful place for scavenging. In some respects, total destruction wasn't possible—the Marine Corps just didn't have that much TNT."

Later he showed me an even more intriguing set of caves, hidden in the jungle near his house. They were actually caves within caves. Each was about a hundred feet long, twenty feet high, and forty feet wide, lined with concrete. Inside each was a concrete building of the same shape, with two feet of clearance all around. An airlock led to the interior of the inner shell, which itself was lined with pure copper. "One theory is that these caves were intended for storing black powder," he said, "but there's another theory to the effect that in the event of an invasion of the home islands they were to have been a hiding place for the national treasure."

"Do you suppose the Japanese planned to use Chichi as their last stronghold?" I asked.

"Maybe. The place is fortified far more strongly than one would think necessary," he answered.

From the standpoint of our own forces in the last stages of the war, the island of Chichi Jima was only a secondary target because our seizure of Iwo Jima effectively neutralized the Bonins. Otherwise, Haha Jima would have been preferred for assault since its terrain is more suitable for airfields. The main importance of Chichi Jima as far as we were concerned was its nuisance threat as a radar and communications outpost and as a nest for torpedo boats and midget submarines. In order to keep the enemy from exploiting these potentials, we bombed the place repeatedly.

American flyers over Chichi reported antiaircraft fire worse than anything they had experienced elsewhere. "The sky was black," one of them told me afterward. "I never expected to finish my run. My wing[man] went in and never pulled out of his dive. I yelled at him, but he was gone."

The first raid took place on 4 June 1944, "D-Day" on Saipan. Planes from the *Essex, Yorktown,* and *Hornet* had the job of neutralizing the islands to the north that day, and Chichi came in for its share of attention. After a second attack eleven days later, the Japanese evacuated the two thousand descendants of the original Bonin Islanders and transported them on the *Nota Maru* to Japan, where they were put to work in the munitions factories.

About seventeen thousand others remained, under the tactical command of Vice Adm. Kunizo Mori and the administrative command of Lt. Gen. Yosio Tachibana.[5] The latter officer, together with Captains Nakajima and Yoshii, Colonel Ito, and a Major Matoba, eventually met death not in battle but in a hangman's noose on Guam in payment for a crime which, as Robert Sherrod has written in his *History of Marine Corps Aviation in World War II,* staggers the twentieth-century imagination. It is not a pretty chapter in Chichi's history, nor yet one that should be passed over: it should be written and read in honor of certain brave Americans. Sherrod recounts these events as follows.[6]

The two raids in June 1944 were followed with four more in July and then three in August, with intermittent drops later in the year by bombers returning from raids on Japan. When D-Day on Iwo Jima rolled around on 19 February 1945 the navy struck again. And again on 23 February.

Occasionally airmen were lost in the vicinity of the island, but whether they survived as prisoners of war was indeterminate, and in most cases they were listed simply as missing in action. Chances were thought particularly good for one marine pilot who parachuted into the sea during the raid on 23 February and was last seen swimming toward a nearby beach.

V-J Day came, and General Tachibana proceeded to comply with instructions from his superiors. He surrendered the Bonin Islands on 30 September to Commo. John H. Magruder Jr., USN, on board the latter's flagship, the destroyer USS *Dunlap* (DD 380). On 5 October, Col. Preley M. Rixey, USMC, a veteran of the Tarawa and Saipan operations, arrived off Chichi with a handful of marines to prepare for the actual occupation of the islands and in due course went ashore with his staff, probably feeling uneasy in the presence of sixteen thousand hostile Japanese who were to be repatriated. Not until some LSTs brought in a battalion of five hundred marines on 13 December was his power more than purely nominal.

One of the first matters Colonel Rixey took up with General Tachibana was the question of the American prisoners of war. "What became of the American flyers captured on these islands?" he asked. The quick reply was, "Yes, we captured six. All navy, I think. They received very kind treatment. Two were sent to Japan by submarine. The last four unfortunately were killed by your own bombers in an air-raid against these islands during the capture of Iwo Jima in 1945. They were blown up by a direct hit. Nothing remains. I am sorry this happened. I was very beloved of them and wished them no harm. We buried what remained of the bodies after cremation. This is Japanese custom."[7]

Major Matoba—cold-eyed, bull-necked, the essential tyrant—was the officer directly in charge of prisoners. Since he had conceived and super-vised construction of many of the defenses, it might well be expected that he would harbor special animosity against those who tried to destroy them. Under questioning, he admitted that his troops may have neglected to pro-vide adequately for the safety of his charges, but he offered no further explanation.

A few days later, Colonel Rixey was escorted to a plot in the old civilian cemetery high overlooking Port Lloyd, to see the alleged burial place. But it didn't look right, considering that the Americans were supposed to have been dead eight months or more. The crude wooden cross implanted at the spot was of *new* wood. Colonel Rixey said nothing.

On 23 October the first shipload of Japanese left the island. Gradually the Bonins were emptied of the people who had overrun them in the past sixty-nine years, and by 10 February the last of them had departed—except for a hundred farmers on Ai Shima and three hundred on Ototo Shima, who were allowed to stay on in order to alleviate the food shortage in the home islands.

During the repatriation phase, a Japanese cutter entered Port Lloyd and landed Frederick Arthur Savory and his three uncles, descendants of the Nathaniel Savory who had pioneered here fifty years before the arrival of the first Japanese. Frederick Savory went to Colonel Rixey and told him he had heard certain rumors in Japan concerning the flyers. "These stories are not nice stories," he said.[8]

Colonel Rixey immediately sought to question one of the key officers of the erstwhile garrison. He already had been repatriated, and when author-ities in Japan went to arrest him, he committed suicide, whereupon the colonel launched a full inquiry into the matter. The case broke when one of the Korean laborers volunteered information. An anonymous letter added further details. Suddenly the mask fell away and the crimes of Tachibana, Matoba, and the others stood revealed.

The American flyers shot down in July 1944 were to first to be captured. After being "interrogated" to the general's taste, they were on 8 August, on his orders, bayoneted to death.

Additional prisoners arrived the following February when a naval pilot, two radiomen, an aviation ordinanceman, two unidentified flyers, and the marine pilot who had parachuted into the sea were captured. The men in this group were apparently farmed out to various units to be played with and disposed of as the Japanese fancied.

One of them was beaten to death.

One of the officers was beheaded under supervision of Colonel Ito in the presence of a hundred troops. It was said that he was very brave.

One of them was beheaded under the supervision of Capt. Yoshii at the radio station on the ridge.

One was executed by personnel of the Torpedo Boat Squadron near Ogiura.

Four of them suffered incredible indignities before being executed.

Major Matoba took personal charge of one of the officers, who was also very brave under "questioning" and never revealed the name of his ship. But the major wasn't satisfied with the torture and death of his captive. He ordered a medic to cut out the American's liver, secretly had it prepared for the mess, and after the meal, disclosed his little prank. Other parts of flesh were rationed out. To some it was a big joke; others vomited. But Major Matoba was pleased with himself and continued so, right up to the day of his punishment.

Thus because of so evil a passage in the evil business of war, Chichi Jima has a taint of horror even on the sunniest days, when the fragrance of its flowering trees and the music of its brooks are sweetest. Sherrod says of this affair: "In extenuation of the Japanese as a race, it may be added that no word of an atrocity reached the people, who were continuously treated to photographs of Japanese soldiers giving candy to children in the occupied areas, or opening schools for them. On the other hand, even if the Japanese people had known, they probably couldn't or wouldn't have done anything about it."[9]

For a year and a half after the Japanese left, the islands were almost deserted. Then in October 1946 the escort destroyer *Keyaki* came down from Japan bearing as passengers the only people having a real right to be called Bonin Islanders.[10] They were 129 members of five families, all that survived of the those who had been deported to Japan in April 1944, with names as un-Japanese as one could imagine, including thirty-seven Savorys, thirty-four Washingtons, eighteen Gilleys, twelve Gonzaleses, and ten Webbs. Their features were in the main occidental, their bloodlines mixtures of American, British, Spanish, Portuguese, Japanese, Polynesian, and African strains. Who, really, were these people, and why did they have a special right to live in the Bonins?

NATHANIEL SAVORY, AMERICAN

The story goes back to 1839, when the British consul at Honolulu decided to sponsor a colony on Chichi Jima to give substance to England's tentative claim of ownership. According to a contemporary report,

> The first colonists of this eastern group were two men of the names of Millinchamp and Mazarro who, having expressed to Mr. [Richard] Charlton, the British consul at the Sandwich Islands, their wish to settle on some uninhabited island in the Pacific Ocean, were by him recommended to go to this group, of the discovery and taking possession of which he had been recently informed. They sailed accordingly in 1830, took with them some Sandwich Island natives as labourers, some livestock and seeds, and landing at Port Lloyd, hoisted an English flag which had been given them by Mr. Charlton.[11]

The record goes on to relate that the little settlement was visited several times by whaling vessels and once by a ship of Britain's China Squadron. Mazarro, anxious to get additional settlers, returned to Hawaii in the autumn of 1842 in an English whaling vessel. He appealed to Alexander Simpson, acting consul in Charlton's absence, for help, describing his little settlement as flourishing: he had an abundance of hogs, goats, and a few cattle; he raised Indian corn and many vegetables; and he had all kinds of tropical fruit—in fact, he avowed, he could supply fresh provisions and vegetables to forty ships annually.[12] Many Hawaiians would gladly have accompanied him, but the Hawaiian rulers insisted on a large fee, well beyond Mazarro's purse, before they would allow them to emigrate. Mazarro then took return passage on an American whaler by way of Ponape, hoping to recruit natives there.

Simpson wrote that Mazarro, by virtue of his first arrival, called himself "governor" but found the task of governing no easy matter:

He applied to me for assistance, and thankfully received the following document:

"I hereby certify that Mr. Matteo Mazarro was one of the original leaders of the expedition fitted out from this port, under the protection of Richard Charlton, Esq., Her Majesty's Consul, to colonize the Bonin Islands; and I would intimate to the masters of all whaling vessels, touching at that group, that the said Mazarro is a sober and discreet man, and recommend them to support him by all means in their power against the troublers of the peace in that distant settlement; recommending also to the settlers to receive Mr. Mazarro as their head, until some officer directly appointed by Her Britannic Majesty is placed over them.

"Given under my hand and seal, at the British Consulate, Woahoo, Sandwich Islands, this 27th day of December, 1842.

Alex R. Simpson
H.B. Majesty's Acting Consul
for the Sandwich Islands
'God save the Queen'"

A small body of enterprising emigrants would find this group a most admirable place for settlement; indeed its colonization I consider to be a national object.[13]

Actually, Mazarro was a washout as a leader, and the de facto governor of the island proved to be Nathaniel Savory, who emerged (much in the manner of James Barrie's "Admirable Crichton") as the one whose industriousness, honesty, and clear common sense earned the others' respect.

The most serious threat to the community came not from the rigors of pioneer life but from the "breakers of the peace"—the whaling crews who came ashore for holiday when their ships stopped for fresh water and green foodstuffs. Rum flowed freely at such times, and Mazarro was prone to become as besotted as any of his visitors, being unable to control them in the name of Her Britannic Majesty or any other name.

On one occasion, a ship's crew took over the entire settlement. They butchered animals, tore down fences, ravaged the gardens, and burned some of the houses. One of the islanders was murdered while trying to protect his wife from being raped. The others, led by Nathaniel Savory, took refuge in the mountains. The sailors settled down to an orgy of rum and destruction, but their revelry had a price. Every morning, one of their number would be found dead, having been killed in the night. Savory and his men struck silently and surely, never killing more than one, as they might easily have done. The interlopers soon learned the futility of trying to pursue their tormentors into the thickets and after four days withdrew to their ship and sailed away.

But others came, and the island was in constant turmoil. Savory, who was not a man to relish bloodshed even in a righteous cause, became increasingly impatient with Britain's failure to furnish any real protection. The place was at the mercy of all comers. So he appealed to his own country for help. The United States had never acknowledged Britain's claim to the Bonins, but the State Department shied away from asserting one of its own. The nation was oblivious to the importance of the island of Chichi Jima as a coaling and watering stop en route to China, despite the fact that until Japan was opened to foreign trade a squadron based on Chichi could have controlled most of the trans-Pacific trade with the Orient. But Savory did not give up. Every Sunday he ran up an American flag in front of his cabin while Mazarro fumed impotently at the other end of the village. And he kept bombarding Washington with proposals and complaints.

The arrival of Commodore Perry in 1854 furnished an opportunity for Savory to press his cause, and he succeeded in convincing Perry of the potential usefulness of the island to the Stars and Stripes. Perry executed a ninety-nine-year lease on a strip of land called "Ten-Fathom Hole" and for the next few months used Chichi as his main base while prying open the gold and vermillion gates of Nippon.

To men of the American squadron, this jewel of an island was a paradise. Master's Mate Lewis wrote:

> There are about thirty inhabitants on the island Americans and Kanakas. They came first from the Sandwich Islands. A man by the name of Savory lives up at the end of the Bay is the head man. Commodore Perry had bought some land here. It is intended for a Coal Depot I believe. A man by the name of Horton who is discharged from the Plymouth is the one who generally pilots vessels in. He generally has a number of fine Turtles. He has a pen made in the water so you can always have them fresh.[14] At the head of the Bay on the left Side facing up is a fine place for hauling the Seine. . . .
>
> I might say in conclusion that this island is capable of being made a most beautiful spot on account of its advantages as a stopping place for Whalers because it is exactly on their cruising ground and also for Men

of War. At this place Vessels might be supplied with fresh Grub which is so much wanted by Sea going persons. Independent of this, the monotony of Sea life is so much relieved by the sight of land. And when you leave, You are invigorated, giving you much confidence and strength. The same as boys who when at School enjoy so much the sight of home and familiar faces, just So with land as a familiar thing relieves and gives us strength to continue on. (Finis)[15]

Lewis's remarks after all these years are still fresh and true, particularly his feeling for land as a source of strength when, as sometimes happens, life afloat seems intolerable.

Convincing Commodore Perry of the value of Chichi Jima turned out to be easier than convincing the United States government. In fact, Perry was sharply criticized for undertaking a long-term lease of Savory's land, and his action was repudiated.

The Shogunate soon took advantage of the situation, and in 1862 a shipload of colonists arrived at Port Lloyd. Their samurai leader planted the Japanese flag and persuaded the islanders to acknowledge Japan's control. However, within a year the policy was changed, the colony was dismantled, and the colonists were sent home.

With the Meiji Restoration in 1868, Japan embarked on fresh expansion. The continued indifference of both Britain and America to the fate of Chichi and its orphan settlement presented an opportunity too good to pass up, so on a fateful day in 1876 a Japanese transport arrived from Yedo bringing soldiers, farmers, fishermen, teachers, artisans—a balanced Oriental community. These were not particularly happy people; they had been plucked from their homes in utmost secrecy, crammed on board ship, and brought away without even being told their destination. Nathaniel Savory had died two years earlier, but his son, Horace Perry Savory, led in signing away the island's independence.

The first expedition failed in the sense that they were unable to establish a permanent community in the Bonins, and they were withdrawn after only two seasons. But the real object had been attained, a fait accompli by means of which Japan extinguished both Britain's and America's interests, and neither of those distant nations cared to make an issue of the matter. The Japanese could now exploit their new property at leisure.

In 1880 a larger and better equipped expedition descended on the islands, and this time they stayed. They did not molest the original inhabitants but merely inundated them in an impersonal, highly regimented tide of immigrants. The Japanese worked harder than anyone properly should in paradise. They built roads, government offices, a sugar mill, a fish cannery, a whaling depot, a bank, stores, Buddhist shrines, a hotel, and numerous small shops and other business establishments, monopolizing the land and the sources of fresh water. Over seven thousand people poured into the Bonins in the years that followed, and paradise became a little sinister. For one thing, few were ever permitted to leave. Two men who tried to stow away on a whaling ship were apprehended and flogged to death as an example to the others. The mother of one of the miscreants, going out to gather his corpse, was visited with a similar fate to complete the lesson in official justice.

Survivors of the original community clung together, preserving their language and keeping aloof from the swirling thousands around them, and continued so until World War II erupted and they were hustled off to Honshu.

Just below the lip of ridge overlooking the village of Omura, I found the old cemetery facing the harbor and the heaped-up hills beyond. Behind it, on the other side of the ridge, the land dropped away to the crashing ocean. It was a beautiful, peaceful spot, which even the weedy thickets of Japanese ginkokai (*Leucaena glauca*) could not stifle. There were many scalloped oriental tombstones, but a group of simpler monuments, looking as if they belonged in a New England churchyard, stood apart where the moss was deepest. There, beside an old hibiscus tree, stood the gravestone of Nathaniel Savory. Pausing there, I could see the American colors flying over the little administration building far below. He would have liked that.

Before we left the island, I met a living representative of the pioneer—his great-great-grandson, also named Nathaniel Savory. In a kind of justice rare in this world, he and other direct descendants of the original settler had had their island restored to them—temporarily, anyway. But in their minds was a question: for how long? When would the United States withdraw its hand and let the Japanese rush in?

Speaking faultless English, with a slight New England twang, Savory voiced his concern. "There is a 'Return to Chichi Society' in Japan, you know," he said. "I understand there are over twenty thousand members and they are exerting great pressure. And if the Japanese government makes it an issue, and asks a price for its friendship, will the Bonins be part of that price?"

"It's quite possible," I replied. "After all, there is a vacuum here because you have so much land and so many fine resources, and not enough people to exploit them."

"But we cannot bring in the white people who might want to come here," he answered, "even from America. It is so unreal. If we could fill up the land with people like ourselves it would not be so tempting. But," he shrugged and smiled, "the navy has said only Bonin Islanders may live here, and there are only a hundred of us in the world!"

I learned later that in 1951 he and the other descendants of the pioneers presented a petition to the military government authorities, asking that the Bonin Islands be made part of the United States, ending with a promise: "We are willing to offer our best to America and ask as little as possible in return."[16]

Washington deferred action, for "diplomatic reasons," and all that Admiral Radford could tell the islanders at the time of his visit was that their petition had been reviewed by the chief of naval operations, the secretary of the navy, and the secretary of state. He well knew how scant were its chances of being approved.

6

Places without People

We spent the first week of February 1954 in Japan sightseeing and making minor repairs to the ship at Yokosuka Repair Base. We then reentered the ComNavMar area and resumed our task of poking, prying, and policing, never knowing what we might run into. The first island on the southward trip was an uninhabited "orphan" sixty-five miles east of the Bonin chain. After our visit there, I wrote:

> A day of rocks, rocks, and more rocks. . . . First Nishino Jima alias Rosario alias Disappointment Island. After a sleepless night on account of rough seas en route, I didn't feel too well pleased with the object of our surveillance: a 200-by-700-yard excrescence of cinders, lava-rock, and bird droppings. Two 75-foot poles, object unknown, stick up in the middle of the island. My guess is that they were used for landing supplies for the handful of watchers the Japanese kept here during the war. We circled the island and departed, calling it worse names than any of the above.
>
> About noon arrived off Muko Jima, the northernmost Bonin, a pair of islands consisting of a jumble of rocks and spires poking up out of the

ocean, the domain of a few forlorn wild goats. Once a couple of villages clung to a strip of land at the water's edge, but they are gone. Choto, the larger, is supposed to have had 46 inhabitants in its heyday, and I feel sorry for all 46. Continued on our way, stopping the night in Chichi.

We left Chichi Jima at first light because I wanted to do a thorough job at Haha Jima, the largest uninhabited island in our parish and one we had slighted on our way north. During the day we made four landings, the first in a beautiful landlocked cove called Higashi Minato, at the northern end of the island. Although it was so small we had scarcely room to turn the ship around, its depth was so profound that we had to lie to without anchoring. There were tunnel openings high above us, but the landing party never found the lower entrances—only an abandoned village and a shrine. They soon returned to the ship, and we proceeded counterclockwise around to the southwest side of the island. Along the shore, every possible landing beach was heavily fortified, with rusty gun muzzles peering at us malevolently from deep embrasures. I had to keep reassuring myself that the island was deserted.

We anchored in eight fathoms off a promontory named Oki Misaka and deposited three separate landing parties on the beach: one at Okimura Town, one at Kofuji-Ya (the fortress I'd noticed several days before on our way north), and one at a point halfway between the other two. I conducted the third of these, with a "staff" of three good men.

Fields that had looked like meadowland from offshore proved to be thickly matted sugarcane, which ten years without harvest had made virtually impassable. We progressed only by following ditches and ravines leading to the top of a large hill. I split our party and took Quartermaster Savage with me. He was a good man to have along on such a jaunt, being as agile as a cat—and as curious.

Along the beach, gun caves were spaced every hundred yards or so, but inland there didn't seem to be any defenses. I had picked a very uninteresting sector to explore, or so I thought until, walking along the crest of the hill, I felt the ground tremble underfoot and heard the ringing of iron. The whole top of the hill was hollow!

In a clump of trees we stumbled onto a 6-inch fieldpiece, its muzzle trained on Okimura Bay, and picked our way around the edge of the pit in which it squatted, looking for an easy way to get down for closer inspection. On this occasion the saint who looks after sailors and fools was with us, for we tramped directly over a thin shelf of earth and rotten boards concealing a vertical shaft. It miraculously held us, and only after jumping safely into the pit did either of us realize the danger. At any rate, the practice of never traveling singly on these expeditions was vindicated.

The shaft was about forty feet deep, with a crazy jumble of planks and spikes—the remains of ladder once descending to chambers below. Camouflage around the gun would have been superb, there being no need for even the lightest foot traffic in the vicinity.

About a quarter of a mile away we found several tunnel openings in a dark gully, some water reservoirs, an electric generator, and an underground kitchen. We could penetrate only a short distance into any of these tunnels because we lacked flashlights and because of the danger of cave-ins. Rather than struggle back through the cane thickets, we tried a more direct route and came eventually to a bluff down which we bumped and scrambled to the water. The boat appeared in due time, and we waded out through waist-deep water and climbed aboard.

The Okimura landing party had already been retrieved. They had found the ruins of a town that according to intelligence had once had 1,486 inhabitants, with a branch administration office, a post office, a court, a telephone office, a restaurant, a radio station, elementary and high schools, a sugar mill, two Buddhist temples, a Shinto mission and shrine, and some shabby hotels. On a subsequent visit I inspected the place myself and unearthed a few grubby treasures deep in a hidden tunnel—seeds, insect spray, fertilizer, chinaware, and other items awaiting the return of some forgotten nurseryman. We never found the entrance to the vehicular tunnel that was supposed to run the length of the island, and I doubt very much if it ever existed.

Haha Jima was a ghostly place to visit, as if still haunted by the thousands who thronged there so recently. It was silent, with a stillness that jarred with its fertility and beauty. And I sensed danger in its heart.

Party number three, the last to be recovered, had been accompanied by William Waugh, a journalist with the Associated Press, for whom we were providing transportation from Chichi to Guam. That party found little at Kofuji Ya or anywhere else at their end of the island, so that by the time we steamed away, I was willing to swear that there was no human being on Haha Jima.

ISLES OF SULPHUR: THE VOLCANOES

The following morning, 8 February, we reached the three Volcano Islands. Situated in a north-south row about eighty miles south of the Bonins, the

Volcanoes consist of Kita Iwo Jima ("North Rock Island"), Iwo Jima ("Rock Island"), and Minami Iwo Jima ("South Rock Island"). We circled tiny Kita at five hundred yards and put a landing party ashore. Izeno Village there had previously been reported as nonexistent, but Bland found it anyway, well concealed in shrubbery. No sign of recent habitation.

Iwo Jima was under the control of the air force and accordingly stood in no need of surveillance, so we pushed on south to Minami Iwo Jima, which, like Kita, is almost as high as it is wide and presents from a distance the appearance of an inverted strawberry. That day an undersea volcano nearby sent up a turmoil of turquoise-colored water, and the seascape for miles around was littered with sulphur flowers. I couldn't help wondering if the volcano might decide to break the surface at any minute, stranding us on a pile of cinders.

The landing party at Minami found traces of a latter-day Robinson Crusoe: assorted ammunition, a towel, a pair of marine fatigue trousers, some signal flares, about twenty-five pounds of rice, some 32mm film, and several cases of C rations. These supplies did not appear to have been in recent use, nor was I ever able to learn the identity of the person who left them there. Maybe someone reading this will know the story.

The Volcano Islands were known long before the existence of the Bonins was established. History relates that the Spanish explorer Ruy Lopez de Villalobos, tarrying in the Philippines in the summer and autumn of the year 1543, sent one of the smaller ships of his squadron to reconnoiter to the northward.[1] This craft, the *San Juan de Letran*, had a crew of eighteen or twenty men on board, commanded by Bernardo de la Torre. To them goes the questionable distinction of having discovered the Volcanoes. They went on to sight "a large, uninhabited island to the northwest" that could have been Haha Jima. They did not land, however, but returned to Manila claiming they had run out of water.

For many years Spain kept its knowledge of the Pacific locked up, and it was not until 1743, two full centuries after Bernardo de la Torre's jaunt to the Volcanoes, that George Anson captured a Spanish chart showing these and other islands previously unknown to the outside world.[2] The resulting publicity sparked general interest in exploring and acquiring title to the remote lands shown on the chart.

The Volcano Islands were sighted again by the Dutch explorers Quast and Tasman in 1639, the Englishmen King and Gore in 1779, and the Russian Krusentern in 1805. John Gore wrote:

On the fifteenth we saw three small islands and bore away from the south point of the largest [Iwo Jima], upon which we observed a high barren hill [Mount Suribachi], flattish at the top, and which when seen from the southwest, presents an evident volcanic crater. The earth, rock, or sand, for it was not easy to distinguish of what its surface is composed, we conjectured to be sulphur, both from its appearance to the eye, and the strong sulphurous smell which we perceived as we approached the point. Some of the officers on board the *Resolution,* which passed near the land, thought they saw smoke rising from the top of the hill. From these circumstances we gave it the name of Sulphur Island.[3]

The islands were neither landed upon nor explored until 1837, when the mayor of Tokyo with a party of dignitaries descended on it in the steamship *Meiji Maru.* Shortly thereafter the Japanese declared them part of their empire and assigned them, like the Bonins, to the Ogasawara Prefecture. A few permanent settlers came to Iwo in 1897, and in 1902 more were brought in to grow cotton. In 1910 they switched to sugar and hogs. After the collapse of the sugar market they switched again, to copra, meanwhile operating a small sulphur mine on Kita. However, there was no effort to make use of Minami, and it has never been known to have an inhabitant save for the mysterious man whose supplies and ammunition our landing party found.

PHOTO OPPORTUNITIES: MAUG

During the night we slanted across to the northern end of the Marianas chain, and next morning, 9 February, we raised the volcanic island known as Farallon de Pajaros. On our way north sixteen days earlier we had seen it on the horizon, erupting violently. Now we could examine it at close range.

As we approached, a continual stream of smoke and vapor trailed from the island's summit, dissolving slowly and sometime coagulating into clouds, while every two or three minutes a black column of heavier material would shoot up toward the zenith like a gigantic piston shedding cinders, boulders, and molten lava. While the amateur photographers among the crew recorded the scene, I made some sextant measurements of the island and found that it had grown considerably since the last official figure given in *Sailing Directions.*[4]

Next we turned south toward Maug, another island which we had missed on the trek north, and reached it about midmorning. Actually, Maug is three islands, each being part of the rim of a drowned volcano. A ship can easily enter the "lagoon" thus formed but will find it almost impossible to anchor because of the depth of water—or so I thought at the time. So we lay to while the landing party went ashore.

At the summit of the eastern island of the three, the ruin of a large concrete building looks out over the ocean, I directed the landing party to examine this installation, which had not been checked for almost a year. Unfortunately they got stuck about a third of the way up the mountainside, having missed the old Japanese route of ascent. The lava rock of which the island is composed was treacherous, and as the party ascended, handholds and footholds crumbled beneath their weight and tumbled down hill. Able to go neither up nor down, they were finally forced to halt. They had nothing to hang on to, not even grass.

Thanks to handie-talkie radio I soon learned their predicament. In fact they could be seen clearly through binoculars, huddled on a ledge about three hundred feet up. They asked for two men and two hundred feet of line, so I sent four men and four hundred feet, with a line-throwing gun to boot. At the last minute, Bland came up and said, "Captain, are you going to send an officer along with landing party number two?"

"OK, go along, Dick," I said, knowing how he liked to take part in anything spectacular.

The second party landed and, finding the Japanese route of ascent marked by white stones every fifty feet or so, quickly reached the top. Bland and Savage (who was also in on the rescue) looked like monkeys on an ashheap. They were unable to bridge the gap between them and the stranded party, so they had to return to the base of the mountain. Savage couldn't be bothered to come down the same way he went up and instead rappelled over the face of the cliff, then found he couldn't retrieve his line—a loss for which I scolded him roundly afterward. (Any taxpayer's heart will be gladdened to know that on a later visit I made him retrieve it.)

Party number two then tried a new, more direct route. Really worried as hell, I dissembled. Bill Waugh must have thought us an offhand lot because while the rescue attempt was going on ashore, our motor whaleboat sashayed back and forth trolling for fish, many of the crew sunbathed, and I occupied myself popping away at tin cans and frigate birds with a .45 caliber pistol.

In due course party number two got a line to party number one and both returned to the ship. The officer in charge of the first party, Lieutenant (jg) Lee, was considerably lacerated in soul and body but cheerfully assumed his upcoming watch, and as we bade a not-too-reluctant farewell to the scene of his tribulations and headed south again, he remarked, "And remember: Maug, backwards, spells Guam!"

THROUGH OTHER EYES

It will be recalled that during the SAR incident we had discovered, by fathometer, an undersea mountain that we dubbed "Mount Keim." Soon after leaving Maug we relocated it and spent a couple of hours surveying its invisible shape beneath us. It proved to be roughly three miles in diameter at 600 fathoms, with a sheer 1,200-foot precipice on its southwest side. The monster stretched up from the ocean floor a full two miles, and we wondered if it would eventually push the remaining 350 feet to the surface.

The vagaries of volcanoes lend an air of constant surprise to this area. Many volcanic islands are quite young, as time is reckoned by geologists, and we have in our day seen them appear and disappear in various parts of the world. Farallon de Pajaros is one whose character has completely changed since Magellan's time, yet no particular notice of the change has been made.

I believe the same has happened in the case of Asuncion Island, the place which so depressed me when I first saw its black, cloud-wreathed shape in December. This belief is confirmed by La Pérouse and Hawkes. Their separate reactions to this same island differ widely because, I think, the island actually *was* different when each looked at it. La Pérouse records:

> On the 14th of December [1786], at two o'clock in the afternoon, we made [the Mariana Islands]. I had directed my course with an intention of passing between Mira Island and Desert and Garden Islands; but their idle names occupy spaces on the charts where no land ever was, and thus deceive navigators, who will one day or other, perhaps, meet them several degrees to the northward or southward. This Assumption Island, which forms part of a group of islands, so known, upon which we have a history in several volumes, is laid down on the Jesuits' chart, copied by all the geographers, 30' too far to the northward: its true position is on 19° 45' north latitude, and 143° 15' east longitude. . . .[5]
>
> The Jesuits have been unfortunate in their judgement as to the size of Assumption: for it is probable that they had no other means of ascertaining but by their reckoning. They attribute six leagues in circumference

to it: but from the angles we took it reduced one half, and the highest point is about two hundred toises [1,269 feet] above the level of the sea.[6] It would be difficult for the most lively imagination to conceive a more horrible place. The commonest view, after so long a run, would have seemed delightful to us: but a perfect cone, the surface of which, to forty toises [256 feet] above the level of the sea, was as black as coal, while it deceived our hopes, could not but afflict our sight, for during several weeks we had feasted our imagination with cocoanuts and turtles, which we flattered ourselves with finding in the Marianne Islands.

We perceived, indeed, some cocoanut trees, which scarcely occupied one fifteenth of the circumference of the island, in a hollow of forty toises, and which were thus sheltered in some measure from the east wind; this in the only place where it is possible for ships to come to an anchor, in a bottom of thirty fathoms, black sand, which extends at least a quarter of a league. This anchorage had been gained by the *Astrolabe*;[7] I had also let go within an anchor shot of that frigate; but having dragged it half a cable's length, we lost all bottom, and were obliged to weigh it with a hundred fathoms of cable out; and to make two tacks in order to reach the land. This trifling misfortune but little afflicted me, because I saw that the island did not deserve a long stay. My boat went ashore, under the command of M. Boutin, lieutenant of the ship, as did that of the *Astrolabe*, in which M. de Langle himself embarked, with Messrs. de la Martinière, Vaujuas, Prévost, and father Receveur.[8] I observed, by the help of my perspective glass, that they found it very difficult to get on shore: the sea broke all around, and they had to take advantage of a smoother interval, and jumped into the sea up to their necks. I was much afraid that the reembarking might prove still more difficult, the billows appearing to increase every moment: this was from that time the only event that could induce me to come to an anchor, for we were all as eager to leave it as we had been ardent in our wishes to arrive at it. Fortunately at two o'clock our boats returned, and the *Astrolabe* got under way. M. Boutin informed me that the island was a thousand times more horrible than it appeared at a distance of a quarter of a league; torrents of lava formed ravines and precipices, bordered by some stunted cocoa trees, very thinly sown, with a few matted creeping plants, through which it was almost impossible to walk a hundred toises in an hour. . . . The lava which flows from the crater overspreads the whole side of the cone, to within forty toises of the sea; the summit seems in some measure to be vitrified, consisting of a dark, soot-colored glass; we did not once get sight of the summit, as it was always capped by a cloud; but though we had not seen it smoke, the smell of sulphur which it emitted to the distance of half a league at sea gave me reason to think it was not quite extinct, and that it was probable that the last eruption of it was at no great distance of time: for there did not appear to be any decomposition of the lava in the middle of the mountain.

Everything announced that neither human creature nor quadruped had ever been so unfortunate as to have only this place for asylum, upon which we perceived nothing but large crabs, which might be very dangerous in the night, if they found any person asleep. . . . M. de Langle killed a bird, that was very black, very much resembling a blackbird, which did not however increase our collection, because it fell down a precipice. . . . M. Boutin, who was obliged to throw himself in the sea, in order to debark and get on board again, had received several wounds in his hands, which he had been obliged to lean upon the sharp-edged rocks with which the island is bordered. M. de Langle had also run several risks, but these are inseparable from all landings on such small islands, and especially of so round a form as this, the sea, coming from windward, glides along the coast, and makes a surf on all points, which renders the landing very dangerous.[9]

How ardently I sympathized with the determined Frenchmen, having nursed my own cut hands and bruised feet from similar landings on rocky shores!

Sixty-eight years later, one of the ships of Perry's squadron paused at Asuncion and found it considerably changed, with vegetation nearly to its summit and palm trees skirting its base. The volcano appeared to have become extinct.

An interesting item in the short and simple annals of Asuncion is found in Burney's *A Chronological History of the Voyages and Discoveries in the South Seas or Pacific Ocean.* Referring to the early missionaries, Burney relates how a certain Padre Morales in 1669 was favorably received at Asuncion and Maug, "many of the inhabitants of which two islands he baptized."[10] Morales may have exaggerated somewhat, because the two islands together could not have subsisted more than a few dozen inhabitants. Burney, of course, would not know this: he wrote in 1812, long before the Marianas had been properly surveyed, and although he participated in the second and third voyages of Capt. James Cook, he never laid eyes on either of these islands.

Padre Morales escaped the fate of his colleague Padre Luis de Medina, S.J., who was killed on Saipan 29 January 1670, the first Spanish cleric to lose his life in the futile uprising of that year.[11] To understand what happened it is necessary to touch on the story of Spain's expansion into the Pacific.

7

White Men and Black Deeds

The Marianas, among the first islands of Oceania to be known to the white race, were discovered by Ferdinand Magellan on 6 March 1521 after he sailed westward from the tip of South America, a voyage rivaling in duration and hardship that made by any explorer in human history. With three ships—the *Trinidad* (110 tons), *Concepción* (90 tons), and *Santiago* (75 tons)—he took departure from Patagonia on 28 November 1520 seeking a westward route to the Orient. He set a northwesterly course and sailed for ninety-seven days without seeing land of any kind except two barren islands. His crew were reduced to such straits that they ate all the old leather they could salvage; nineteen men died and about thirty were so weak they could do no work. But Magellan held course and passed through the heart of Micronesia without seeing any one of those islands where he could have found refreshment.

At last in twelve degrees of north latitude Magellan sighted the Marianas. Near Guam, the natives swarmed on board the ships and started carrying off everything movable—not exactly the kind of reception the mariners had hoped for. Most outrageously, they stole Magellan's own skiff from under the stern of his flagship. This so irritated the captain-general that he went ashore with a party of forty armed men and killed seven natives, burned a village, and destroyed several canoes. The skiff was recovered.

Thus the men who first set foot in the Marianas did so in anger. It was not a good beginning. Finding no good to be done there, Magellan sailed away to the west, labeling the place which had been such a disappointment *Las Islas de los Ladrones* ("Islands of the Thieves").

The best account of the voyage was written by one Antonio Pigafetta, an Italian gentleman who happened to be in Seville when the expedition was being prepared and who decided to go and see with his own eyes the wonders of the new world. Concerning the inhabitants of Guam he wrote:

> Those people live in freedom and as they will, for they have no lord nor superior, and they go quite naked and some of them wear a beard. They have long hair down to their waist. . . . Those people are as tall as we, and well built. They worship nothing. And when they are born they are white, then they become tawny. . . . [The women] are handsome and delicate, and whiter than the men. . . . The pastime of the men and women of that country, and their sport, is to go in their boats to catch flying fish with hooks made of fishbones. . . . And there is no difference between the stern and the bow in the said boats, which are like dolphins jumping from wave to wave.[1]

Magellan met death in the Philippines soon after, but one of his captains, Sebastian del Cano, completed the circumnavigation and two years later set out on a second such expedition. He died en route, but his ships reached the Marianas on 4 September 1526, after a voyage that rivaled the hardships of the first. Three years later Alvara de Saavedra—another of the doughty navigators that Spain and Portugal turned out in quantity in those days— landed on Guam itself and took possession in the name of Charles V.

For two generations the Marianas were left alone, until Miguel de Lopez de Legaspi brought several ships from Mexico with orders to conquer the Philippines and the Ladrones as well. He landed on Guam 25 January 1565 and made the standard proclamation to the uncomprehending natives. The name assigned by Magellan did not seem appropriate, so he renamed the group *Las Iljas de las Velas Latinas* ("Islands of the Lateen Sails"), in recognition of the speed and grace of the native canoes. The Spanish changed the official name to Marianas in 1668. However, derogatory names have a way of sticking, and until quite recently the islands continued to be called the Ladrones.

After Legaspi proclaimed possession of the Philippines, he sent his flagship, the 500-ton *San Pedro,* under command of Felipe de Salcedo, back to Mexico to report his success. The *San Pedro's* pilot was Rodrigo de Espinosa, and the chief pilot of the expedition, Esteban Rodriguez, was also on board, but a third pilot, Fray Andres de Urdaneta, was really in charge. Legaspi ordered them to sail east, rather than by way of the Indies and the Cape of Good Hope.[2]

Urdaneta sailed north in an effort to get out of the trade winds, which were as much of an obstacle going east as they had been helpful in going west. He finally found favorable winds in latitude 40° north and continued along that parallel until reaching the coast of North America, a very long voyage, filled with trial and error. He reached Acapulco only to learn that another of Legaspi's ships, the *San Lucas,* under Alonzo de Arellano had beaten him back to Acapulco by three months. Arellano had hastened on to Spain to claim a reward, reporting that Legaspi and the other ships had been lost.[3] The good Urdaneta followed, demolished the story, and was duly recognized as the discoverer of the eastern route. Nevertheless, Arellano stands as the first navigator to sail from the Orient to North America.

Urdaneta kept an accurate journal and made many scientific observations leading to establishment of a practical system for two-way traffic between the Philippines and American segments of Spain's dominions, a traffic which was to flourish for over two hundred years. Enormous, slow, and ungainly, the Manila galleons were built for endurance and payload. They sailed with crews of as many as four hundred men and could carry up to fifteen hundred passengers and great quantities of cargo. Their hulls of thick Philippine hardwood were stout enough to weather any gale and even to turn a cannon ball. As a precaution against boarders (for the stings of buccaneers like Francis Drake and Thomas Cavendish were being felt as early as 1578) the galleons carried well-trained companies of marines.

By 1600 the galleon system was in full swing, with Guam an important way station on the route westward. However, no effort was made to establish a permanent colony there for another sixty-eight years. In that time there were a few settlers, including several survivors from the crew of the *Concepción,* wrecked at Aguijan Beach, Saipan, in 1638, and a Chinese man named Choco cast ashore by the waves ten years later.[4]

THE PADRES

The impetus to found a colony in the Marianas came not from military or trade motives but from the religious zeal of one man: Padre Diego Luis de

San Vitores, a passenger on board a patache (a kind of fleet tender about the size of a modern tuna boat) named the *San Damián,* which paused there in June 1662. He was so horrified by the nakedness of the "indios" that on reaching Manila he clamored for their conversion and the founding of a mission for the purpose. He made such a nuisance of himself that he was told to discuss it no further.

Meanwhile San Vitores wrote a memorial to Philip IV, as well as a letter to the queen regent's confessor, and prevailed upon his own father, then a member of the Treasury Council, to intervene—a move that resulted in a royal *cédula* dated 24 June 1665 approving the project and relieving the governor of the Philippines and other officials who had opposed it. San Vitores then recruited two survivors of the *Concepción* as interpreters and returned to Guam in 1668 with a contingent of clerics and soldiers, bent on converting the entire Chamorro population.

Pigafetta's original observation that the natives acknowledged no superior and adored nothing was wide of the mark. After all, Magellan's men were too busy burning and killing to collect much information about local culture. As a matter of fact, there existed in the Marianas an elaborate society, with an aristocracy as sharply defined as any to be found in Europe.[5] For example, any ruling-class Chamorro who had sexual relations with a commoner was usually punished by death. Local customs and traditions were based on complicated taboos, the same as persist today in some of the Caroline Islands. Flouting these taboos was unheard-of until the missionaries came along.

At first the ruling classes took to Christianity with enthusiasm, as an interesting addition to their own demonology. But they were offended when San Vitores insisted on initiating prince and pauper alike in its mysteries, and he soon lost their support. He further alienated them with his preachings of equality, his insistence on the wearing of clothes, and his way of baptizing children without their parents' consent. As for the average convert, the excitement of building a mission quickly palled, and those who had foolishly volunteered now found themselves forced to continue the drudgery. Then too, the brutality of the soldiers earned for all Spaniards a brimming cup of hate and fear. The break came in 1670, when Padres San Vitores and Luís de Medina ventured to interfere in factional strife on Saipan and Tinian, an effort that resulted in the death of Medina.[6] Soon a full-fledged rebellion was rolling toward Guam.

Perhaps if San Vitores had abated his zeal even temporarily and had come to an understanding with the chiefs then and there, the debacle would have been averted. After all, the Chamorros were a friendly lot, understandably averse to having their lives made over by strangers. But the missionary was inflexible. Finally Matapang, the one chief who had consistently supported him, bowed to the will of the majority and consented to San Vitores's assassination. This was the crest of the rebellion, and the year 1672 found the few surviving whites huddled in the mission stockade, afraid to go forth even in daytime. Thus matters stood when a relief ship jammed with soldiers arrived from Manila.

Restoration of order on Guam came first; the northern islands could wait. The new governor, Don Damien de Esplana, set out to prove the superiority of Spanish muskets over native lances and succeeded with a thoroughness amounting to massacre. Esplana died a natural death on 6 August 1694 and was succeeded by one Don José Quiroga, who had come out of retirement in the Spanish army. Quiroga combined within himself a degree of religious fanaticism and ruthlessness that is ideal in one with such an assignment.[7] Wherever he went, those who refused to surrender died, and those who did surrender were remanded to the priests. It was a very efficient operation.

Many years later Charles Le Gobien, S.J., wrote his *History of the Marianas, Newly Converted to Christianity, and of the Glorious Death of the First Missionaries Who There Preached the Faith,* in which he rejoiced over the step-by-step subjugation of the Chamorros. Later still, the English historian James Burney used the account as basis for a seething indictment that would have dismayed poor Le Gobien.[8]

Esplana had wiped out resistance on Guam itself; Quiroga turned his attention to the other islands of the archipelago. Rota, being nearest and most susceptible to influence from Guam, capitulated in October without a struggle, and Padre Basilio Roulso celebrated by baptizing a hundred and fifty of its children.

The following July, Quiroga left for Saipan with a frigate and a flotilla of twenty canoes. There the natives tried to prevent his landing but fled when fired upon by muskets and cannon. With the beach under control, Quiroga disembarked the rest of his force, penetrated the interior, and captured all the inhabitants. Next the little armada sailed to nearby Tinian, where they found only a few old people, the others having withdrawn to Aguijan for a last stand.

A nineteenth-century historian, Luís de Ibáñez y García, describes Quiroga's assault on Aguijan:

Street scene, Guam (1819). Engraved from a drawing by Jacques Arago, artist with the expedition of Louis Claude Desaulses de Freycinet in the corvettes *Uranie* and *Physicienne,* 1817–20.

In this island, which is three miles long by two miles wide, there are only two entrances, both very difficult, up two narrow defiles which the natives were determined to defend to the death. Governor Quiroga could not induce them by threats or cajolery to submit, so he resolved to attack it in force, even though the undertaking was a frightful one. He divided his troops in two groups covering both defiles. Nicolas Rodriguez attacked the western one with great heroism, but the natives threw down so many rocks from above that it was necessary to withdraw to avoid being buried alive. Juan Perez Vello could not tolerate such inaction, however, and, together with a Filipino captain Pablo de la Cruz, began to climb over the sharp rocks, disdainful of danger. This example of heroism so encouraged the others that they attacked fearlessly, gaining the enemy entrenchments, and secured the whole area.

So brilliant was the Spanish advance that it amazed the rebels, who quickly surrendered their weapons and asked for quarter.[9]

Quiroga spared them on condition that they all come to Guam, "there to be instructed in the truths and maxims of the Christian religion," as Le Gobien put it.[10] Burney put it another way: "In short, they were carried into abject slavery; and all this was perpetrated under the unrighteous assumption that it advanced the cause of religion."[11]

In the next few years, some of the natives deported to Guam filtered back to their home islands, and in 1698 Quiroga's successor, Don José Madroza, got together a new expedition to recapture them, together with any inhabitants of the northern islands who might have escaped Quiroga's dragnet three years before. It was really just a mopping-up operation, accomplished in due course by Capt. Don Sebastian Ruiz Ramon with a dozen Spanish soldiers and many "Indians."

AGUIJAN

So this was the cliff-girt island we had seen on our way north—an island that defied access, an island comfortably ignored. At least it had been that way until the morning of 18 February 1954, when we boiled on down past Saipan and Tinian and beheld it again, looking—as I'd said before—like a wedding cake on the horizon. I positioned the ship about five hundred yards off the southwest tip of the island and called out the landing party, which this time consisted of Bland, Sheffler, Savage, Baker, Theiss, and me, with Ledford to "cox" the boat. It was Rayner's turn to remain on board in temporary command.

We climbed in the boat and made for the shore, whose deeply carved and hollowed cliffs gave some hope of access. There was just enough surge in and out of the caves to make entry impossible, however, so we coasted around the west end of the island looking for a strip of sand or even a crevice in the rocks wide enough for us to use. The windward side was out of the question; there the booming waves tore at huge rocks where the beaches mentioned by Garcia once had been. The only possible landing place was at a remnant of stairway leading up directly from the water, a place where the Japanese had placed a small breakwater many years ago. The breakwater had been broken up by the sea, and its fragments lay strewn at depth offshore, scarce giving pause to the waves that curled and rushed around the lee of the island.

If the following excerpt of my journal seems confusing, it is because the events it recounts were themselves confused. Everything seemed to happen at once:

The water by the cement steps was too rough for the boat, so we all piled in the rubber raft which trailed astern, with our equipment consisting of a pair of binoculars, a handie-talkie radio, a thermos of drinking water, three .45 caliber pistols, a sheath knife, a battle lantern, a set of signal flags, and a hundred feet of one-inch line. The boat cast us off and we paddled up to the rock.

Savage and Baker hopped ashore on the first pass. Then, as the swell worsened, we got a line to them and Sheffler and the chief made it. Perhaps I should have gone first—it's a nice point of protocol. Anyway, when I tried to scramble onto the rock a swell came up and knocked me and the chief back into deep water three times in a row. The chief regained the rock, then was carried away again, this time coming up under the raft. One moment the raft would be flung violently upon the ledge. The next it would be swept off and wallowing far below the rim. The chief got into the raft (I had tumbled out by now and got my feet tangled in some line), then I got in too and rested a bit. Then we both jumped in the water and made the rock together—this time with diminishing surf and a couple of good helping hands from above. I didn't get a scratch, but the chief's back was rather bloody.

At this point I radioed the ship in the style of the U.S. Marine Corps to the effect that the landing had been accomplished "according to schedule." Later I had the motor-whaleboat pick up the raft, which had got away from us. The only casualty was loss of our thermos and one of my shoes.

We scrambled to the top of the cliff and found ourselves at the site of headquarters of a sugar plantation, with foundations of several buildings, and two derricks which at one time must have been connected by cable to the former breakwater, for transfer of cargo. A narrow-gauge railroad ran off into the bush, and a processing plant stood at the edge of the cliff, where a deep notch provided a chute down which waste could be jettisoned into the ocean. Apparently the entire island had been devoted to sugar. There wasn't a coconut tree in sight, and the only edibles we found were some unripe bananas, papayas, and oranges.

We struck inland, working around to the right in order to reach a road we'd seen from offshore. Baker, who was somewhat in the lead, suddenly yelled "Look at 'im go!" A green creature streaked up the trunk of a banyan tree, and I brought him down with one lucky shot—a giant iguana lizard, apple green all except for pea-sized brown speckles on his back. Long graceful neck. No fangs. He was equipped with inch-long claws to account for his tree-climbing ability. Overall length was about four feet, but I radioed the ship eight to give the crew something to talk about.

We surprised a herd of goats sidling through the brush and stalked them for a time. Later we saw several more; I guess there must have been about a thousand on the island. They were all colors—black, beige, white, and red, and in magnificent condition. Even the females had formidable horns lying well back over the shoulders. The forage being so abundant, I suppose they could increase tenfold without running short of food. Their presence helped, in a way, because we could follow their trails through the densest thickets. Also their bedding-down places of well-crumbled black earth felt good to my shoeless feet.

I didn't see the big black he-goat until Bland shouted "Captain! Look out!" and ran to one side. The beast was about three and a half feet high at the shoulders and six feet long, and his beard swept the ground: a real grand-daddy. He charged and I shot him somewhere up forward, knocking him back on his haunches. As he scrambled up I put two more bullets in him, but he kept coming, crying something like "Angus! Angus!" in a voice of human pain. He swerved away and Sheffler shot him again, but he staggered on and disappeared over the edge of the cliff where we could not follow. His mate appeared, trotted fearlessly through our midst, and joined him somewhere below.

He was a noble fellow.

We found a road and followed it to the top of the island, where more cane fields luxuriated. This was strictly machete country, and since we had neither machetes nor time to linger, we returned to our beach-head. Another time, we might have found the radio station and big guns I am sure were located somewhere near.

Leaving the island was fully as complicated as our landing had been. The affair went thus, as nearly as I can remember:

(1) A boatman brought the raft to the landing, and Chief Theiss embarked. They were swept out by the surf, but not without first having secured a line to the shore.
(2) Bland swam out to the raft and carried the end of another line from the raft to the motor whaleboat.
(3) Sheffler swam out to the raft, using the shore line, and climbed in.
(4) Savage and Baker made up a bundle of equipment with my life-

jacket and tied it to the end of the shore line; they then swam out to the boat by way of the raft.

(5) I jumped in and swam directly to the boat, then pulled the raft alongside. Its occupants then transferred to the boat.

On the way back to the ship we broke the no-smoking rule, reviewed our exploits, and teased Savage with a description of a huge barracuda which someone said had made a pass at his flashing feet during the swim. Rayner ran up a BZ ("well done!") at the halyard, and we dragged ourselves and the dead lizard on board. Baker was anxious that his shipmates see the monster, even though it wasn't quite eight feet long. For me, the high point of the day had been seeing him dive into the ocean with the reptile tethered to his belt. It had followed, legs and tail waving, in what seemed the better dive of the two.

On the way to Guam that evening, after a good dinner and a hot shower, I was sitting in the captain's chair on the bridge when Sheffler came up and confided, "You know, Captain, I haven't had so much fun since I've been in the navy!"

THE AGE OF THE BUCCANEERS

The fate of the Chamorro race was sealed by the capitulation of the last defenders of Aguijan, and the revolt that had flared and flickered for twenty-eight years died out. The slaughter cannot be set at a particular figure. Early estimates of the population range from 44,000 to 100,000— probably much exaggerated.[12] Suffice to say that only 3,678 people were left alive by 1710. Except for a few who escaped to the Carolines, the rest either died of smallpox or were massacred by Esplana, Quiroga, and their like.

Concurrent with the campaign of pacification, the governors of Guam undertook to fortify Agaña, Umatac, and Apra Harbor. Since the dwindling supply of native labor was insufficient for the work, drafts of Filipinos were brought in, and before long, the original Chamorro strain had been eclipsed.

As soon as the forts were completed, Guam sank into lassitude. The Manila galleon came only once a year. And in some years it failed to show up at all—something that often signified a disastrous encounter with buccaneers, who themselves would occasionally appear in the Marianas to alarm and mortify the Spaniards. For a long time these marauders were the outside world's only source of information concerning the far Pacific.

The first of these interlopers was the Englishman Thomas Cavendish in the treasure-laden *Desire,* who paused off Rota in 1588 to barter for fresh fruit and vegetables. A few years later, in 1600, came the Dutch admiral Oliver Van Noort, who left the following day. Then in 1616 came Joris Spilbergen, whose naval successes in the Pacific increased Dutch prestige, and in 1625 the Nassau Fleet under Vice Admiral Schapenham, whose ineptitude lowered it. Schapenham's force, comprising eleven ships with 294 guns in all, was the most formidable to be seen in that part of the world in the entire three-hundred-year span from Magellan to the nineteenth century. Schapenham could have had Guam for the taking but contented himself merely with conducting a review of his fleet, in which the number of men amounted to 1,260, including thirty-two Spanish prisoners and "Indians."

The first of the out-and-out pirates to pose a threat was one John Eaton, of London, in the 26-gun *Nicholas.* Meeting little success off the west coast of South America, he crossed the Pacific to Guam, arriving in March 1685. Governor Esplana, being busy with the rebellion, was hardly in a position to deny anchorage. Eaton decided to act as friend rather than foe and even helped the governor by hacking up a few natives. For this favor he was presented with greens, rice, and some thirty hogs. One of Eaton's crew observed that the natives died hard and that the governor "gave us tolerance to kill them all if we would."[13] Refreshed, the *Nicholas* sailed off for Macao.

Later that year another buccaneer came along: Edward Swan, in a ship he had named the *Cygnet.*[14] On board was William Dampier, who afterwards published a detailed account of the voyage. While they were at Guam, wrote Dampier,

> The Acapulco Ship arrived in sight of the Island, but did not come in sight of us; for the Governor sent an Indian Proe, with advice of our being here. Therefore she stood off to the Southward of the Island, and coming foul of the same Shole that our Bark had run over before, was in great danger of being lost there, for she struck off her Rudder and with much ado got clear; but not till after three days labour . . . which put our Men in a great heat to go out after her, but Captain Swan persuaded them out of that humour, for he was now wholly averse to any Hostile action.[15]

Dampier estimated fewer than a hundred "Indians" on the island.

Back home, Dampier's *Voyage round the Terrestrial Globe* made a great impression, so that a few years later we find him in command of an expedition of his own: two ships, the *Saint George* and the *Cinque Ports Galley,* fitted out as privateers by some merchants of Bristol. The *Saint George,* with Dampier in command, mounted twenty-six guns and carried a crew of 120. The *Cinque Ports Galley,* a smaller vessel with sixteen guns and a crew of sixty-three, was commanded by Charles Pickering. They sailed for the Spanish Main on 11 September 1703. Dampier soon showed that he had little talent for leadership. His officers were constantly quarreling among themselves and with him. Pickering died while the ships were still in the Atlantic, and his first lieutenant, Thomas Stradling, became skipper. After rounding the Horn in January, things got so bad that Dampier detached the *Cinque Ports Galley* to fend for itself.

He fared better with the *Saint George,* for a time, at least, and even captured a few prizes. However, his chief mate, John Clipperton, absconded with the best of them, taking with him twenty-two men and allegedly Dampier's own commission document. William Funnel became chief mate. Things got worse, and after a failed attempt to take the Acapulco galleon in December, thirty-five men of the remaining crew elected to go with Funnell in a captured bark, while twenty-eight men remained with Dampier in the rotten old *Saint George.*

Funnell set out for the Orient in February and sixty-six days later, on 11 April 1705, reached "Magon" (Rota). Trading with the natives, he described them as "tall and large-limbed, of tawny complexions, with long black hair reaching to their middles, and all were utterly stark naked." "On mature deliberation," Funnell further recorded, "we resolved to proceed directly from this place to New Guinea, without putting in at the island of Guam, which was in sight."[16] But in the Moluccas Funnell's frail bark and feeble crew were seized by the Dutch. After enduring more than a year of confinement and abuse, eighteen of the original thirty-five adventurers made it home to England.

Dampier and his crew of twenty-eight men abandoned the *Saint George* and likewise headed west in another prize. On reaching the Moluccas they met the same kind of treatment as Funnell and his people and likewise returned to England penniless.

The Bristol merchants lost their entire investment in the *Saint George* and *Cinque Ports Galley* venture. Nevertheless three years later they sponsored two new ships, the *Duke* and the *Duchess,* and obtained a commission from the lord high admiral to war against the French and the Spanish. This expedition proved somewhat more successful—possibly because Dampier was engaged as pilot rather than commanding officer. The *Duke* (320 tons, 30 guns, 117 men) was captained by Woodes Rogers, the *Duchess* (260 tons, 26 guns, 108 men) by Stephen Courtney.[17] Rogers and Courtney sailed from England on 11 September 1703 and made their way to the west coast of Mexico, pausing at Juan Fernandez to pick up Alexander Selkirk (the prototype Robinson Crusoe).

They soon captured two fine galleons—one of which, the *Nuestra Señora de la Encarnaçion* (400 tons), they rechristened the *Batchelor.* But a third galleon, the *Begonia* (700 tons, 40 guns, 400 men) proved too tough for their 6-pound shot. By the end of thirteen months Rogers and Courtney had seized twenty ships, yielding as much plunder as their own four ships could carry. They were shorthanded, and it was time to head home. So on 10 January 1710, they set out westward from Mexico.

The expedition reached Guam on 10 March 1710 and anchored under Spanish colors at Umatac. The governor was not very happy with his visitors but managed to retain his composure till they revealed their intentions. Since Rogers's and Courtney's need for provisions outweighed any temptation they might have had to plunder, an amicable exchange was concluded whereby all parties were satisfied. After eleven days' dalliance, the four ships left for the Moluccas and reached home a year and four months later, intact and richly laden. Rogers wrote up his adventures, a standard practice for freebooters, and published them under the title of *A Cruising Voyage round the World.*

John Clipperton came that way again in 1721 in the 36-gun *Success,* which had originally sailed from Plymouth in 1718 in company with the 24-gun *Speedwell* under one George Shelvocke. Although the two were bent on similar missions and met frequently during the ensuing months, they never exchanged a friendly greeting.

Off the coast of Mexico, Clipperton captured the Spanish ship *Prince Eugene,* taking prisoner the Marquis de la Villa Roche, former president of Panama, who he hoped would bring a splendid ransom when they reached Guam. However, the governor of Guam temporized, and Clipperton realized there was no chance of succeeding without a show of force, so he decided to seize a Spanish ship moored close inshore in Apra Harbor. He weighed anchor in order to run alongside the intended victim, but—drunk as usual—he ran aground instead and lay for several hours under the fire of Spanish batteries at Fort San Luis. One of his officers and several men were killed in this affair. As soon as Clipperton could get clear, he gave up in disgust and sailed for China. Although he appears not to

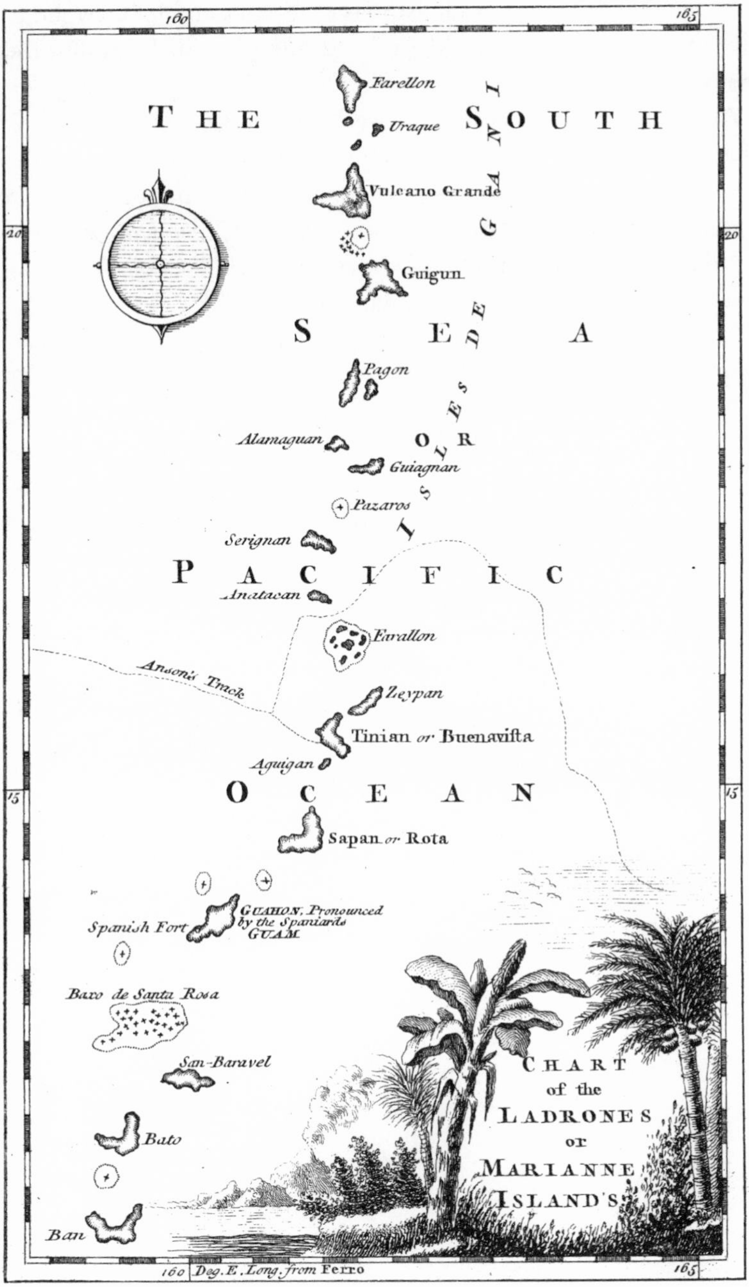
160
165
THE SOUTH
SEA
PACIFIC
OCEAN
ISLES DE GANI
OR
Farellon
Uraque
Vulcano Grande
Guigun
Pagon
Alamaguan
Guiagnan
Pazaros
Serignan
Anatacan
Farallon
Anson's Track
Zeypan
Tinian or Buenavista
Aguigan
Sapan or Rota
GUAHON, Pronounced by the Spaniards GUAM
Spanish Fort
Baxo de Santa Rosa
San-Baravel
Bato
Ban
20
15
CHART of the LADRONES or MARIANNE ISLAND'S
160 Deg. E. Long. from Ferro
165

Chart of the Mariana Islands showing Anson's track in the *Centurion* in 1742 (from the *London Magazine,* 1748).

have gained a peso from his illustrious captive, he and his crew did get a nice price for the *Success* at Macao, which they divided amongst themselves before dispersing.

As for Shelvocke, his adventures were marred by poor discipline, rotten luck, and excessive sickness among his crew, which he attributed to the quantities of sweetmeats they were continually eating. In August 1721, from a position off the California coast, he set sail for China in a 300-ton prize called the *Sacra Familia* (the *Speedwell* having been wrecked the year before). When still eighty leagues from Guam, he had only six men fit for duty, and rather than risk capture he sailed between Guam and Rota without stopping and eventually reached Canton.[18]

In 1739 the Englishman George Anson, commanding six ships sent out during the war between Spain and England, bypassed Guam in favor of Tinian, which was uninhabited save for a herd of wild cattle.[19] Noting the fertility of the island and bearing in mind the value of a replenishment station in the area, he is said to have left off several Hawaiians to cultivate gardens and husband the livestock. The benefits of his foresight were later reaped by his countrymen John Byron (1765) and Samuel Wallis (1768). The Spaniards on Guam at length became suspicious, sent an expedition to Tinian, indignantly rounded up the settlers and hustled them off the island.[20]

Although privateering flourished in the Pacific for many years, Guam was left in comparative peace until the Spanish-American War, possibly in the belief that its defenses were too stout to justify direct assault.

Sketches from the Author's South Seas journal

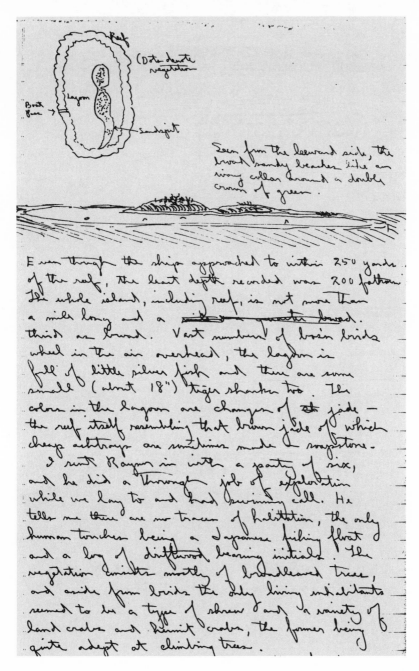

Reef

(Dense vegetation)

Lagoon

Boat Pass →

Sand spit

Seen from the leeward side, the broad sandy beaches like an ivory collar around a double crown of green.

Even though the ship approached to within 250 yards of the reef, the least depth recorded was 200 fathom. The whole island, including reef, is not more than a mile long and a ~~little~~ ~~quarter~~ third as broad. Vast numbers of basin birds wheel in the air overhead, the lagoon is full of little silver fish and there are some small (about 18") tiger sharks too. The colour in the lagoon are changes of jade — the reef itself resembling that brown jade of which cheap ashtrays are sometimes made & soapstone.

I sent Raynor in with a party of six, and he did a thorough job of exploration while we lay to and had swimming call. He tells me there are no traces of habitation, the only human touches being a Japanese fishing float and a log of driftwood bearing initials. The vegetation consists mostly of broadleaved trees, and aside from birds the only living inhabitants seemed to be a type of shrew and a variety of land crabs and hermit crabs, the former being quite adept at climbing trees.

Arrived off NAMA about 1030 and went ashore
with the landing party. NAMA and LOSAP nearby
are unique in being almost uncharted. My impression
of the former is about as follows

Sand & broken coral beach & reefs

Heavy vegetation, mostly coconut
breadfruit, pandanus, &
"hang" Trees. Some
banana & papaya

Narrow
reef

Practically no lagoon

ship

canal passage

Shoreward, where the landing was made,
we saw what may be one of the most
fantastic rock formations in the world

The pinnacle at the right is 456 feet high,
the pierced rock about 300 feet. Deep water

as close an inspection as possible in view of
our reduced time available. This permitted
us one pass one way only, and because of
the prevailing wind and sea I chose
the relatively sheltered route indicated:

The coasts of
these islands are
generally very
craggy, often
cut, and in
many places
the rocks
are cut
through
with
monumental
arches and
caverns.
The south —
west slopes
of

the
main
island,
and portions
facing HIGASHI
MINATO are beautiful
once farmed intensively, with
terraces and lines of

YAP FALU
(PHALLU?)

Backwater →

...foliage keeping up a loud, fairly musical...

Practically all the women of this small village gathered at the "dispensary", and the CHM had a busy session with stethoscope and aspirin. Though some complained of chest pains, he said they were all sound as a drum (although their shape belied the simile.) They were all casually dressed, i.e., grass skirts period. On this island a man's wealth is gauged by the girth of his mate, and there are no poor men in NGULU. Most breasts were staggering in their immensity. Seated, a NGULU woman is pyramidal, and looks as if she could never get up. One such proved to be 14 years old!

Next to the dispensary is the house of the number two chief, whom I had entertained during our

23 February

Enroute SOROR ATOLL on course 072°T opgc,
068° psc, speed 15 knots.

24 February

Arrived Sorok at 1200 I and sent landing
party ashore at 1230. Unfortunately the break in
the reef has a least depth of 1 fathom, so
that it was out of the question for us to
take the HANNA in. A little judicious
blasting would of course
open this gem of a
lagoon up for
ships of
this
size.

Rayon officiated
today, and on return said it was the
cleanest, most unspoiled island so far. Only
Soron I is inhabited, and by only sixteen
people of whom he saw only the men. "They
were round and solid," he said, "looking
enormous in the distance but in reality just
5×5, and hard. I happened to touch one
of them on the arm and it was like rock."
The Japanese had a seaplane base here at

The cliffs rise   to a height
of about 75 feet,
but does not
present an unbroken
front. At the pier
landing one
walks inland
up a gentle
rise.

This landing
is the only
one usable by boats.
The natives bring
their canoes right up
to the village beach
at high tide, but there
is no break in the reef
there.

The southern end of the island is flat
tableland where the _____ who built the

FAIS

cliff

REFINERY

M.B.
Site ⊕

Cliffs

Stone
Pier →

RR

COPRA

cliff

cliff

Village

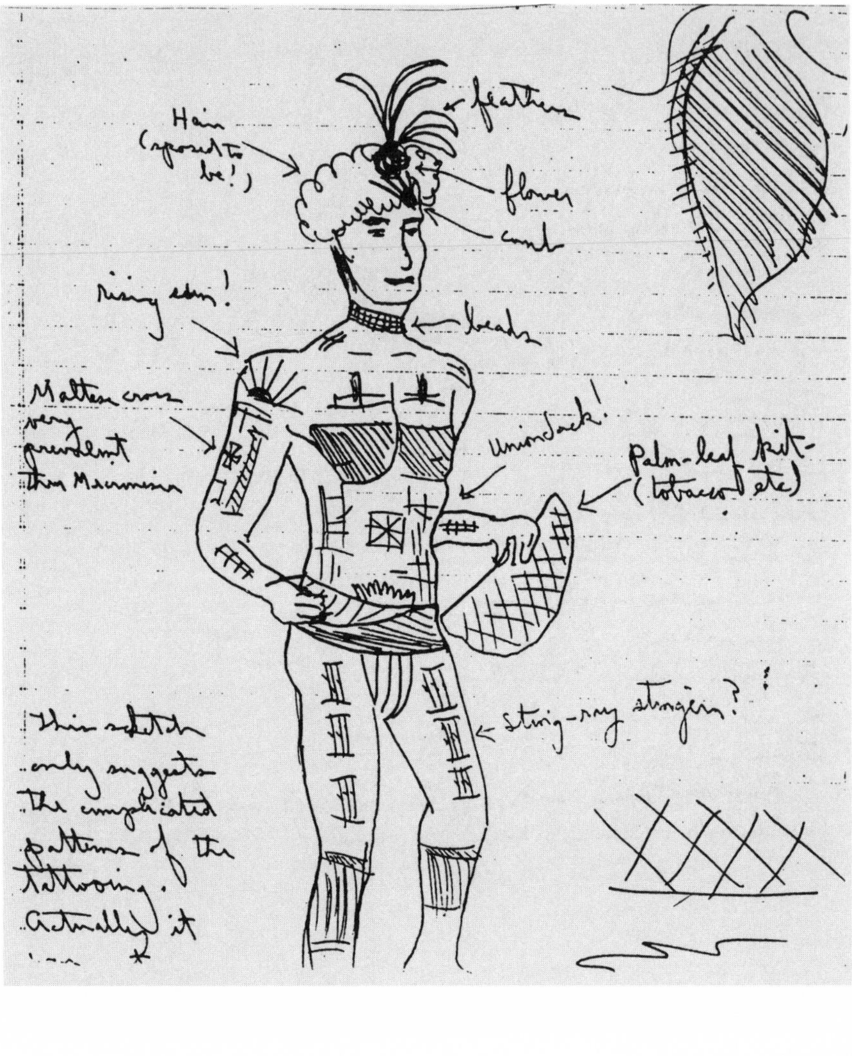

Hair (supposed to be!)
& feathers
flower
comb
rising sun!
beads
Maltese cross very prevalent thru Micronesia
Union Jack!
Palm-leaf kit (tobacco etc)
sting-ray stinger?
This sketch only suggests the complicated patterns of the tattooing. Actually it

8

Haunted Islands

Our mission to the north having been completed, we remained at Guam for a few days to catch up on paperwork and liberty. The *Hanna* had already traveled thousands of miles without covering its entire parish. There remained the western Carolines—an inviting unknown, sprawling south-west of Guam. I arranged with Captain Klinker and Admiral Murphy to make a jaunt through that sector, stopping at Yap, Ngulu, Palau, Merir, Pulo Anna, Sonsorol, Sorol, and Ulithi, in that order. Of these, Yap and Palau would be the most important but not necessarily the most adventuresome.

The western Carolines differ little from those in the east, and in fact there is no gap or dividing line. The people are also Micronesian, although per-haps a shade darker than in the "isles of Ku," and even more scantily clad, down to nothing. Native structures are larger and more elaborate, reaching a kind of phallic splendor on Babelthuap Island in the Palau group. Again we were to sail through ghost-ridden waters, and again the ghost of the Japanese Empire had to be exorcised in order for past or present pleasures to be validated.

My first questions in any new place were what did the Japanese have here, what was their strategy, and in what measure did it succeed? The opportunity for studying firsthand our recent enemy's tactical arrangements

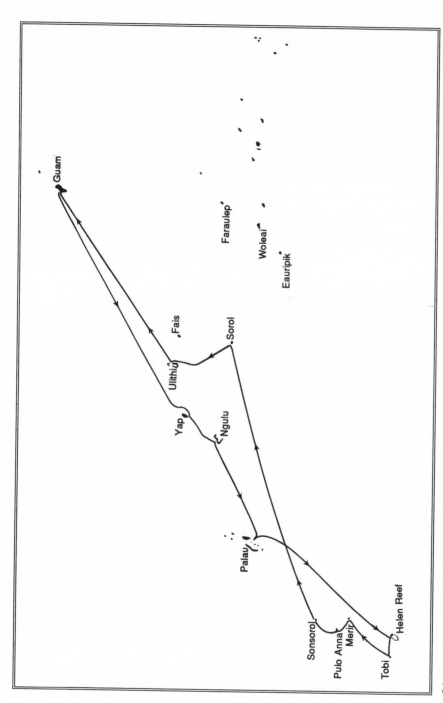

Itinerary in western Carolines 19–26 February 1954.

was too good to miss; it would yield information not to be come by in any other way. We found our late adversaries by no means unskilled, as bramble-covered remains of their fortifications testified. Here as elsewhere we needed to exercise caution, for there was still quite a lot of unexploded ordnance lying around.

YAP, HOME OF THE GODS

We reached Yap our first day out, 19 February 1954—Yap of the stone money, Yap legendary and remote, Yap the place bypassed by the river of American sea power flowing toward the Philippines in 1944. The group consists of a half-dozen hilly islands jammed together in the shape of a slender papaya, with a common reef and lagoon forming a veranda on the sea. Entering Tomil Harbor, the *Hanna* passed within yards of the rusted hulk of an LST perched on the reef beside the channel where it had been tossed by a typhoon two years before. Like the 1,000-ton German *Adler* at Samoa in 1889, it got under way too late to escape. The sight of such a wreck is enough to sober any commanding officer, for he knows that a small miscalculation may, some day, bring him to the same pass. I always made a wordless, split-second prayer that my ship and I be spared, before taking my post on the bridge to conn the ship through some narrow passage.

When a naval ship approaches harbor, the word to "station the special sea and anchor detail" is passed over the loudspeaker. Immediately the normal steaming watch is replaced, and a complex organization involving practically everyone on board takes over.

In the case of the *Hanna,* this process would go something like the following. A quartermaster known for his ability to bring the ship quickly to a given heading, and to keep her there, would report to the pilot house and take the wheel. Other quartermasters would spread charts and select landmarks to guide us into port. A man would emerge on the open bridge and don a telephone headset to relay messages instantly to or from the radar operators. In the Combat Information Center below, the most experienced radarmen and plotters would go to work under the watchful eye of an officer. The fathometer, if not already in use, would be turned on, sending a series of depth readings to the bridge. Radiomen would tune into harbor circuits, if any, and signalmen would man the signal lights and "flag bags" ready to communicate ship-to-ship or ship-to-shore as might be needed. The ship's navigator (in our case the executive officer) would begin "cutting us in" with minute-by-minute plots of our position using visual bearings, radar ranges, and depth information furnished him and would, in turn, recommend the best course to steer.

At first the officer of the deck would continue as conning officer, but before long I would either assume the conn myself or assign it to some junior officer in training. Meanwhile the officer of the deck would be relieved by an officer regularly assigned to that duty in the ship's "Watch, Quarter, and Station Bill"—the chart of all personnel assignments on board.

While this bustle and preparation were going forward in the realm of ship control, elsewhere on the *Hanna* men would hurry to their posts. In each of the engine rooms an officer would station himself, while extra men would show up to watch critical gauges and to whirl handwheels on split-second demand. An electrician and a quartermaster would set up shop in the steering-engine compartment, ready to take local control if anything should happen to the remote system.

On deck, swarms of seamen would break out mooring lines and fake them down for easy running through the chocks, and those up in the bow would release the stoppers on the anchor chain so that the anchor could be dropped at any time. The crew of the motor whaleboat would climb into their craft and ready it for lowering. Even the men whose sole duty was to shift colors the moment we moored would go to their stations well ahead of time and await the shrill note of the quartermaster's pea whistle as if they had the most important job on the ship.

Nothing was left to chance; each man had a prescribed duty for which he had been trained and in the performance of which he had been observed. The entire crew were devoted to the object of furnishing the commanding officer with quick, reliable information and bending the ship to his decisions.

The special sea detail on the *Hanna* had attained, long before we reached the Carolines, the kind of responsiveness to the captain's will which gave me confidence to take her anywhere. In the two and a half years of my command, never did the *Hanna*'s engines fail me, never did my men. Successfully entering and coming out of harbor, threading narrow channels, delicately going alongside other ships to transfer oil, stores, ammunition, and human beings—things easily mentioned and dismissed—have their origin in the competence, energy, and discipline of many men. In over six months of operations in some of the most dangerous waters in the world, never did we come to grief. For this and other things I was intensely proud of the *Hanna*.

Tomil Harbor. "Just about *Hanna*-size," I thought as we squeezed into it. No wonder the Japanese never made it a fleet base; we even had trouble finding an anchorage where we could swing freely on the hook without smashing our stern into the surrounding coral. As soon as we were secure, I went ashore to pay my respects to the district administrator, an official responsible for the entire western Carolines, occupying an area the size of Mexico. Don Heron, once a stockbroker, was now a specialist in human relations. I found him a ruddy, dedicated man with a wry sense of humor. I liked him at once.

The office of District Administrator Don Heron occupied an airy pavilion once used by the Japanese as an officers' club, on a knoll jutting out into Tomil Harbor. After initial amenities, he made the usual request that my men not molest the natives. I was no longer offended by such admonitions, knowing that previous visitors had made them necessary. Soon a steady influx of sailors into Yap Town began. For the remainder of the day, one was likely to encounter camera-toting "whitehats" along any leafy lane.

Yap Town—or Kolonia, as the Germans called it during their stay—still bore the scars of war: the tonnage of bombs rained on the island in 1944 by carrier aircraft must have been enormous. Although direct seizure of the island was not attempted, the Fifth Fleet made it worthless to the garrison of 4,123 army and 1,161 navy personnel sequestered here. Unfortunately there was nothing we could do at the time to help the 5,500 natives. A year later, when notified by Tokyo that all resistance was to cease, the Japanese commander cheerfully surrendered to Capt. J. L. Wyatt, USN, on board the destroyer USS *Tillman*. Later he fully cooperated, particularly in clearing the harbor of its six mine fields.

During their twenty-year hold on Yap, the Japanese did very little. For one thing, their German and Spanish predecessors had already brought the island to a level of activity commensurate with its limited resources. Yap Town came to their hands ready-built, and the German-laid cables to Guam, Shanghai, and Menado in the Philippines fitted readily into the imperial communications network.

Another factor was the Yapese aversion to work in any form. Only one man in history has succeeded in overcoming their passive resistance to toil: a Yankee trader named David O'Keefe, virtual king of the island for many years. He hit on the idea of helping the natives obtain their stone money from far-off quarries in Palau, then impounding it until they should perform for him a certain amount of work producing copra and dried bêche-de-mer. He owed his success to the semireligious fervor that would seize these strange people when bent on adding to their island's collection of stone money.

One sees quantities of this indestructible currency strewn along the pathways around Kolonia. Each piece is connected somehow with ownership of a plot of ground and belongs in one sense to a certain individual and in another sense to that individual's tribe. The seemingly casual way in which these stones are positioned on edge or lying in heaps is deceptive. I saw one such stone lying in three feet of water near a deserted council lodge, and Don Heron told me that even this one had a recognized owner who was content to leave it there.

The Yap jungle is like a garden. A thick, sweet carpet of moss stretches away under the trees, and everywhere are retaining walls and platforms of black, gray, and copper-green stones having a look of contented great age. Some of these sites appear to have been unused for generations. As F. W. Christian remarked long ago, the island is full of the relics of a vanished civilization. Trees have broken through the ancient pavements, and rows of stone backrests dignify imagined councils.

Abundant papaya and taro lined the path, with flimsy bamboo railings lashed to living staffs of hibiscus gently demarking each man's land from that of his neighbor. A small, jade-colored lizard decorated an overhanging bunch of bananas, and as we passed, a pair of jet-black birds darted up through the foliage, sounding a loud, musical note.

"Where is everybody?" I asked.

"Oh, there are plenty of people back there," Heron waved at the green thickets, "but they don't like strangers. The women are very shy. And the men are snobs. They know their way of life is best, their stone money the soundest, and their island the most beautiful in creation. Maybe they're right. Anyway, to these people, we are just another version of the Spanish, German, and Japanese regimes." A surprise encounter with a trio of Yapese belles gave point to his words. They scattered like quail in the underbrush.

Because of their reticence, the Yapese have managed to preserve their old customs and beliefs to a surprising degree. When the moon is full, they still dance and make love all night long. Away from the mission the shark god is remembered, and the counsel of the *machamach* respected. It used to be said that in Yap bad men never die but disappear somehow.

We visited a group of male clubhouses, or *fallu*, which together serve as Yap's Grand Hotel. Two are for visitors from outlying districts, and the others for men of Yap and guests from satellite atolls of Ngulu, Sorol, and Ulithi. Their high, prowlike gables overlook the lagoon and seem like great ships about to sail off into some spirit world.

NGULU, ISLAND OF FAT WOMEN

One can pronounce the name of Ngulu best by swallowing hard and saying "glue" at the same time. It is an atoll with a lagoon so enormous that it could hold all the navies of the world but so ill-protected that neither the Japanese nor the Americans used it during the war. Having no commercial or military importance, Ngulu was left to its own primitive devices. The houses we saw in the one tiny village were innocent of the scrap lumber and sheet metal so prevalent elsewhere in Micronesia. Fantastic gables similar to those observed in the Yap fallu adorned even private dwellings.

On the day of our visit, 20 February, I found ample opportunity to study the real estate because at first the inhabitants avoided us. One old man proved less circumspect than the others, however, and accepted a cigarette, but he turned out to be a little daft. He was wonderfully tattooed; on his sparse locks he wore a wreath of yellow and brown flowers and in his earlobes tiny bouquets of the same.

At length a squat little fellow came forward and gave me to understand that he was "number two chief," "number one" having gone to Yap for a few weeks. In greeting me, he interlaced his fingers in mine and slowly pumped my hand high and low much as teenagers in America used to do before the war. He agreed to escort me around the island, and before long we gathered quite a following. Even the women ventured out of their huts. And what women! They must have outweighed the men three to one, and standing or sitting they loomed like pyramids of flesh, with breasts the size of footballs and untold steatopygic marvels below. On Ngulu, the fatter the wife the richer the husband, and by this token it was a rich island indeed.

"Number two" (I never did learn his name) later came out to the ship to return my visit and quaffed Kool-Aid in the shade of an awning stretched over the main deck. At one point he selected a betel nut from a pandanus pouch and offered it to me. I declined with thanks, so he prepared it for his own consumption, first by bruising the nut, then rolling it up in a small green leaf and sprinkling it with coral lime from a bamboo tube. As he popped the confection into his bloodred mouth, the sight didn't much recommend the practice, but at any rate our photographers had a field day.

Ngulu welcoming committee.

My own snapshots had to be mental ones, but they were nonetheless vivid. The most striking for me was the sight of the chief hopping from one foot to the other on the hot deck, his tough soles not tough enough for him to do otherwise. In leaving, he presented me with several coconuts "for the children"—that is, for my brood of two hundred rather grown-up men.

We checked the entire lagoon, including two uninhabited reef islands, and sortied by way of Dobutsuoruniiga Pass—which, by the way, nobody on board tried to pronounce.

PALAU, JEWEL OF EMPIRE

On the morning of 21 February 1954 we came to Palau—once a prize possession of the Mikado, but at the time of our visit the western anchor of the Trust Territory. Palau consists of a jumble of reefs and weirdly contorted high islands—with equally contorted names, such as Babelthuap, Uruk-thapel, Arakabesan—all centered on the island of Koror, where administrative headquarters are located. Common access is by way of Malakal Passage, a narrow, winding way from Koror Road to Malakal Harbor. From a vantage point atop the pilothouse I watched the colors that told of lessening depths: from blue-black to cobalt to aquamarine to turquoise to gold and brown—the last being coral awash at low tide. A ship is perfectly safe, as a rule, over anything darker than dark green.

Once inside Malakal Passage, there is no turning. On this day a vicious crosscurrent poured off the shallows, contending with the ebb of deeper tides running along the channel itself. So clear was the water that we seemed to be levitated in air, and the men looking over the side were startled by the apparent nearness of coral heads and amused by the schools of tropical fish skittering in fright at the throb and pressure of our advance.

Finally, and with unbounded relief, I brought the ship safely into Malakal Harbor—the most beautiful harbor I have ever seen, formed by the encircling arms of Urukthapel, Ngargo, and Auluptagel Islands, much as the portico of St. Peter's curves to receive the devout. Koror itself is reached by a boat canal carved out between Ngargo and Auluptagel, which brings one to Madelai landing a few yards beyond.

On every hand there is evidence that the Japanese had meant to stay. Soon after they seized the Carolines from Germany at the outset of World War I, they established here their administrative headquarters for the entire archipelago. Colonists poured in; stores, banks, hotels sprang up. Millions of yen were spent on public works and harbor improvements. As a final touch the Japanese erected a magnificent Shinto temple on the highest hill.

Economic development went swiftly forward. The main part of the South Seas fishing fleet, numbering 360 vessels, made Palau home port, and the annual catch of bonito ran as high as 30,000 tons, in addition to large quantities of tuna, bêche-de-mer (for the Chinese trade), and trochus (whose pearly shell makes the finest buttons). The mining of phosphate, which the Germans had begun in 1909, was stepped up to 70,000 tons per year and reached a high of 200,000 tons in 1936.

To accomplish all this, the Japanese had to import thousands of laborers —Formosans, Okinawans, Chinese, and "kanakas" from Yap and elsewhere in the Carolines—leavened with hordes of their own peasants to set a standard of industriousness. Daily wages in the mines ranged from 3.19 yen for a Japanese to .77 yen for a native, so that the latter group cannot be said to have benefited much from the exploitation of their land.

True, there were schools and hospitals, but their value was meager compared with the mortality rate imposed by this kind of work. In 1783 the population was estimated at about 50,000. The number dwindled to around 10,000 by 1862, 4,000 by 1882, and 2,748 by 1901. In 1897 Christian reported 151 deserted villages out of a total of 235. The native population was close to dying out altogether even before the Japanese came along, and the Japanese all but finished it off.

Japan put its labor practices in the best possible light, claiming that the number of voluntary workers was slowly increasing. However, in the phosphate mines on Angaur, daily pay for a "Chamorro" still amounted to less than half a yen, compared with over three for a Japanese worker.

In the 1930s, the Japanese fortified the Palaus. The white soldiers who came to fight and die on Peleliu and Angaur encountered only the southern fringe of these defenses. For them to have seized Koror, at the heart of the island complex, would have cost ten times as much in men and material—a fact that can be appreciated by anyone who examines the ruins of the fortifications. At the time of surrender, the garrison still intact on Palau consisted of 18,493 army troops, 6,404 navy personnel, and 9,750 Japanese civilians. By the time these aliens were sent packing, the population of Palau had been reduced by 85 percent. The remaining survivors of a once-proud race were left to wander in a field of ruins. And although to me they seemed locked in lethargy, as if the imperial juggernaut had crushed out their wills, they were once again their own masters. It was theirs again, this island world.

During the morning, Rayner and I prowled the ruins of Koror and nearby Arakabesan Island, joined to it by a causeway. We found that our chart was sadly out of date. For example, it showed on Arakabesan two villages and an offshore island that the Japanese long ago had flattened to make a seaplane base, which in turn was bombed out of existence by the Fifth Fleet. Its acres of concrete now were littered with demolished planes and other scrap. But who knows? After time completes its cycle, the chart may again be correct, and one will find those two villages and an offshore islet.

At another place we found a vast ammunition dump, with piles of artillery shells and horned mines. The mines were of a type that the Japanese planted on the shores of Peleliu, where they caused many casualties among marines of the 1st, 5th, and 7th Divisions.

In the afternoon I went in the motor whaleboat to look over a Japanese warship sitting on the bottom near Urukthapel. It was the repair ship *Akashi,* a converted cruiser from World War I, which our first carrier air raid on Palau had bombed out of service on 31 March 1944.[1] The ship lay on an even keel, with its main deck three feet above water, and its pagoda-like superstructure still sound, though marred by fire and rust. The ship's twin 5.5-inch guns pointed blindly skyward, as they had at the moment death arrived for their nameless crews. In the crannies where dust had lodged, frivolous plants now bloomed and promised in another ten years to festoon the ship from stem to stern. I later sent a working party back with an acetylene torch to cut away a fine reel for stowing manila lines that had caught my eye. Readers who imagine that the Japanese used inferior materials may be surprised to learn that the galvanized steel of this reel was in excellent condition after a decade of the most corrosive weather imaginable. And incidentally, the salvaged item saved American taxpayers about $750, which was the best estimate I could get from a home shipyard for duplicating it.

Following a suggestion offered by Don Heron at Yap, I decided to diverge from my schedule by adding Helen Reef to our itinerary. Based on certain rumors, there seemed a possibility that we might surprise an encroaching fishing fleet since the price of trochus (with which the place abounds) had reached a high of $450 per ton, and to poachers the temptation would be well worth the risk of arrest.

So we left Palau somewhat earlier than first planned, in order to be off Helen by first light the following morning. Actually, the place is more than just a reef—it is a rather large atoll, with a bona fide island at its northern extremity. Heron wanted to eliminate the poachers before they seriously depleted the shell beds in the lagoon, for he hoped to revive the trochus industry along native lines.

AT SEA

During the night of 22–23 February, we experienced a strong northeasterly sea that somewhat delayed our arrival. When we did come up to the reef, there were no intruders to be seen except one battered hulk stranded there long ago. We didn't take time to go ashore on the islet, but I made a mental note to check Helen again the next time we came this way.

Helen, Tobi, Merir, Pulo Anna, and Sonsorol form the western extremity of the Carolines. Beyond lie the East Indies—a different world altogether. The five small islands named are too insignificant to have been of any economic or strategic value to the Japanese, and as watching posts they had only minor tactical usefulness. In the roll-up after V-J Day, the Americans found on Tobi only 439 Japanese soldiers, on Merir 261, and on Sonsorol 639. None of the garrisons knew the war was over until so informed by the ships that came to take their surrender.

The *Hanna* visited Merir, Pulo Anna, and Sonsorol during the remainder of the day, putting landing parties ashore at the first two. It was late when we checked Sonsorol, but the moon was high and made a magic sight, enhanced by pinpoints of firelight along the shore. Here the violence of the ocean current that characterizes the area was most explicit: great boiling patches, riffles, even breakers lifted the ship this way and that as the poor helmsman grappled with the wheel. Certainly there could be no intruders at this place, so we struck out toward Sorol Atoll on the homeward half of our patrol.

At the end of a thirty-six-hour jaunt, we raised Sorol on the horizon. The entrance to the lagoon being too small to accommodate us, I sent a landing party ashore in the motor whaleboat, coaching it around hazards by radar and radio. At the time of our visit, the only available chart of Sorol was a rough four-by-five-inch plat dated 1926, based on an early Japanese sketch. I decided to resolve some of its discrepancies while waiting for the landing party to return, and so I summoned the "hydrosurvey team" to the bridge. We moved slowly around the reef, recording bearings and soundings later to be collated and reported to Washington. Along the way were three islands in addition to Sorol itself: Bigelimol, Bigeliwol, and Bigelor. Bland and his assistants took great pleasure in shouting out their names and bearings. We found a ten-fathom anchorage in the lee of Bigelimol, outside the reef, but it was too small for our use.

Some of the men not otherwise employed went back to the fantail and trolled for fish. They were grateful for our going so slowly and hauled in a prize catch including a nineteen-pound wahoo and one of sixteen pounds. The wahoo, a great fighter that will hit anything at 8 knots, often managed to escape with the men's fishing tackle.

The hydrographic information assembled at Sorol revealed that the orientation of the atoll shown on the official chart was about eight degrees in error, in addition to minor distortions of the various islands. The cause of this could only be that those who made the original survey had failed to allow sufficiently for compass error.

At length we completed our work and retrieved the landing party. Rayner, who had been in charge, reported sixteen natives, all of one family. For some reason no other inhabitants had returned after the war. "They are proud and solid," he said, "real five-by-fives. They are so healthy they didn't even ask for aspirin!" The little community had only one worry—what paradise would be complete otherwise?—an unexploded 500-pound bomb right in the center of their village.

The Japanese had a weather station here and a radio transmitter whose tower still showed above the treetops. American planes destroyed the installation in 1944 and ignored Sorol from then until V-J Day.

On 8 September 1945, the destroyer escort USS *Booth* appeared off the atoll, carrying a Japanese lieutenant and a corporal from the Yap garrison as well as a native interpreter from Ulithi. They saw one Japanese on the beach, but he dodged into the brush and refused to reappear. A landing party came ashore, posted notes in conspicuous places, and then returned to the ship. The *Booth* went away for four days, and when it returned, a single Japanese emerged from among the trees and surrendered. Another five who were on the island had committed suicide as soon as they read the notes. In addition to these six men (all civilian radio operators) there were ten natives on the island, probably including those we found there.

Ulithi Atoll, our last stop on this trip, came in sight at 0700, and we entered the lagoon by way of Mugai Channel at 0830 on 25 February 1954.

9
Mogmog Revisited

Ulithi Atoll features several reef islands, one of which will long be remembered by navy men: the island of Mogmog.[1] Many years ago, when the lagoon here was the scene of comings and goings of the greatest striking force in naval history, Mogmog was dedicated to one purpose—recreation. To the thousands of men and officers who poured ashore here it was, for many months, the only land they walked on. So Mogmog would be remembered, even if were not unique.

But it was unique. A native village had been taken over intact by the Seabees, who, instead of bulldozing it to one side and building a half-dozen Quonsets on the site, used existing structures as a basis for an elaborate recreation center. The huts, on their neat platforms of crushed coral, were refurbished, their sides opened up to the breeze and their interiors furnished with chairs and tables. Here small groups could establish themselves for the day with beer, cards, and assorted delicacies from home. To provide a central gathering place, an airy pavilion was built overlooking the water.

At the east end of the island was a baseball diamond flanked with a small mountain of cases of beer. Even though the beer was warm, it was a beverage not to be had afloat, and therefore it was rare and wonderful.

Each morning early, working parties would come ashore and police every foot of the island, so that it always had a pristine look: green shrubbery and white sand laced with neat, shady paths. Two pontoon jetties gave access to the island on the lagoon side, and a banner proclaimed "Welcome to Mogmog—Paradise of the Pacific." Although some who landed here might not agree with that slogan, at least it was an oasis of relaxation during the long drive to crush the Japanese Empire.

As one of those visitors, I sometimes wondered about the people whose homes we had appropriated—what they were like and how they were getting along on nearby Fasserai Island, to which they had been moved. What did they think of the staggering power displayed before their eyes? Would they ever come back to Mogmog, and if so, would they ever revert to the way they were before the upheaval?

Returning here now, 25 February 1954, I had opportunity to answer these questions and to think back on long-vanished shipmates, extravagant sea stories, and crucial poker pots. Recent surveillance landings had taken place at off-lying Falalap Island, where the U.S. Coast Guard maintained a loran and weather station, but as far as I knew no navy ships had entered the lagoon since 1949. So Mogmog was a worthwhile subject for reconnaissance, apart from the element of my personal interest.

We entered the atoll by way of Mugai Channel, no longer the simple matter it was when six buoys marked its limits. The buoys were long gone, and I was obliged to depend on visual tangents, notoriously unreliable where coconut islets are concerned. The reef in the vicinity of the channel is well submerged, so its colors are not as distinct as the one could wish. Finding the passage consisted of selecting the darkest shade of blue and heading over it. Once inside, we did find a rusty buoy watching Roriparakku Rock, the only marker of any kind left in Ulithi. And thanks to the men who had blasted and dragged great areas of the lagoon to minimum depths of fifty-five feet, it was possible to make good time covering the eight miles from that point to Mogmog. Not far from where the destroyer tenders once lay, we anchored in seven fathoms, and I went ashore with a landing party. One of the pontoon jetties installed there long ago was still serviceable, though requiring nimble footwork.

Ashore we were greeted by a crowd of boys in scarlet loincloths who led us gravely to their village, where we encountered one of the most interesting people we were to find in the Trust Territory: Father William Walter, S.J., missionary of Ulithi. He was barefoot and sported a faded pair of blue shorts and a bushy red beard. In fact he looked more like a beach-comber

Landing party at Mogmog Island, Ulithi. (Note the old boat jetty built by Seabees.)

than a priest, and it was only after talking with him for a while that I realized the scope of his understanding and wit and his devotion to the people of Ulithi.

The erstwhile parklike simplicity of Mogmog Village had given way to the normal clutter of Micronesian habitation—piles of coconut husks, festoons of fishing gear, and so on—but the huts were the same, and their mossy stone retaining walls looked as timeless as ever. The Officers' Club was gone, and in its place a lofty fallu arose. It was thatched and timbered in the traditional way but was eked out at the ends with sheets of corrugated iron. Aside from this touch, there was only Father Walter's ancient Quonset chapel and the skeleton of what may have been a bulldozer to show that modern "civilization" had ever come near the place. The millions of empty beer cans had long since been turned to red dust, washed away in the sand.

Nor could one surmise from the Ulithians themselves any past upheavals or strange visitations. There seemed to be no past as far as they were concerned, and very little future. In 1954 this special branch of the Micronesian race numbered about four hundred—a small, handsome people. At the time of our visit, about a hundred lived on Mogmog and the remainder on Falalop, Fassarai, Sorlen, and Potangeras Islands. Their language,

With John (wristwatch) and friends on Mogmog.

according to Father Walter, was different from any other in the world, and he admitted that after five years he still had not mastered it. "For one thing," he said, "they will never tell you when you make a mistake because they don't want to hurt your feelings. I learn mostly from the children, because when I say something wrong, they giggle, and then I get them to tell me. A very complicated language, with lots of subtleties. I am working on a dictionary, but it takes a long time."

I remarked on the absence of Western dress, for on a majority of the Trust Islands the natives were markedly clothes-conscious, wearing them daily for the sake of prestige or putting them on when we arrived in deference to a supposed white man's taboo against nudity. Not so on Mogmog. Here it was actually against the rules to wear more than a *laplap*, or grass skirt. "The reason is simple," Father Walter explained. "If a man goes to Yap and comes back with a pair of pants for himself and a skirt for his wife, before long, all the others would all want pants and dresses no matter how impractical, and the expense would be ruinous to a majority. After all, the average income here is only twenty dollars a year. They have nothing to trade. The economy is self-contained and is adequate as long as the people aren't led to buy a lot of stuff from the outside."

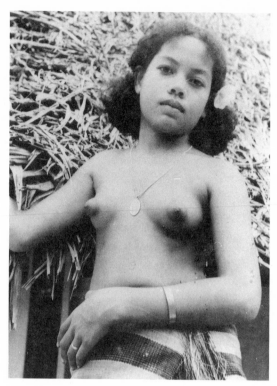

Young woman of Ulithi Atoll, western Carolines.

Fish and taro form the staple diet, and only the missionary was dependent on supplies from the outside—a fact that bothered him because he had wanted to adopt the native life completely. "But," he said, "I almost died trying to eat their food, and I had to decide between doing so and continuing my work. The difficulty is that a Ulithian always shares. They are the most unselfish people in the world, so they do not understand, and it is awkward." Father Walter was the sort to feel this: during the war he tramped with the infantry through New Guinea, the Philippines, and Okinawa. Even when his major's rank would have made a desk job at division headquarters available, he chose to remain with the smaller units. Back in civilian status he welcomed his assignment to the Caroline Islands.

Apparently a kind of tribal socialism still prevails in Mogmog. Every morning the chief calls a meeting at the *fallu* and announces the community project for the day, for which each clan furnishes a designated number of men, whether it be for fishing, copra gathering, boat repair, or (as is often the case) simple holiday routine. The most important joint enterprise is the building of a canoe, and fortunately the local canoes are so well built that they last for generations. I say "fortunately" because the breadfruit trees essential to boat-building grow nowhere in Ulithi, and for this enterprise the natives are obliged to send a deputation to Yap to cut a tree and hew it into shape. In payment for accommodating one of these working parties for several months and for taking one tree, the Yapese exact a fee in pandanus matting, coconut honey, laplaps, and other produce totaling in terms of labor value about six man-years. Small wonder the Mogmog canoes are not only the best built but also the best cared for in the area!

While we were on the island, one of these great oceangoing canoes returned from a five-day expedition on nearby Mangejang Island laden with pandanus fiber, cooking pots, men, women, and children. It was a magnificent craft, black with orange stripes, and it carried its ton-and-a-half burden as gracefully as a leaf on the water. About a hundred yards from shore its crew lowered the sail, unstepped the mast, jumped in the water, and pushed it the rest of the way to the beach—because it was taboo to sail a boat in the vicinity of the Seabee's old jetties.

DEATH OF A PRELATE

The oceangoing canoes of Ulithi played a part years ago in giving the world its first intimation of a vast archipelago south of Guam. It is believed that long before the white man came to the Pacific, trading expeditions from the Carolines occasionally made the seven-hundred-mile round-trip to Guam and back with Ulithi as the point of assembly, departure, and return.

One name stands out in ensuing developments: Padre Juan Antonio Cantova, S.J., who gained the confidence of a group of these Micronesian vikings. They had landed on the east coast of Guam 29 June 1721 in a huge canoe—so huge, in fact, that a Spanish soldier mistook it afar for a frigate. From them he gained a wealth of information about their island world.

Already there had been vague reports of land to the south. In 1625 the Nassau Fleet sighted both Ulithi and Yap. In 1686 Don Francisco Lazcano discovered a large island, probably Yap, and named it "La Carolina" after King Carlos II. From the simple defect of not knowing one island from another, the Spaniards came to call all of them the Carolines. In 1696 Juan Rodriguez sighted Faraulep, and in 1712 Bernard de Egui rediscovered Ulithi and named it "Garbanzos" because the profusion of reef islands reminded him of a scattering of chickpeas.

Padre Cantova resolved many of the perplexities raised by these sporadic discoveries and rediscoveries by persuading one of his dark visitors to lay out, with pebbles in the sand, a diagram of the Carolines whereby he was able to prepare a rough map of the entire area from Truk ("Torres" or "Hogeleu") on the east to Sonsorol ("Sonrol") on the west. He then applied to the authorities for permission to accompany the voyagers back to their islands to learn more about the people and bring them the "saintly truths." The governor was agreeable, but the local Father Superior vetoed the plan, saying such a project would be distasteful to Manila. This prompted Cantova to send a long letter, with his map, to the king's confessor in Spain, Padre d'Aubenton, who passed the information to his sovereign.[2] Here, within the grasp of a devout monarch, lay fresh fields for conversion. The royal consent was immediately forthcoming, sanctioning an expedition to the mysterious southern isles. We learn next that Cantova made one trip to the Carolines, from 11 May to 6 June 1722, of which there remains no further record, and that he was preparing to set forth on another.[3]

The second expedition, nine years later, consisted of Padre Cantova and another priest named Victor Uvaltec—more commonly known as "Walter"—along with a party of soldiers, interpreters, and others departing Guam on 2 February 1731. Thirty days later they reached Falalap, in the Ulithi group, and erected a large wooden cross on its southern shore. At first the project succeeded, perhaps because of its novelty. At the end of three months Padre Walter returned to Guam for additional supplies and equipment, it appearing that Catholicism had secured a firm foothold in the Carolines. Padre Cantova remained with eight Spaniards, five Filipinos, and a slave.

But Padre Walter never reached Guam. Contrary winds forced his small ship to the Philippines instead, and there he had to wait a year for an opportunity to return to the Marianas. The ship in which he embarked was wrecked even before it got clear of the Philippines. The church authorities in Manila built and provisioned another vessel and sent it to Ulithi, with Padre Walter on board. Going by way of Acapulco—the only practical route—it arrived 9 June 1733, two years from the time he had left. A memoir written by Don Fernando Valdéz y Tamón, governor of the Philippines, tells the rest of the story:

> They fired a cannon to inform P. Cantova of their arrival. The same was done repeatedly, but no bark of the island appeared, which gave

suspicion that the barbarians might have killed him. They took resolution to enter a bay formed by two islands, the largest of which is Falalap, and when they came within a musket shot of the shore, they observed that their former habitation had been burnt, and that the Cross which had been erected near the sea side was no longer there.

After some time four small canoes of the Islanders approached the vessel, bringing cocoa-nuts. They were questioned in their language concerning P. Cantova and his companions; they answered, but with symptoms of embarrassment, that he had gone to the great Island Yap. Their countenance at the same time expressed fear, and they refused to come on board, although offered biscuit, tobacco, and other things of which they are fond, which left no doubt that our people had perished by the hands of the barbarians. At length it was contrived to seize one of these Islanders, and to get him in the ship, whereupon the others took to their barks, or threw themselves into the sea, swimming away with loud cries.

The vessel stopped the night in this bay, and the next day sailed with the design to go to the Island Yap; but not knowing in what degree it was situated, nor the course it was necessary to follow, they were not able to discover it. During this time they repeatedly questioned the Islander, giving him every assurance that no harm would be done to him if he would speak the truth. At length he confessed, that a short time after the departure of Father Walter, the natives killed Father Cantova and all his companions.

P. Cantova, it seems, went with his interpreter and two soldiers to the Island Mogmog to baptize, whilst the rest of his company remained at Falalap. Scarcely had he set foot on Mogmog, when the natives came around him armed with lances, and setting up great cries. Cantova demanded mildly why they wished to take away his life who had never done them any harm: "You come," they said, "to destroy our ancient usages." With these words they pierced him through and through with their lances. They afterwards enveloped the body of the father in a mat, and buried him under a small house, which among them is an honorable form of interment, and given only to their principal people. They killed at the same time the three men who were with him, whose bodies they put in a canoe and turned loose to the will of the waves.

They afterwards went to the Island Falalap where the other persons of the mission were. The soldiers, seeing the Islanders approach, and that they were transported with rage, put themselves on their defense, and fired some small cannon which they had placed before their house, by which four of the Islanders were killed, and they continued to defend themselves with their sabres till they were overcome by numbers. There perished on this occasion, besides the Father Cantova, eight Spaniards, four natives of the Philippine Islands, and a slave. A young native of the Philippine Islands was spared, because one of the principal people took compassion on him, and adopted him for his son.[4]

No one offered to revive Padre Cantova's scheme. A parallel attempt launched by the Manila mission to evangelize the western extremity of the archipelago had similar results. And in the inertia that crept over mission-ary affairs in the next century and a half, it seemed best to leave such ungrateful heathen to their heathen fate. For this, at least, the heathen had reason to be grateful. In more recent times the picture has entirely changed. Today the people of the Carolines have been blessed by the presence of churchmen like Fathers Walter, Rively, and Costigan. This is not a para-dox: the early priests, with soldiers at their beck and call, came to the islands with the taint of blood upon them, and the islands repaid them with blood. Their modern counterparts have succeeded through humility, under-standing, and unselfishness—which are, after all, Micronesian qualities.

Father Walter and his people crowded the jetty and lined the shore as we hoisted anchor and made our way out to sea, and at our last sight of them they were still waving palm fronds in farewell.

1o

The Seizure

On Guam 27 February 1954 we learned that the *Hanna* would have to leave again within twenty-four hours. The USS *Whitehurst,* the destroyer escort sharing our duties, had been diverted to take part in a search and rescue mission near Kwajalein, and as a result, we had to make the trip originally scheduled for that ship, retracing the same itinerary through the Marianas, Bonins, and Volcanoes that we had completed only five weeks before— hardly a suitable reward for good performance. The crew were understandably dismayed, particularly those who happened to be in the duty section the day of our arrival and thus were denied all liberty. The trip could have been postponed or canceled had it not included, as before, a rendezvous with an itinerant submarine near where we had met the *Pickerel* on the previous occasion. "I don't want these DES to miss any chance of training with a live submarine," said the admiral, and that was that. So off we went, moaning low. Having already covered the area, we expected no surprises.

Shortly after midnight on 28 February we circled Aguijan and, eight hours later, Anatahan. No interlopers. We then pointed our bow northward to Maug and cranked the engines up to 18 knots. I wanted to try something I had had in mind ever since the day Lee and his "mountaineers" had been

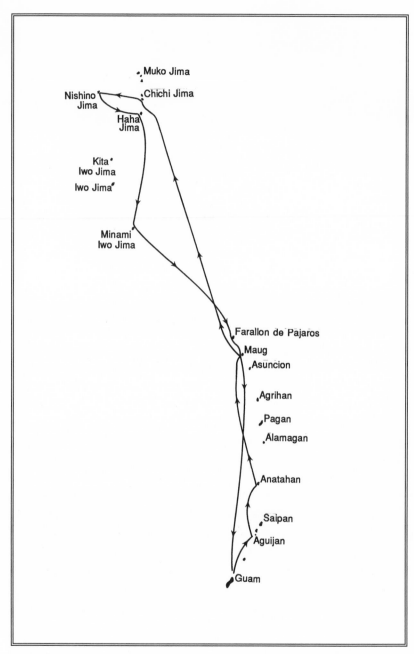

Itinerary in Northern Marianas, Bonins, and Volcanoes—27 February–8 March 1954.

marooned on those crumbling volcanic slopes. According to the chart, the depth of water over the drowned crater of Maug averaged 125 fathoms (750 feet), far too deep for anchoring. But in the center a pinnacle rose to within fifteen fathoms of the surface. Could we possibly anchor to it? And if we hit the spot, would the anchor hold or would it just tumble downhill? I wanted to find out.

We reached Maug just after last twilight, the black masses of the three islands distinct against a sky of stars. We easily located the pinnacle, but it was so small I couldn't depend on the depth of water under the bow to be the same as that registered on our fathometer about a hundred feet aft. The current and the breeze kept setting us forward over the pinnacle. The leadsman kept calling out "no bottom at twenty" even while the fathometer was indicating fifteen. Changing tactics, we "walked the anchor out," that is, lowered it by windlass to fifteen fathoms and held it there. Then I let the bow drift down on the pinnacle. As soon as the anchor snagged, we let the chain run out to sixty fathoms. It dragged. We let out another thirty and it held. However, we couldn't relax completely during the night, for if the anchor had dragged, we would quickly have found ourselves under way again and in danger of running aground on one of the three islands formed by the drowned crater. Engines had to be ready for quick action, likewise the crew. Anyway, it was better than rocking about in open sea, which had begun to kick up a bit that afternoon. And so we wove another strand in the *Hanna* legend by being one of the few ships in history to anchor in the crater of Maug.[1]

At sea, 2 March—our friendly submarine, the USS *Menhaden* (SS 377), was somewhat off in his navigation, so we failed to get together until mid-morning and the time spent on exercises turned out to be less than planned. We parted ways at two in the afternoon—the submarine for Midway, the *Hanna* for Chichi. We reached Port Lloyd about noon the following day and spent the afternoon consulting with Jack Frost and indulging in further explorations. We even found some Japanese installations the local residents didn't know about.

CHICHI JIMA
At 8:45 the following morning, we got under way again, to continue reconnaissance of the Bonins. I planned to go through the strait that separates Chichi from Anishima, its next neighbor to the north, in order to have a

look at the eastern side of that island and little Ititi Shima next door. As we swung into the narrow passage we glimpsed a medium-sized vessel at its far end and gave chase. He dodged out of sight around a cape, but we found him a few minutes later in one of Anishima's eastern coves. It was the *Seiyo Maru* "fisheries inspection vessel" (144 tons) out of Tokyo, and clearly within territorial waters. We ran up a "κ" flag, meaning "stop your engines." He complied, and we followed the "κ" with another signal meaning "follow me into port," and he came along with us into Port Lloyd.

As soon as we made fast to our accustomed buoy, I sent a boarding party over to the *Seiyo Maru,* whose captain asserted that he had been granted clearance to enter within the three-mile limit to search for a missing fishing boat. However, neither Jack Frost nor I knew of any such dispensation, and the fact that the "Fisheries Inspection Vessel" was privately owned made us suspicious. Within minutes a coded message was on its way to ComNavMar, and a few hours later an answer came back, directing me to release the *Seiyo Maru* with a warning.

I took advantage of the interval by going to the deserted south end of the harbor, in order to sort out how I felt about Chichi Jima and why I was there. I remembered a simple statue in the overgrown remains of a park that I had seen on our previous visit, and I hoped to capture in charcoal something that had eluded the camera—a sense of dignity and loneliness. I sent the boat back to the ship with instructions to return in two hours— or sooner, if word from Guam came in before that.

The sketch was a bad job, and I tore it up and looked around. Chichi was afflicted with a plant called "ginkokai," introduced by the Japanese early in the war to provide concealment from the air. In Japan it was cherished in gardens; here it ran wild, forming a dense cover at a height of ten feet or so. A screen of the shrub hid everything beyond my statue, and curiosity led me to penetrate a short distance beyond. I was rewarded with a broad path ascending a knoll, through a beautiful *tori,* to a flight of stone steps leading to a summit, where I found two monuments—tall stone slabs, highly polished, bearing hundreds of oriental characters. There was a deep springy carpet of moss around them, a view of the bay, and pine trees angling over: the kind of setting the Japanese excel in creating. In one corner of the terrace a stone lantern lay on its side, and I gently righted it.

Sitting in the shadow of the two monuments and looking out over the quiet waters of Port Lloyd, I wondered if the spot were dedicated to the legendary Ogasawara, who the Japanese believe discovered the Bonins. Musing on the past, I wondered about all the contending claims swirling around me—claims of discovery, national interests, commercial interests, and perhaps the most valid of all, the lives and loves invested here, entire.

According to the Japanese, Ogasawara discovered the islands in 1593 and called them *Mu-nin Sima* ("Isles without Men"). The emperor is supposed to have bestowed them on him in fief, following which he founded a colony that lasted only briefly. Later visits are asserted—in 1670, in 1675, and in 1728. In 1785 Shihei Hiyashi published a chart of the group. Explorers from the West were inclined to scoff at these claims because the earliest Japanese account placed the islands three hundred miles *east* of the Izu Islands (which are strung out south of the Tokyo area) instead of *south,* a discrepancy that could of course have been intentional. Then, too, though it correctly locates the group, Hiyashi's chart does not give it the shape and orientation readily recognized by Western eyes. Be that as it may, we can discount the Ogasawara story and still concede that Japan, whose people have always looked seaward and whose fishermen take appalling danger for granted, must have known of the islands so near at hand before any white man set foot on them. This is not the same as assimilation, or ownership by foreknowledge, but only part of the mosaic.

Spain, to be sure, could assert claims even antedating Ogasawara, beginning with Bernard de la Torre, and there can be little doubt that the Spaniards from time to time saw the Bonins from the decks of their galleons in the sixteenth century. But they were not in the habit of broadcasting their discoveries, and in that particular area they were less interested in minor islands than in pursuing their northerly course back to the coast of America. The Spanish chart Anson acquired amid the booty of the *Nuestra Señora de Covadonga* in 1743 showed a cluster of islands labeled *Arzobispo* ("Archbishop") in the approximate location of the Bonins and a similar cluster 320 miles to the eastward. Of course they could have been one and the same, so unreliable were contemporary estimates of longitude, but later navigators could not be sure and, in the face of a general proliferation of nonexistent islands on Spanish charts, were inclined to reject them all. Gore, Colnett, Broughton, La Pérouse, Kruzenstern, and many others plowed the sea north, south, east, and west of the true location of the group, seeing nothing but land birds and occasional floating branches (and fog), so the Arzobispos were dropped from the charts, although they were there all the time.

＊

No information could be expected from Japan, the forbidden land where unauthorized visitors were summarily executed, where the Shoguns out-lawed Christianity and underscored the decree by executing some thirty thousand converts, where the only foreign contacts were with Dutch traders permitted to visit Nagasaki from time to time. Strangely, however, it was through this channel that early Spanish discoveries were substanti-ated. In 1785 one of the traders, Isaac Titsingh, managed to smuggle out a copy of a geographical treatise entitled "Description of the Three King-doms." He kept it locked up as long as he lived, but after his death in 1812 it fell into the hands of a French scholar named Abel Remusat.

Fascinated with the description of Mu-nin Sima and the explicitness of the chart, Remusat studied the known tracks of seafarers who had passed in the vicinity; he concluded that the Arzobispo Islands existed after all and that they would in time be found somewhere south of Japan. Remusat pub-lished his views in the *Journal des Savants* in July 1817 and lived to see his theory proven six years later by the American Captain Coffin, master of the English whaling ship *Transit,* who landed on Haha Jima and gave his name to its "principal bay" (probably Okimura).[2] Within two years another ship stumbled onto Chichi Jima—the British whaler *Supply,* in September 1825. Other whalers came and went, but their skippers were a casual lot and sel-dom rushed into print at the end of a voyage.

Then came Capt. F. W. Beechey, RN, FRS, commanding HMS *Blossom* on a four-year voyage "to the Pacific and Beering's Strait to cooperate with the Polar Expeditions." Finding himself near the islands as shown on Arrow-smith's chart (following Coffin's report) but without sighting land, he was on the point of calling them invisible when one morning he saw "several islands, extending in a north and south direction as far as the eye could discern":

> They all appeared to be small, yet they were high and very remarkable; particularly one near the centre, which I named after Captain Kater, V.P.R.S. . . . As the islands to the southward appeared to be the largest; and finding they were fertile, and likely to afford good anchorage, Lieu-tenant Belcher was sent in shore with a boat to search for a harbour. In the evening he returned with a favorable report, and with a supply of fourteen large green turtle.

Wind, current, and fog prevented finding good anchorage, and the *Blossom* was forced to stand off and on, with one or two close calls, until the following day, when they spotted an opening that appeared to offer haven. They sent a boat in to explore, and it returned with news of a good harbor within, where the ship would be safe in any winds.

We were a little surprised, when he came back, to find two strangers in the boat, for we had no idea these islands had been recently visited, much less than that there were any residents on them; and we concluded that some unfortunate vessel had been cast away upon the island. They proved to be part of the crew of a whale-ship belonging to London, named the *William*. The ship, which once belonged to His Majesty's service, had been anchored in a rather exposed position (the port being then not well known), and had part of her cargo on deck, when a violent gust of wind from the land drove her from her anchors, and she struck upon a rock in a small bay near the entrance, where in a short time she went to pieces. All the crew escaped, and established themselves on shore as well as they could, and immediately commenced building a vessel from the wreck of the ship, in which they intended to proceed to Manila; but before she was completed, another ship, the *Timor*, arrived and carried them all away except our two visitors, who remained behind at their own request. They had been several months upon the island, during which time they had not shaved or paid any attention to their dress, and were very odd-looking beings. The Master, Thomas Younger, had unfortunately been killed by the fall of a tree fifteen days prior to the loss of the ship and was buried in a sandy bay on the eastern side of the harbour.

We entered the port and came to anchor in the upper part of it in eighteen fathoms, almost landlocked. . . . Almost every valley has a stream of water, and the mountains are clothed with trees, among which are the *areca moleraca* and fan-palm conspicuous. There are several sandy bays, in which green turtles are sometime so numerous that they quite hide the colour of the shore. The sea yields an abundance of fish; the rocks and caves are the resort of crayfish and other shellfish; and the shores are the resort of plovers, snipes, and wild pigeons. At the upper part of the port there is a small basin, formed by coral reefs, conveniently adapted for heaving the ship down; and on the whole it is a most desirable place of resort for a whale ship.

Naturally this led to assertion of ownership:

Taking possession of uninhabited islands is now a mere matter of form; still I could not allow so fair an opportunity to escape, and declared them to be the property of the British Government by nailing a sheet of copper to a tree, with the necessary particulars engraved upon it. As the harbour has no name, I called it Port Lloyd, out of regard for the late Bishop of Oxford. The island in which it is situated I named after Sir Robert Peel, His Majesty's Secretary of State for the Home Department.[3]

Beechey goes on to describe other islands of the group, bestowing names with a prodigal hand. He honors a professor of geology at Oxford, the president of the Astronomical Society, a Mr. Walker of the Hydrographic Office, and a host of others. At length, after spending as much time in the area "as was consistent with my orders" (he probably hated to leave), Beechey departed northward in pursuit of his primary objective, which was to link up with John Franklin and William Parry in the Arctic.

Britain's claim led to Consul Charlton's attempt to establish a colony on Chichi, which as we know was followed by violence, rum, and blood in the next hundred years. Seeing Chichi Jima quiet at last, so beautiful and so vulnerable, I wanted to remember it in terms of the delight expressed by Beechey and by Matthew Calbraith Perry's cabin boy and in terms of Nathaniel Savory's dream, standing like a promontory facing the ocean, symbolizing one man's hope, love, and pride in and for an island.

Then I thought of the hands that had fashioned my hidden shrine and of the Japanese settlers of times past, whose farthest of degree was that they might live here humbly as farmers, fishermen, shopkeepers. I knew they had loved this island too.

The sun was high toward noon when I heard a whistle blast from the ship and saw the motor whaleboat heading my way like a busy water beetle. Back on board I was handed a message directing that the *Seiyo Maru* be released with a warning. This done, we headed out to sea again, checked Nishino Jima with negative results, and spent the night on southerly courses slowly closing Haha Jima. Daylight showed no change in its fertile desolation, so we set off for the Volcano Islands.

That evening we spotted an unidentified vessel in territorial waters off Kita Iwo Jima, and it proved to be our old friend the *Seiyo Maru*. This time he claimed to have received a new clearance, through 9 March. Again, I had no knowledge of such permission, and it seemed to me that if he were truly concerned about a missing fishing boat, the *Hanna* would already have been directed to participate in the search, consistent with our mission. Fuming, I arrested him a second time and directed him to follow me to

Saipan, where his violation—if it were a violation—could be adjudicated. We set off at 8 knots, the *Seiyo Maru*'s top speed, groaning at the prospect of wallowing along with him for the next two days. Meanwhile there were messages among the *Hanna,* ComNavMar, and certain luminaries in Japan, and I seemed to be caught in the cross fire between two admirals. Eventually the matter was ironed out, and at 2:30 A.M. I received instructions to release my companion. We notified him by flashing light, and without so much as a "roger" he flipped around and departed northward. I'm sure we were both relieved. Two days later the *Hanna* arrived at Guam for a week of rest and relaxation.

11

Barefoot Baseball

When first assigned to patrol duties in the Trust Territory we were expected to follow itineraries set for us in three major sectors—the eastern Carolines, the western Carolines, and the island groups north of Guam—even though circumstances often upset the prescribed schedules. Early on, detailed instructions were appropriate and necessary, but now that our novitiate was over, it began to appear that the admiral's operations staff, cloistered on Guam's Nimitz Hill, were not in the best position to grasp the realities of our island world. I found I could better judge how and when to approach certain islands in order to take advantage of light conditions and, once on the scene, how long to remain.

I wasn't sure if I would be allowed to take the initiative in planning our trips, but it was worth a try. My immediate superior, Capt. Roy Klinker, USN, agreed it was a good idea, and so did Adm. Murphy's operations officer, Capt. William Jonson, USN. We worked out a procedure, and a few days later Captain Klinker informed me that our next junket would be in the eastern Carolines. "Work up a schedule to include Ponape and Truk, and I'll shoot it up the hill for approval. Can you be ready by the tenth?"

"Yes, sir, and if it's all right, I'd like to hit Kapingamarangi this time; none of our ships has gone there yet."

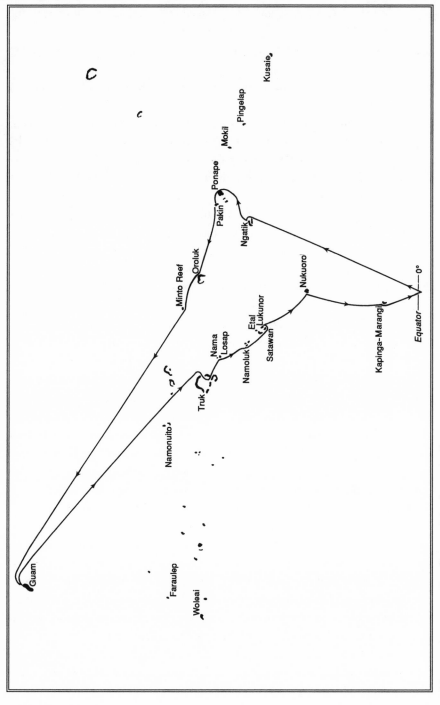

Itinerary in eastern Carolines 12 March–10 April, 1954.

"Well, it's pretty far south," he glanced at his wall chart, "almost on the equator. Do you want to go over the line?"

"Yes indeed. There are entirely too many polliwogs running around loose on my ship."

"OK, Joe, if the admiral approves of Kapingamarangi I'll suggest that you be allowed to dip below the equator for five minutes!"

Kapingamarangi—the name alone evokes rhythms of dancing feet—is an atoll far off the beaten track, on the southernmost edge of Micronesia. Its people belong to the Polynesian race even though separated from the "Polynesian Triangle" by thousands of miles. On Guam little was known about the place, only that its natives made wonderfully fine lauhala matting.

The admiral not only bought the idea; he sent along a newspaper correspondent, Robert Miller, to cover the formalities of our crossing-the-line ceremony. On the agreed-upon day in March 1954 we set forth from Apra's inner harbor and slipped past Orote Point (where old Fort San Jago is only a memory) and out to sea. We would call first at Truk, then Nama, Namoluk, Satawan, Lukunor, and Nukuoro, working our way down to Kapingamarangi, thence back north to Ngatik, Ponape, Oroluk, Minto Reef, and Guam—a full schedule. We hoped there would be no typhoon this time.

We entered Truk lagoon by way of the northeast pass on the morning of the 12 March. Salat Pass lay over the horizon in the southeast quadrant so we could not see whether the *Romance* had been freed from the reef. This time we anchored off the west side of Moen Island, district headquarters for all the eastern Carolines except for the Ponape sector. As I headed ashore in the motor whaleboat, the district administrator's picketboat came out to meet me, with "Distad" Moeller himself offering the services of his boat for ferrying our liberty party—a mark of courtesy not often encountered in the shore establishment. Later he showed me around the Island Trading Company, which boasted a large general store, a bakery, a cinema, and a factory where some old German machinery had been restored to squeeze oil out of copra and further process it into soap. I bought a few trade carvings at the store, and we wound up at the official guest house.

Over a cold beer Moeller confessed to being discouraged with his situation: responsible for a million square miles of ocean area and about sixteen thousand natives but without money for a host of things that needed to be done. "It's a dead-end job, because the deputy high commissionership is a political appointment, so whatever I do here is mainly for my own satisfaction." He smiled. "But the people are wonderful."

"I'm impressed with what you have done with the Island Trading Company."

"Yes, it's been my pride and joy. But I just had to fire some of my best workers because they are Quakers and—can you imagine?—they're considered security risks by somebody higher up who doesn't want to have any potential conscientious objectors around!"

When the time came for our forty-man liberty party, laden with more trade carvings, to return to the ship, the picketboat's diesel engine refused to start. Down in the engine compartment a native mechanic shuffled and clanked for half an hour while we waited, but there wasn't even a cough from the motor. At length he steeled himself to emerge and tell us that it was "broke." So catastrophic was his loss of face that we did all we could to conceal our impatience under a cover of nods and smiles (islanders have been known to commit suicide over such trifles). Finally we returned in our own trusty little boat, making three trips instead of one.

That afternoon we shifted anchorage southward in the lagoon to the place off Dublon Island where we had anchored on our previous visit, and I left the ship again with a small landing party, making for what appeared in the fading daylight to be a splendid boat jetty inshore, a little west of the parade ground that we had visited before. The water proved to be shallow all the way out to the end of this stone structure, and before we could circle and extricate ourselves, the boat hit a forest of coral. Nobody needed to be told what to do: we all jumped out and started pushing the boat to deeper water. Miller, who had come along for the ride, took part enthusiastically, and we all climbed back in. All this happened within a few yards of the ship, to our embarrassment, so without further ado we went to the one landing place we were sure of, where Bland had built his bonfire three months before.

Miller was delighted with Dublon's parade ground, opening on vistas of palm and hibiscus, and wondered why it wouldn't have been a better location for the district headquarters than dusty Moen. Some youths were playing an odd sort of ball game in a dusky clearing with a ball that was actually a green oblong of interwoven palm leaves—the object of the game being to knock this ball as high as possible in the air without allowing it ever to touch earth. It was like playing volleyball with a badminton bird and no net. I took part long enough to drop the ball one time, to the great glee of the natives.

This time the people of the island seemed to know they could trust us, and they were much more friendly than on our first visit, even affectionate.

When darkness came and we had to leave, the only islander who spoke English asked me to come again, and I promised I would, knowing in my heart, and to my sorrow, that it was a lie.

Next morning we hoisted anchor and sortied through Salat Pass. The *Romance* was gone, having been hauled into the lagoon by volunteers conjured up by the mission and towed to a repair basin at Moen. Noon found us off Nama, where we traded more of our aspirin and ice cream for more coconuts and papayas. Thence to Losap, hoping this time to enter the lagoon. Bland went off in the motor whaleboat to check the depth of water in Morappu Channel. Although our chart showed just sufficient depth for the *Hanna,* I could not be sure, for the chart was based on a very old survey, and coral grows at a rate of about one inch per year. Bland found suitable depths on the left-hand side of the channel, except for a 2.5-fathom bump, which ruled out the project because the ship drew 12.5 feet, leaving too little margin for error. "I'm sorry," I told Miller, "but I hate writing reports." So we ran around to the south end of the atoll and settled for a brief landing on Pis Island instead.

Off Namoluk Atoll late that night we found nothing amiss that our radar could discern. I lingered for a while on the southwest side, in the lee of the reef, hoping to entice some visitors, but they were either too busy fire-fishing or too awed by our dim and monstrous presence to come out to us. There was no moon, only soft blackness and stars, and along the rim of coral between us and the lagoon, the water lay glistening still. Near the submarine wall of the reef shone scores of orange fires of coconut husks, borne on the platforms of outrigger canoes like offerings to the god of the sea. Dim figures moved near the fires, and when the flames were stirred into up-soaring sparks, there were golden reflections on poised bodies and on up-stretched sails of canoes, and more reflections in the dark water below. What fish—or for that matter, what bird or beast—could resist such beauty?

More Island at Satawan was next, and we reached it in the morning, anchored in the lagoon, and went ashore at a place where about a hundred natives had arranged themselves—providentially and cleverly, I thought— in two lines at right angles to the shore in order to guide us to a safe landing place. This enabled us to step ashore dry-shod over the bow of the boat to be greeted by the chief and his retinue. After the first handshakes someone in the crowd gave a signal (never, in the Carolines, an order), and a hundred voices shouted a phrase of welcome. We all went immediately to the village under a cathedral-like vault of very old breadfruit trees and entered an open-sided meetinghouse where the welcomers, now doubled in number, seated themselves on the ground, facing our party.

As usual, the local schoolteacher acted as interpreter. He said the people would like to sing something in my honor, and at an imperceptible cue the song burst forth—deep organ tones from the men, perfect harmony and rhythm from the women and children. No one set the pitch or tempo, but there it was. At Lukunor I had been impressed. But here, the flesh of my back tingled and I didn't know for sure if I could hold back the tears. Here were people who had no idea who I might be or if I were kind or whether I hated or was bored with these islands. But I had come, a guest and a stranger, and their hearts were open.

I wanted to do something for them, so I offered transportation (highly irregular!) to anyone wishing to go to Lukunor: a hard day's sail for a canoe, tacking against the wind, but the *Hanna* would be making it in an hour or so. After much giggling it was decided by two young couples that they would go over to be properly married by Father Rively, and the party eventually numbered about ten. While preparations went forward, we toured the immaculate island and admired an old Spanish church that had been spared the fate of its counterpart on Lukunor. Nearby a Lutheran chapel had fallen into sad disrepair, and we were told that there is only one Protestant family left from the days of the Liebenzeller Mission and that the distinction was only hereditary, Satawan society never having been ravaged by sectarian conflict. Not these gentle people.

Wherever we went, they followed us—not to gape but because they liked to see someone admire their homes and because they liked to be near us. Before leaving we bought some of the unusual *kutu* figures for which Satawan is famous, and one of them now sits, hands on knees, watching me with his mother-of-pearl eyes as I write.[1]

In leaving I had to pause in the channel, while canoe-loads of exuberant islanders came out from the beach and clambered on board to say farewell to the wedding couples. It was an uneasy time for me, waiting for them there in the 4-knot current ebbing out of the lagoon, but good practice in ship-handling.

A GAME TO REMEMBER

At Lukunor we debarked our passengers and found Father Rively waiting for us on the pier. His first proposal was that we all have a drink of coconut milk.

His second was to challenge our crew, on behalf of his parishioners, to a game of baseball. In short order we had forty men ashore with all the necessary equipment. This is how Miller reported the game to the United Press:

> The Americans invented baseball, the Japanese introduced it to the South Pacific Islands, and the Micronesians showed the Navy how the game is played, defeating a team from the Destroyer Escort *Hanna*, 16 to 9, in as weird a nine innings as has ever been played.
>
> The game featured home runs, stolen bases, two balls lost in the jungle, a women's cheering section, and the old hidden ball trick. It was the second time the barefoot Micronesian champs of this idyllic South Pacific island had ever met an outside team.
>
> Lukunor's batteries were Puas and Fuss; the pitcher, Puas, being a prince of the island's ruling family with a fast-breaking curve and a good change of pace. Palmer Brettingen, of Ogilvie, Minn., did the hurling for the Navy with Jimmy Carper of Los Angeles behind the plate.
>
> The crowd, some 900, was the largest that ever watched a game in these parts. Scores of Lukunor rooters came from off-lying islands in outrigger canoes to cheer the locals.
>
> Seldom has baseball been played in a more remote spot of the world, or under similar conditions. The infield was of coral base with ankle-high grass in the outfield. The grounds were bordered with coconut palms, the Pacific Ocean, jungle, and the Lukunor Catholic mission. A ground rule limited lost balls in the taro patch to two baggers. Flies into the breadfruit trees went for singles. The Lukunorians were short on uniforms but long on ability. There wasn't a pair of shoes on the whole team, and only three of the players owned shirts.
>
> Twice the locals hoodwinked the *Hanna*'s base runners with the old hidden ball trick, choking off rallies that could have tied the score. The Americans out-hit the locals with three home runs, one that bounced off the thatched roof bordering left field that was said to be the longest ball ever hit on Lukunor.
>
> There was plenty of Brooklynese from the sarong-clad lady rooters who cheered the home team with chants and rhythmic hand-clapping interspersed with shrieks of laughter whenever an error was made by either team. The only resident who was unhappy with the outcome was Father W. J. Rively, of Altoona, Pennsylvania, who commented sadly, "There'll be no holding them now. I have been telling the team for several months

that they weren't nearly as good as they thought they were, and that any American team would wallop them. Next thing you know they'll be asking for tryouts with the National League."

We stayed overnight at Lukunor and gave the population a treat with a shoot-'em-up Western movie. They were completely adrift in the conversational parts but went wild over the horses and the gunplay.

The trek to Nukuoro took the better part of the next day's daylight, but I hoped to go ashore there anyway, having been cheated out of a landing by typhoon Doris during our first trip. Like Kapingamarangi, Nukuoro is Polynesian and virtually unknown. Both atolls, too far south to have been sighted from the deck of even the most errant galleon, remained undiscovered until 1795 when Capt. William Mortlock of the storeship *Young William* reported a group of islands in the vicinity of the Lukunor/Satawan/Etal triad now known as the Mortlock Group. I have failed to turn up any particulars concerning either Mortlock's voyage or the next encounter with the islands, which took place during Monteverde's voyage in 1806 in the Spanish frigate *La Pala*. On Lütke's "General Chart of the Carolines" (1828) an island is shown in Kapingamarangi's latitude labeled "Gr. Pyguiame?" Truly one needs to be a detective to unravel old voyages.

The sea off the entrance to the Nukuoro lagoon ran high, threatening to capsize our boat before we even cast off. With me were Bland, Savage, and Mathews, with McCall, that peerless coxswain, at the tiller. (I didn't invite Miller to come along, because of the danger.) In case we were unable to find a suitable landing place inside the lagoon, we planned to transfer to a six-man rubber life raft trailing astern. McCall had to fight a strong ebb current pouring out of the lagoon, but he managed to reach still water inside and landed us at a fine masonry pier on the principal island.

Here was another model village laid out with geometric precision, coral stones defining well-swept paths, neat thatched houses on stilts, a profusion of flowering shrubs, the usual scrawny chickens, but no pigs and no flies. We were met by a band of naked children and the island's "doctor," who sported an armband proclaiming his profession and whose English vocabulary consisted of "hello" and "yes." He led us to the house of Hagatuk, the chief magistrate, who spoke even less English. A personage arrived wearing a sport shirt—bright red, the color reserved for Polynesian royalty—and we all sat around an oilcloth-covered table silently drinking coconut milk until the inevitable schoolteacher-interpreter showed up. He told us we had just missed a Japanese interloper who stopped by recently to trade sugar for fresh water and fruit. Unlike some, the crew of this one refrained from appropriating the women and whatever else they wanted. He also told us about a 30-ton trawler that had foundered on the reef here and was salvaged by the natives, who used it to ply between Nukuoro and Ponape. It was always breaking down, but the islanders were wonderfully proud of it, for every stick and plank now belonged to them.

Hagatuk presented us with several exquisite ghost canoes. Perfect miniatures of the standard native outriggers, these tiny craft originated from an ancient cult practice wherein they would be laden with good things to eat, a priest would make an incantation to persuade evil spirits to climb aboard, and they would then be launched out to sea to drift forever—or to some other island, *any* other island. I tried to reciprocate the gifts with cigarettes and a pocket lighter engraved with the *Hanna*'s likeness, but Hagatuk declined. "He does not smoke; he is a Christian," explained the schoolteacher. Others accepted, though.

It was rapidly getting dark, and by the time we reached the channel, the water was oily black, but by means of some sixth sense McCall stayed away from coral heads as the still-ebbing tide swept us out into the open sea. Where the fast outflowing river met the incoming surf, he slowed to bare steerageway and even though the boat stood on its beam ends, we avoided shipping any water. As soon as we could prudently do so, we paralleled the reef in order to avoid meeting the waves head on. The rubber raft broke away and I ordered it abandoned, an easy decision since not even a hundred-dollar raft was worth the risk of turning toward the reef. The thing could still be floating a thousand miles from nowhere.

KAPINGAMARANGI—YOU CAN'T GO THERE!

Kapingamarangi Atoll is like a slender necklace, and in approaching it next morning I was reminded of La Pérouse's description of an atoll reef in sunshine as resembling a circle of diamonds surrounding a medallion. (He was, I think, a poet as well as an explorer.) Certainly this morning Kapingamarangi glittered like a thousand jewels.

It was Rayner's turn to go ashore, and he and Miller made the most of it. Eventually Miller published an article entitled "Kapingamarangi Is Paradise—But You Can't Go There." During the war the Japanese used the atoll as a seaplane base, and in due course American air attacks sank their seaplane tender, where it was visible even now in the limpid depths of the lagoon. The small islands making up the necklace are connected by causeways so old no one knows when or by whom they were constructed. One island is set aside as community property, where anyone may help himself to coconut or pandanus. Another is reserved for the king and his household, and there our landing party luxuriated under a canopy of fine matting, sitting in chairs carved out of single sections of breadfruit trees and drinking the usual coconut milk.

Meanwhile several natives came out to the ship to trade shells and mats for cigarettes and soap (how ironic the odyssey of a cake of Palmolive!). One canoe capsized in shooting the passage in the reef, and for a time I worried about its occupants. But they managed to secure a footing on the reef, righted their craft, bailed it out, and continued out to see us, as merry as if the accident had been the funniest thing that had ever happened to them, despite the fact that they had lost their entire stock in trade. As Otto von Kotzebue observed long ago, "The Carolinians' boats upset easily for want of precaution, which on their voyages frequently happens twice a day; but as they are good swimmers and divers, it produces no consequence other than that of making them laugh heartily; they then turn the boat up again and swim by the side of it until they have thrown out the water out of it with their hands."[2] I have seen them bail so rapidly as to create a constant stream of water—or make it seem so.

That afternoon we were favored by a visit from the king, attired in a panama hat, sunglasses, and a bright red shirt. Another indication of his high rank was his corpulence, making him as ungainly as his subjects were lithe. I did the honors, and since our men were having a swim at the time, we staged an exhibition of diving from great heights into the blue-purple ocean that amazed and delighted him. He presented us a with a ghost canoe for remembrance and clambered ponderously down the Jacob's ladder to his own craft, almost swamping it. Since we had drifted a considerable distance during the day, we passed a long line to the canoes and towed them all back to the entrance. As soon as they cast off, we headed south again toward that famous imaginary line around the Earth's midriff.

THE POLLIWOG REBELLION

During the night a horrible screech broke the silence. We had crossed Latitude Zero, an event that was the culmination of days of alarms and excursions, and again I will let Bob Miller tell the story as it was carried by the United Press a few days later:

> The navy revealed today that a mutiny of 153 officers and men aboard the uss *Hanna* was beaten down by the ship's captain and seventeen loyal shellbacks while the ship was cruising recently in equatorial waters of the Western Pacific. The revolt broke out on board the San Diego-based destroyer escort, now operating out of Guam, when the rebellious polliwogs attempted to fly a foreign ensign—the polliwog flag—over the *Hanna*. The Navy said the mutineers gained temporary control of the situation under the leadership of a young ensign who identified himself as the chief wiggler. An eyewitness agreed with the report. The traitors were beaten into submission, lost their hair, were doused with salt water, and eventually swore allegiance to Neptunus Rex.
>
> A lack of solidarity among the mutineers caused their downfall. Fifth columnists planted by the shellbacks offered leniency to those who revealed the names of the ringleaders, and bribes were proffered to those who failed to support the mutiny. The promises made by the shellbacks were never fulfilled, for once the mutiny was broken, all those who had any part in it were severely dealt with by the royal party of Neptunus Rex which boarded the *Hanna* at the equator.
>
> King Neptune (Chief Boatswain's Mate A.V. Bell, Eslingdale, Mass.) took personal charge of the mutineer trials from his barber's chair tribunal on the stern of the *Hanna*. From that moment the polliwogs were doomed. Neptune paid high tribute to the *Hanna's* skipper, Lt. Commander Joseph C. Meredith, for his efforts in putting down the mutiny. Several of the renegades were thrown into irons, others put in the stocks, and all were paddled soundly for their part in the revolt, whether guilty or not.

It should be added that Miller himself acted as defense attorney, with magnificent aplomb in a costume consisting of two coconuts strategically placed, and never failed to throw his clients on the mercy of the court.

The next leg of our journey, some five hundred miles to Ponape, gave everyone time to forgive and be forgiven, and took us close enough to Ngatik Atoll to justify checking that place, even though we would have to do so by night. Coming up to its edge in pitch blackness we detected two objects by radar that could have been fishing boats or simply some beacons shown on our chart, except that the echoes were stronger than those usually reflected by such objects. Approaching as closely as I dared and shining our small searchlight in that direction, I could see nothing; a fine drizzle stopped the beam within a few hundred yards. Waiting until daylight would have disrupted the schedule, so I broke off and headed for Ponape. Maybe District Administrator Hedges would be able to resolve the question.

12

On Lütke's Courses

Soon we picked up Ponape on radar and by dawn saw its misty slopes in the distance. I headed for a point on the southeast edge of the island, near Matalanim Harbor, bringing us to a place that embodies one of the enigmas of the Pacific—the ruins of mighty Nan Matal.

There is something of the archeologist in all of us, something deeper than mere lust for treasure. Twist and turn as we will, the not-unfriendly hand of the past is on our shoulders, for we are in essence the same people who built Persepolis and Tihuanaco and the pyramids of Egypt and Shensi. The *how* and *why* of our fluctuating destinies linger in our deepest subconscious. Something like this recognition whetted my appetite to see first-hand the ruins that I had heard about during our first visit to Ponape—and that F. W. Christian, Willard Price, and Walter Karig, among others, have described, telling of a whole city in the lagoon, not an isolated fortress but a kind of Venice with several artificial islands, severely rectangular, covering a large area.[1] Who these people were, whence they came, and what their fate may have been remain mysteries.

As we edged up to the reef that rainy morning we could see, abruptly rising from the water washing over the coral shelf, a city of islands partly concealed under a glistening cover of mangrove, through the openings of which loomed walls of great monoliths, walls whose barbaric immensity made the castles of Europe seem ladylike in comparison. The stones were laid up like logs, with their sheer weight anchoring them in defiance of the jungle. We paralleled the reef, studying the shapes of the fortifications (if that's what they were), the causeways connecting them, and the long protective break-water that had withstood centuries of onslaught by the Pacific. It was easy to identify *Nan Tauch* ("The Place"), the hugest structure of all, as described by Christian:

> The waterfront is faced with a terrace built of massive basalt blocks about seven feet wide, standing out more than seven feet above the shallow waterway. The left side of the great gateway yawning overhead is about twenty-five feet in height and the right some thirty feet, overshadowed and all but hidden from view by the dense foliage of a huge *ikiok* tree, . . . a wonder of deep emerald-green, heart-shaped leaves, thickly studded with tassels of scarlet trumpet-shaped flowers, bright as the bloom of coral or flame tree.

> Here, in olden times the outer wall must have been of considerably greater height, but now had fallen into lamentable ruin, whether from earthquake, typhoon, vandal hand, or the wear and tear of long, long ages. A series of rude stone steps brings us into a spacious courtyard, strewn with fragments of fallen pillars, enclosing a second terraced enclosure with a projecting frieze or cornice of somewhat Japanese type. The measurement of the outer enclosure, as we afterwards roughly ascertained, was some 185 by 115 feet, height varying from 20 feet to nearly 40 feet. The space within can only be entered by the great gateway in the centre of the western face, and by a small ruinous portal in the north-west corner. The inner terraced enclosure forms a second parallelogram of some 85 by 75 feet, average thickness of wall, 8 feet, height of walls, 15 to 18 feet. In the centre of a rudely paved court lies the great central vault or treasure-chamber, identified with the name of an ancient monarch known as Chau-te-Reul or Chau-te-Leur, probably a dynastic title like that of the Pharaoh in ancient Egypt. *Chau* was the ancient Ponapean word for denoting both the sun and the king.[2]

According to legend, a race of giants created this city by the sea and then became soft through luxurious living. A savage invader named Idzikolkol came from far away but was so awed by the fortifications that he gave up the idea of assault and was about to depart, when a native woman came to him in the night and betrayed the secret of Nan Tauch (the small side door?). With her help Idzikolkol was able to enter and take the king unaware; the invaders then overran the city and slaughtered the inhabitants. The old civilization was stamped out, and Nan Matal was abandoned forever because the new masters of Ponape preferred to live in the jungle.

Without trying to assess the basis of the legends or even to advocate any particular theory, Christian draws some startling analogies, citing similarities between ancient Sumerian and modern Peruvian words and suggesting a Carolinian bridge consisting of words too nearly the same to admit coincidence. In the introduction to Christian's *The Caroline Islands: Travel in the Sea of the Little Lands,* Cyprian Bridge ventures that the ruins are not those of buildings erected by races now inhabiting the islands and that in any case the builders must have vastly outnumbered the present population.

Looking on Nan Matal from the deck of the *Hanna* I had to believe that the work could not have been accomplished in this enervating climate without thousands of workers, probably slaves directed by a "master race."

Nan Matal faces the sea and is of the sea. Its founders may have been people who trusted their fate not to jungle glens but to the wide expanses of the Pacific, who drew upon Ponape's fertility for food and workers but had aspirations far beyond the horizon. Could Ponape have been a way station between Peru and Malaya? Did the ancient voyagers know enough about the counterequatorial current running just south of Ponape to use it for passage from the Orient to America? Christian challenges us:

> There are many such stone enclosures upon Ponape, especially upon the island of Tauk, a little southeast of the Mant Islands, off the coast of U, near Nallam-en-Pokolooh Deeps, before you come to Aru on the Matalanim border. It is for future explorers to make them give up their secrets, which I have striven feebly to depict in words. Neither must they, not indeed can they, pass over indifferently these relics of grey antiquity, venerable as dolmen, kitvaen, or kjoekkenmôdding—the work of a vanished people who, Titanlike, have stumbled down into the darkness of a mysterious doom.[3]

We left Nan Matal and sailed clockwise around the south edge of Ponape's barrier reef past the harbors of Lot and Kiti and up along the western shore toward Jokaj, unaware we were following Lütke's course when he discovered Ponape in 1828.

Feodor Petrovich Lütke was sixteen when he enlisted in the tsar's navy, and he was twenty when he won a commission for the bravery he displayed at Danzig in 1817 while serving under Capt. Vassili Mikhailovich Golovnin. The Russians in those days were busy consolidating their discoveries in the northern reaches of the Pacific, and for a time they outshone the explorers of all other nations. When Golovnin was ordered to proceed in the sloop *Kamchatka* to investigate rumors of maladministration in the Alaska colony, young Lütke went along and fell under the spell of the islands.

Soon afterward, we find him a captain-lieutenant with an expedition of his own, consisting of two ships built at Okhta expressly for the purpose—the *Seniavin* and the *Möller.* The former was an 800-ton bark mounting sixteen cannon, a vessel that Lütke considered ideal for such service because it combined features of good warships without requiring too much equipment. The latter was seaworthy enough but lacked the other's ability to maneuver in tight places.

Lütke left Kronstadt in September 1826, reached New Archangel in Alaska the following June, and explored the Bering Sea until winter forced him south. He then visited the Marshall Islands and worked westward into the Carolines.

Much earlier, according to an old account, the Spaniards sighted an island "almost round, about thirty leagues in compass; it is well wooded, and on the sides of the hill there is an abundance of rose-colored flowers, and much tilled land; three leagues west of it are four bare islands, and a great many more close to it, all hemmed in by rocks."[4] They labeled it "La Quirosa" and proceeded to forget the whole thing. Although the description fits Ponape, the location ascribed to La Quirosa does not, and for years it hopped around on various charts on a negative basis—that is, later explorers determined only where it was *not.*

Some other Spaniards saw Ponape but never lived to tell the story: legend tells of a floating island that came up out of the sea, inhabited by men with white skins whom the natives could kill only by piercing their eyes. And an old Spanish cannon was removed from nearby Ant Island in 1839 by the British man-o'-war HMS *Larne;* it has since disappeared.

Lütke tells his own story of the rediscovery of La Quirosa:

Since my advent to the archipelago of the Carolines, I made it an inevitable rule to run short boards during the night, under small canvas, in order not to pass up in darkness some unknown land, nor to tumble on its shores.⁵ Thus I lost ten or twelve hours daily, but this loss was equally compensated by the accuracy of the navigation gained, and by a more exact exploration of the part of the ocean through which we were passing. Just once, on the night of 13 January, I allowed myself to break this rule: we found ourselves at the intersection of the routes of Captains Tompson, Ybargoita, Duperrey, and one other, and it seemed impossible for there to be in this place room for even a small undiscovered island.

We could scarcely believe our eyes the next morning when we saw a great island before us; such a discovery seemed to be out of the question here; the strongest proof (if any be needed) that the discovery of unknown lands is but a happenstance, and whoever disputes the honor of a first discovery disputes nothing. It was certainly strange that the highest and one of the largest of the Caroline Islands was the last to be discovered. Captain Duperrey looked for it 50 miles further north, following the advice of the inhabitants of Kusaie, who told him that an island of "Pouloupa" was situated west-northwest of their island.

If the wind had been blowing a little more freshly during the night, or if the dawn had found us farther north, this unexpected encounter might have been disastrous. But now nothing prevented our rejoicing in a highly agreeable discovery, even though it had been due solely to luck.⁶

Lütke's landfall was near Nan Matal, and it is a pity he didn't notice the ruins there, for they would certainly have doubled his wonder. At any rate, the conduct of the natives in the next day or so kept him fully occupied. No sooner had the *Seniavin* and the *Möller* arrived than a swarm of outrigger canoes set out, loaded with naked men and women who danced, shouted, made faces, and carried on far less sedately than islanders he previously had encountered in the Marshalls. "Their savage faces imprinted with defiance, their large bloodshot eyes, and the vacancy and turbulence of these people made a very disagreeable impression on us," he noted.⁷ Those who climbed on board were given presents, then became so jealous of what they had received that they would permit no one to show them what the objects were intended for. One fellow seized the sextant out of Lütke's hand and almost got away with it—but failing that, he jumped over the side.

Lütke sent a boat in charge of Lieutenant Zavalachine into Lot Harbor to look around, but when stones and lances were seen in the canoes that crowded round, the boat quickly returned to the ship. The canoes dropped behind after nightfall, but on the morning of 15 January 1829 the natives could be seen along the reef barking like dogs.[8]

At Kiti Harbor, Lütke himself headed the scouting party and was immediately surrounded by forty canoes filled with natives who at first showed no hostility, but as they closed in, one warrior stood up and pointed a spear at Lütke. Lütke was not the kind of explorer who enjoyed killing, but he felt obliged to shoot, and the death of the man disconcerted the Kiti people long enough to permit the Russians to withdraw. That night the sound of the triton horn—the signal of trouble on all the islands of the sea—could be heard echoing in the jungle. Next day the wind died and the *Seniavin* was almost carried onto the reef. The natives danced and howled in anticipation, but a breeze sprang up in the nick of time and the ship managed to work clear.

Lütke observed that the Ponapeans much resembled Papuans, which is significant because unlike Micronesians the natives of Melanesia have an unpleasant trait of regarding every visitor as legitimate prey. This and a persistent negroid strain in Ponape even today may be a clue to their origin—or to the invaders who destroyed Nan Matal.

The *Hanna,* benefitting from the changes of the past 126 years, sailed peaceably along the shore without being barked at, and without our hearing any triton horns. The natives spearfishing along the reef scarcely looked up as we passed. That afternoon I called on Henry Hedges again and told him about the mysterious radar pips in the lagoon at Ngatik. "The beacons are gone," he told me, "so maybe you had an intruder there after all."

"In that case I'll go back tomorrow and have a look by daylight. So far we haven't nabbed a single trespasser red-handed."

"That's because we stopped letting them go with just a warning. They used to be a great nuisance, but warnings mean nothing to them—their life is so dangerous anyway."

Ngatik is not a very accessible piece of real estate because the only pass through the reef is too narrow for ships of any size. It was discovered long before Ponape, first by Capt. Savaria y Villar of the merchant ship *Nuestra Señora de la Consolación* in 1773.[9] Then came the Englishman Musgrave in the *Sugarcane* in 1793 and (probably) the Spaniard Lafita in the *Principe de Asturias* in 1802. Somewhere along the line, the natives earned for this small ring of islets the interesting name of the "Passion Islands," with the main island being called the "Island of the Brave Ones."

When we arrived, the lagoon was innocent of anything larger than a canoe, but I decided to send a boat ashore anyway to see what information we might pick up. The water was so calm that the landing party were able to step onto the reef from the ocean side, direct from the motor whaleboat. We could even have moored the ship alongside the wall of coral had there been a fender or two to protect our paintwork. Rayner headed the landing party this time, and he and Miller toured the island while the ship waited off the reef in the center of a covey of native canoes. Rayner reported that the dwellings bore a startling resemblance to those of a New England town: four-square, neatly whitewashed, in some cases even two-storied. The paramount chief overwhelmed our men with hospitality, and even the women seemed enthusiastic—an attitude that was possibly a holdover from the times during the war when we dropped supplies and even landed seaplanes in the lagoon here, right under the noses of the enemy. Now the roles were reversed: a Japanese fishing boat had just spent a whole week there, leaving only three days before our arrival!

Darkness came long before the landing party returned, and when they did come away from the shore, the scene resembled a water pageant, with flashlight beams bobbing along the surface of the water and a backdrop of torches on the beach. Later that night the quartermaster on watch, who had been one of the lucky ones to go ashore, confided that while he and another sailor were waiting for the others, two Ngatik maidens had come along and offered themselves. He said also that the offer was declined, and though he may have told the truth, I would hesitate to observe, as Lütke did, that in all the time we cruised the Carolines, not one of my crew fell under the tropic spell.

We headed back toward Guam by way of Oroluk Atoll and Minto Reef, diverging from Lütke's track, which took him southwest to Lukunor before he too sailed for the Marianas. His work in the Carolines was by no means at an end, however, for he returned in the next winter season and made new discoveries, besides fixing more precisely the positions of older ones. This time he bypassed Ponape (understandably) and sailed straight through the reef-infested area south of Truk, via Woleai, Olimarao, Fais, Ulithi, and thence to Guam and the Philippines, from which he sailed home in the spring.

The *Seniavin* and the *Möller* arrived intact at Kronstadt on 16 September 1829, and Lütke found himself a hero. The rewards of successful voyagers in those days were substantial, and he was elevated to rank of senior captain and then to vice admiral—and then to the title of Count Lütke. In our time the Soviets have canonized him as a "People's Pioneer," a title for which one may assume his relatively humble origins made him eligible.

Pursuing our own course, the *Hanna* reached Oroluk in the morning and found it deserted except for hundreds of thousands of sea birds, whom a blast from our whistle sent spiraling upward like a cloud of confetti in the sky. Later in the day we came to Minto Reef and were indulging in a little target practice on the 4,200-ton hulk lying there, when we were suddenly interrupted by word that there was a Japanese fishing boat on the far side of the reef. We raced around to intercept and found a 35-ton craft lying on the reef itself, with not a soul on board. All navigating and radio equipment had been removed, a calendar in the pilot house had been checked off to 7 February 1954, and all indications pointed to an orderly abandonment. It would have been easy to salvage the craft, except for the fumes from tons of rotting fish in the hold. So we turned away and headed back to Guam.

Before leaving the subject of the eastern Carolines, I should touch on the voyage of another Russian explorer, Otto von Kotzebue, who took an interest in the Carolines even before Lütke. The Kotzebue expedition, sponsored by the incredibly rich Count Romanzoff, left Finland 23 May 1815 in a spanking new 180-ton brig christened the *Rurick,* bent on discovery. On board were a number of distinguished persons such as the artist Louis Choris and the poet Adelbert de Chamisso as naturalist. The ship carried eight guns and a mass of scientific equipment, with ample quarters for officers and men, "from a conviction that on this the health of the entire crew depends."

After rounding Cape Horn and reaching California the Kotzebue expedition touched at San Francisco, where they were entertained by the Spanish garrison. They then proceeded to Hawaii, where they met "King Tamea-mea," and to Guam, where Gov. Don José de Medinilla y Piñeda did the honors. Though his courage and good seamanship were undoubtedly an inspiration to Lütke ten years later, Kotzebue became hopelessly muddled by the early charts when his expedition sailed down among the Carolines:[10]

I knew from experience, that the depth near the coral reefs is always very considerable, and I was therefore bold enough to overlook the danger;

besides, this is the only means of examining them, since at the distance of a half-mile the passage would no longer be visible. This navigation requires the greatest precision; there must always be a man at the mast-head, a second on the bowsprit, a third on the ship's head, and the pilot (provided with a good telescope) in the scuttle, in order to ward against danger; and Captain Flinders justly observed of these places that "a man who has weak nerves should leave such investigations alone."[11]

13

Treacherous Waters

GUAM

It was the evening of 12 April 1954, and we had been in Guam only a few hours. Those of the crew who had not gone ashore were sprawled on deck watching one of the old movies that circulate endlessly among navy ships and shore stations. I had donned fresh slacks and an aloha shirt and was just leaving the ship when a call came from Captain Klinker: "Joe, how soon can you get under way?"

I tried to sound matter-of-fact. "Well, I have only one boiler lit off, and a lot of the crew are on liberty, but I think we can be ready to go in an hour"—the absolute minimum for warming up the main engines.

"How soon can you be at full power?" I consulted the chief engineer, who had come running.

"One o'clock."

"Okay, here's the pitch. There's a British freighter north of Guam whose skipper has been badly injured, and it's up to you to get him to the hospital. I'll be down to give you the details."

During the next fifty minutes we scrambled to retrieve the liberty party, while more information filtered in: the captain of the ss *Avonmoor*, bound for Fiji, had fallen through a cargo hatch; the ship could not reach Guam in less than twelve hours; his first mate was afraid the injured man would die sooner than that.

We got all but three of our crew back on board. Bob Miller showed up to cover the story, and we were away from the dock exactly fifty-five minutes from the time of the first telephone call. I cleared harbor cautiously, it being my first night sortie and better to lose five or ten minutes doing so rather than to run aground before even passing the breakwater. The night was moonless and none of the buoys was lighted, but I had a dozen pair of eyes to supplement my own, and soon we emerged safely upon open sea. The engines began drawing steam from both boilers, and by midnight we were ready for full power an hour ahead of promise. I rang up 24 knots (a forbidden speed except in emergency because of the strain on our plant and the prodigious fuel consumption) and held it there.

Our first radar contact on the *Avonmoor* was at twenty-four miles straight ahead, showing her dead in the water, somewhat to my surprise—I expected that at least she would have been headed for Guam. It turned out that in addition to other troubles her engineering plant had broken down. By 2:45 A.M. we were alongside and had put a doctor on board, and about a half-hour later we completed the highline transfer of the patient (Capt. Francis F. Gilbert) to our ship.

It was daylight when we passed the entrance buoys of Apra Harbor, still at 24 knots, and I slowed to 15 lest we swamp nearby small craft. In the inner harbor we backed down full and sidled into our berth like a cat on a cushion, within ten minutes of original estimate. I went down to the quarterdeck to witness the patient's transfer to the ambulance. He was yellowish gray, almost the color of death. I was sobered by the sight but glad the *Hanna* had performed well, even though the performance might prove futile. Later I learned that our midnight dash had indeed saved the man's life.

On 17 April we got under way for our second and final patrol of the Western Carolines, stopping at Yap on 19 April and striking southwest from there directly toward Helen Reef, where I hoped to find a poacher or two, the season for gathering trochus shells now being well advanced.

On the twenty-first, hidden in early morning rainsqualls, we swept down like a wolf on the fold. Up to that moment we had maintained radio silence so that trespassers, if any, would have no hint of our approach.

The lagoon was empty. I sent a landing party ashore on Helen Islet. Finding only an abandoned hut and two concrete tanks used for leaching out the shells, they soon returned to the ship. Disappointed, I set off for

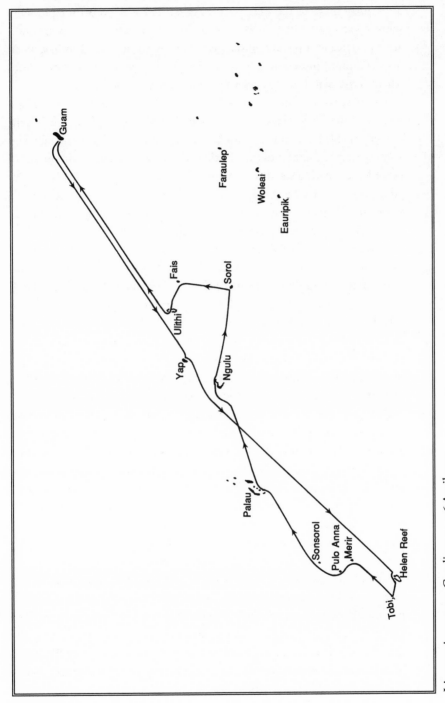

Itinerary in western Carolines 17–26 April 1954.

Tobi, forty miles to the west-northwest, while I worked off my pique by shooting at flying fish with a .45 caliber pistol, an excellent form of small-arms practice and posing no danger whatever to the fish. Tobi had been neglected until our coming: tiny, remote, said to be "of no interest." Still, where is the island in the ocean that doesn't have a good story?

The first white man to see Tobi was the English freebooter Woodes Rogers, of the *Duke*. He sighted the island 11 April 1710 and logged: "Nothing remarkable has happened worth noting, but that we have generally had a strong Current setting to the Northward. At Two Yesterday Afternoon we made Land, bearing s.e. distant about 5 Leagues, being a low flat Island, all green, and full of Trees. Lt. 2.54.n. This Island is not laid down on any Sea Chart; our Ship continues very leaky."[1] Rogers did not bother to name his discovery, nor did Philip Carteret, who sighted it sixty-seven years later. In 1782 William Hambly also sighted Tobi and named it after his ship, the *Lord North*. That same year a Deutsche Handelsgesellschaft ship, the *Iphegenia*, effected a landing and bestowed on it the name of Johnstone's Island. Seven years later Commo. Joseph Dorrin came along in the *Duke of Montrose* and called it Neville Island.

This proliferation of names was due not entirely to explorers' conceit nor to their ignorance of each others' work. The ocean current in these parts is so swift that it was impossible to get a good "fix" in order to locate the island accurately. Each therefore believed he had made an original discovery.[2]

Perhaps it was just as well that landings on Tobi were seldom attempted, considering the experience of a handful of men who were forced to spend the years 1832, 1833, and 1834 there, cut off completely from the civilized world.

The New Bedford whaleship *Mentor*, in which these unfortunates had sailed, fetched up on a reef in Palau on 21 May 1831. The survivors established friendly relations with the natives and would have been wise to wait for eventual rescue, but instead they set forth in the ship's remaining boat and a native canoe, hoping to reach the Dutch settlement of Tidore in Halmahera. Three Palauans accompanied them.

One of the castaways, Horace Holden, tells of how the expedition was marred on the third day when the canoe upset, with loss of most of their provisions and fresh water. They divided what was left, four coconuts each, and continued for nine days facing almost certain starvation. To their joy they then saw land about ten miles off and exerted all their strength to reach it. When within about six miles, they could see coming out to meet them a fleet of canoes, filled with naked blacks. Holden narrates the episode:

They attacked us with brutal ferocity, knocking us overboard with their clubs, in the meantime making the most frightful grimaces, and yelling like so many incarnate devils. They fell on our boat and immediately destroyed it, breaking it into splinters, and taking the fragments into their canoes. While this was going on we were swimming from one canoe to another, entreating them by signs to spare our lives and permit us to get into their canoes. This for a long time they refused, beating us most unmercifully, whenever we caught hold of anything to save us from sinking.

After they demolished our boat, and kept us in that condition for some time, they allowed us to get on board. They then compelled us to row toward the land. They stripped us of all our clothing immediately after we were taken in.[3]

Once ashore amid a crowd of yelling females they were paraded around the island while their captors contended to see who should have them as his property. This was only the beginning. The abuse heaped on the captives during the next two years was such that most of them died. In a bitter outburst Holden declared, "This island, unlike the Pelews, is one of the most horrible and wretched on the face of the globe. . . . The character of the inhabitants much resembles that of the island itself. Cowardly and servile, yet most barbarous and cruel, they combine in their habits, tempers, and dispositions the most disgusting and loathsome features that disgrace humanity."[4]

But Holden admitted that his existence was no better or worse than that of the islanders and that they themselves were incapable of comprehending a better one. His "owner" was the only one who befriended him, hiding him under some thatch after an earthquake had shaken the island and the natives had concluded that the white men must die in order to placate their god "Yarrow" and keep him from sinking the island into the ocean. The crowning indignity came when they tattooed Holden and the others from head to foot, missing nothing, but again he concedes that in the eyes of an islander the undecorated body was shameful and offensive.

On 3 February 1833, just fifty-nine days after the capture, a prospect of rescue appeared off the island in the shape of a British trading vessel. Two of the Americans managed to get out to the ship in a native canoe and win their freedom. But the others ware not permitted to show themselves, and the ship's cowardly captain sailed away.

Eight men remained: Horace Holden, Benjamin Nute, Charles R. Bow-kett, William Siddon, Peter Andrews, and the three Palauans. Only Holden and Nute survived the horrible eighteen months that followed. When finally the British got around to sending the bark *Britannia* to their rescue, these two climbed aboard stark naked, tattooed and pitiably emaciated.

The experience these men suffered, one notes, does not conform to the usual tales of Micronesian hospitality. The most reasonable explanation is found in Tobi's Melanesian character—the island being only two hundred miles north of New Guinea—for as I have mentioned, Melanesians usually dealt with visitors as legitimate prey.

In spite of this grim background, I found I had nothing to fear in landing on Tobi. The people were Melanesian all right—black and homely as sin, with great mops of frizzy hair topping male and female alike. But they greeted us like long-lost kinfolk and even insisted on carrying me the last fifty feet from shallow water to the beach.

A young dandy stood before me, clad only in a necklace of yellow shells. "My name Ferman," he said. "I am nineteen years."

"I am captain," I replied. "Take me to chief."

Grasping my hand, he led me a short distance to the village, an untidy mélange of shanties and thatched huts among piles of coconuts. The only presentable structure was an open pavilion reminiscent of the bandstand in Feeney Park back in my hometown. There I met the chief.

Chief Tuarmo spoke no English at all, and Ferman's understanding of the language was so sparse that I finally gave up any attempt to communicate other than by the customary signs, nods, and smiles. The gift of a carton of cigarettes caused a yell of delight, and I was duly presented with a pair of beautifully carved "monkey men," the squatting figurines that seem to peer fixedly at one from every angle. Each island follows its own particular style of carving, but I noticed that the closer one came to white influences and the lure of the district trading store, the cruder that style became.

Two massive platforms occupied the center of Tobi's main village. We were told they had been used by the Japanese to mount antiaircraft guns. I am inclined to believe they may have been older, from a hint given in F. W. Christian's 1899 book, *The Carolina Islands: Travel in the Sea of the Little Lands,* wherein he mentions "Tobi, her massive platforms topped by stone images of her *Yari,* or ancient heroes, gazing out upon the deep."[5]

We shoved off for Merir that afternoon (22 April) and reached it after nightfall. It was too dark for anything but a radar check, for which I was glad because I had been on the go since four in the morning and had no urge for further investigations that day. We then headed for Pulo Anna and Sonsorol.

The current was so strong that we had to steer five degrees to the right of the track needed to get us to Merir, two degrees to the right to get to Pulo Anna, and four degrees to the right to get to Sonsorol. There is something unnerving in being thus pushed about by a huge silent river, far from any coast, answering not to wind or weather but to forces set up by the rotation of the earth. It must have been even more unnerving in the days of sail.

Weaving thus, we came to the twin islands of Sonsorol and Fana. After breakfast I took landing party number two ashore on Sonsorol, where the village of Tamagl sprawls among the coconut trees. Sonsorol, together with Map Island at Yap, once comprised the kingdom of "His Majesty O'Keefe," that most colorful of entrepreneurs. During our two-hour stay on the island, I could find nothing there to ascribe to him, for much had happened on Sonsorol since his disappearance in 1809. He may have been responsible for the ruined cement pier that once extended to the edge of the reef, but it was impossible to tell, for erosion of concrete depends so much on the original formula and on the temper of the sea.

O'Keefe had had special entree on Sonsorol because on one occasion he saved the natives from starving. It seems that in 1779 or shortly before— well before Spain moved formally to establish title to the Carolines—a Spanish warship landed a party of sailors and marines on the island, and their behavior so offended the native elders and priests that they destroyed the brightly colored cloth the interlopers had set up on a tall stick. The Spaniards then proceeded to burn and pillage the island, even destroying the coconut trees, before sailing away. O'Keefe happened along soon afterward, distributed food to the natives, and transported some of them back to Yap, where they had a better chance of surviving.[6]

The Spaniards' reaction may have derived, in part, from their memory of something that had happened on Sonsorol a century and a half earlier, when the existence of the Caroline Islands was only suspected—a story that merits telling at this point.

THE SANTISSIMA TRINIDAD STORY

In 1696 a group of some thirty natives drifted ashore at Samar in the Philippines and, upon being questioned by a Jesuit priest named Paul Clain (originally Klein), were able to name for him eighty-seven different islands in the region whence they came. Clearly these islands represented a vast new field for conversion to the faith. Indeed, these particular castaways seemed quite gentle and eager to learn civilized ways. Father Clain's idea intrigued his superiors, including the Jesuit procurator of the Philippines, Father Andres Serrano, S.J., who won for it the support of Pope Clement XI and, through him, the backing of the Spanish Crown—a fact that led to three successive attempts to reach what Serrano called the "New Philippines." The third of these efforts set forth in a patache called the *Santissima Trinidad,* under command of Sgt. Maj. Don Francisco Padilla, with José Somera as chief pilot, two priests, a lay brother, eighty-six soldiers, and a Palauan family they hoped to repatriate.

Fifteen days after leaving the Philippines they sighted two islands, which Father Duberron named the Isles of San Andreas—doubtless Sonsorol. Somera relates that he sent his assistant to take soundings offshore and that when the ship's boat came within a mile of the island, two canoes came out to meet it: "One of the islanders, seeing a saber, took it, examined it, and jumped overboard with it."[7]

The sounding party found no suitable anchorage, the depth being everywhere very great, but they learned from the natives that two other islands, Poulo (Pulo Anna) and Meriers (Merir), lay to the south and a large island they called Panloq (Angaur in the Palau Islands) to the northeast. Somera recounts the experience:

> The current carried us away to the Southeast so violently that we were unable to reach land until six in the morning of the fourth. . . . I sent the boat to search for an anchorage, but it was useless. The boat returned at four in the evening to report nothing but rocks, at great depth, and it would be impossible to anchor. At nine in the morning of the fifth, Fathers Duberron and Cortil formed a plan to go ashore and plant a cross. Don Padilla and I told them of the dangers to which they would expose themselves, from the islanders of whom they knew nothing, and also from the risk of the ship's being carried off by the current and being unable to regain position to rescue them. In their zeal they refused to listen. They persisted in their resolve. They left Brother Baudin in the ship and embarked in the boat with the quartermaster and the ensign. They also took along the Palauan of whom I have spoken, with his wife and children.
>
> The two missionaries having departed, we held our ground all day under sail against the current, but in the evening the wind died and the current

drove us off. We hung a lantern at the bowsprit all night, and another at the mizzen, to show our position to those on the island. . . . At dawn the large island lay about eight leagues to the north-northwest. Until noon on the ninth we made every effort to approach the land, with no success.[8]

At this point Padilla made a much-criticized decision, under pressure from pilot Somera and the lay brother Baudin, to try to carry out the main object of the expedition by locating "Panloq" and other islands of the Palau group so as to open them for conversion. He expected that winds off Sonsorol might improve in a week or so, and meanwhile the priests who had gone ashore there would be able to take care of themselves.

So the *Santissima Trinidad* sailed off and did in fact reach Angaur on 9 December, where they remained four days—during which time they shot a few natives. (Somera's casual mention of this fact speaks volumes about Spanish methods used "to introduce the Holy Religion among the Islanders.") On the eighteenth they were back at Sonsorol and plied back and forth all day, and again the next day and the two days following, without a sign of their boat. On the twenty-first a storm drove them off to the westward, "and considering that we had no boat and were short of water, without knowing where to get any," explains Somera, "we were all of the opinion that the only course we could pursue was to return to Manila with the sad news."[9]

It must be conceded that aside from his ineptitude in risking his only boat on a strange shore without first coming to some sort of understanding with the natives, Padilla was correct in deciding to abandon the vigil. There was no point in waiting any longer for a sign from the island, for Father Duberron and Father Cortil had probably been felled soon after they stepped ashore.

In the year following the disappearance of Duberron and Cortil, Serrano sailed from Manila in a vessel fitted out to rescue them, but it foundered in a gale even before getting clear of the Philippines. Many of the crew managed to get in the boat but were so flustered they forgot to cast off and were pulled down by the ship. Only Serrano and two Filipinos survived this disaster, which for a time discouraged any further attempt to Catholicize the Palaus from a base in the Philippines.[10]

On the shore of Songosor, the larger of the two islands comprising Sonsorol, stands a high wooden cross facing the westward sea. It bears no inscription, nor does it need any, but if I were to compose one, it would read:

To the memory of two brave men,
Cut off from their own kind,
And cut down alone.

We reached Sonsorol at six in the morning, steering crabwise four degrees to the right of our intended course, as I mentioned above. While the ship lay off, I went ashore at Songosor with Bland, Savage, and others, using a narrow channel cut through the coral leading to what had been a concrete pier but was now so broken and scattered that we had to wade the last hundred yards.

Songosor has a land area of about 330 acres, compared with 130 acres for little Fama half a mile away. But despite their small size the two islands managed in the old days to produce much copra. Traders like Andrew Cheyne, Alfred Tetens, and "King O'Keefe" found the place useful as an entrepôt, as did the Germans and the Japanese. With this kind of acculturation it is hardly surprising that we encountered none of the generosity met with elsewhere in the Carolines. Every trinket had a price: usually two dollars or two packs of cigarettes—except that a banana fiber *laplap* (*lavalava, maro*) cost a full carton. In other respects the natives seemed to be completely disorganized. The only one who understood English took me to see "number two chief," who had nothing to say—even in his own tongue.

We looked around the village, in the center of which stood a chestnut tree towering twice as high as the palms, within whose branches innumerable terns resided, making it clatter with their comings and goings. The remains of a narrow-gauge railway circled the island, but there was no way of telling whether it dated from the German or the Japanese era, or whether the Japanese had fortified the place in any way.

An air of indecision hung over the island. Some of the natives wore clothes, and others were naked, though all seemed to be tattooed from head to toe. The only purposeful activity I noted was that of a solitary old man splitting coconuts. It remained for an old woman we met along the way back to the landing to make me feel I might be welcome in this corner of Micronesia. Doubled over with age, she hobbled up and pressed my hand to her face—the ancient greeting on Sonsorol.

TRADER TETENS

Lest Sonsorol be thought hopelessly dull, I should tell about Alfred Tetens, master of the brig *Vesta* in the employ of the J.C. Godeffroy firm of

Hamburg in 1865. As in our own case, he had to wade ashore, but he was immediately surrounded in the water by men, women, and children waving palm branches. Forming a litter with canoe paddles, eight stalwarts carried him into the village for a real celebration:

All those who were close enough stretched out their hands to touch my body: it took all my strength to remain upright. Mothers held up their children so that they could stroke my face; where maternal discipline was lacking, inquisitive offspring tried to climb up my legs. While the men and children wondered about my clothes, my beard, and my hair, and especially about the white color of my arms and face, their feminine counterparts could not restrain their even greater curiosity and persisted in trying to take off my clothes or at least shove them aside. As soon as they were convinced I was the same color all over, the women danced around in such a frenzy that I really became very uncomfortable. Naturally I received the signs of friendship and endearments of the ladies with apparent nonchalance; I had no desire to go against the customs of the country. The enmity of the men would be an inevitable consequence, and in that case I should never leave the island alive.[11]

(Does this give a clue to the fate of Duberron and Cortil, who may have offended the natives by spurning such familiarity?)

By the time formalities of greeting ended, Tetens's white linen suit was so besmeared with the turmeric used by the natives that he decided no soap in the world could get it clean. Divesting himself of the garment, he handed it to the chief, who "under the pardonable delusion that this was a usual form of greeting among white men, seized the trousers and into them tried to force his conspicuously generous bulk." At length, with the help of his retainers, the chief succeeded, and Tetens brought forth gifts of tobacco, fishhooks, flint, and steel. The men ran off to gather gifts in return: coconuts, bananas, chickens, fish, taro, and other delicacies, while the women began a kind of caressing that robbed Tetens of the last vestige of his dignity. "As soon as the bearers of the gifts arrived, I thanked this peace-loving people and returned to my ship. At the promising sight of the delicious fruits, my crew hardly noticed the absence of my clothes. After an interval of five months during which we had had only ship's rations, these fresh fruits tasted superb."[12] Unlike Tetens, I returned on board fully clothed; otherwise, the crew would have had one more wild story to add to their collection.

Tetens proved a skillful trader and excellent seaman. He seemed somehow able to read natives' thoughts and thereby to sense and deflect trouble before it happened—and thus to escape the fate of some his contemporaries, such as Andrew Cheyne and Philo Holcomb. Instead, Tetens's career in the islands was cut short by a gun accident, following which he returned to Hamburg and was appointed to the most honorable office the city could bestow on a merchant seaman: the post of *Wassershout,* literally "overseer of the water," a kind of arbiter of matters maritime.

We set off for Palau at ten o'clock. During the day a cormorantlike bird flopped exhausted on the main deck and Gunner's Mate Larry Ledford brought it to the bridge: eyes like black buttons in a white-feathered head, long beak, brown cap, and "snood," light brown wings. He hissed bravely at us as I had Ledford put him in a box for release near land. The next entry in my journal, alongside a sketch of the creature, says, "Ledford reports the bird has escaped. Blood on the box, etc. Poor thing." I don't know why, but the incident depressed me. It isn't true that life at sea hardens men. Other things happen to the spirit, but not that.

By 0715 next morning we were off Malakal Passage, with a strong current flowing off the coral shelf at right angles to the narrow channel, so I had to proceed at 10 knots in order to get adequate rudder-response in following its twists and turns. After anchoring with a sigh of relief, I went ashore to confer with District Administrator Don Heron (who split his time between Palau and Yap), and we got to talking about Palau and its fascinating history, well deserving a separate chapter here.

14

The *Antelope*

Although Drake is believed to have discovered Palau in 1579, and José Serrano most certainly saw it in 1710, the real credit for making the group
known to the world goes to Henry Wilson, and this is his story.

At the hour of 1500 on 20 July 1783, the 300-ton packet *Antelope,* Henry
Wilson, master, cast off from the British East India Company dock in
Macao and headed out to sea, bound for an unspecified destination. On
board besides her master were four officers, a crew of twenty-seven, and
three passengers including the captain's own son and a half-caste Bengalese
"linguist." The ship worked through Bashi Channel between Formosa and
the Philippines, then headed southeast. On Sunday, 10 August, they ran
into trouble. The sky became overcast, with much thunder, lightning, and
rain. The chief mate judged the weather would break and clear up, so he
did not consult with the captain or call up extra hands, but about midnight
he had the men who were on duty reef some of the sails. Suddenly the
lookout shouted, "Breakers!" and the ship struck.

George Keate, Wilson's scribe, depicts the scene in his *Account of the
Pelew Islands:*

> A moment convinced them of their dreadful situation; the breakers
> alongside, through which the rocks made their appearance, presented the

most dreadful scene, and left no room for doubt. The ship taking a heel, in less than an hour was filled with water to the level of the lower hatchways. . . . Orders were in consequence instantly given to secure the guns, powder, ammunition, and small arms, and that the bread and other provisions as would spoil by wet should be brought on deck and secured by some covering from the rain; while others were directed to cut away the mizzenmast, the main and fore-top-masts and main yards, to save the ship and prevent her from oversetting, of which they thought there was some hazard, and that everything should be done to preserve her as long as possible.

The boats were hoisted out and filled with provisions and water, together with a compass in each, some small arms, and ammunition; and two men were placed in each boat, with directions to keep them in the lee of the ship, and be careful they were not staved, and to be ready to receive their shipmates in case the vessel should break to pieces by the dashing of the waves and the violence of the wind. . . . The people now assembled aft, the quarterdeck laying highest out of the water.[1]

The captain gave a pep talk, stressing that shipwreck was something to which all mariners are liable and that such occurrences were often rendered worse by the despair and discouragement of the crew, to avoid which he urged everyone not to drink any "spirituous liquor." Everyone agreed, whereupon they all had a couple of glasses of wine. As Keate continues, "The dawn of day discovered to their view a small island to the southward, about three or four leagues distant, and soon after other islands were seen to the eastward. They now felt apprehensive on account of the inhabitants."

The choice of a place to land, as land they must, fell on a small island to the south that appeared least likely to harbor large numbers of hostile natives. Fortunately the *Antelope* was lodged on a leeward reef, or she would have broken up long before her crew could have abandoned ship in so orderly a fashion. Fortunately as well, Henry Wilson's leadership was such as to suspend for a time the old law of the sea whereby the crew of a ship cast up on a foreign shore are free to fend for themselves as individuals.

The island (apparently Aulong, otherwise known as Apurashokuru) proved to be uninhabited and was blessed with a sandy cove, a lush growth of palm and breadfruit, and a stream of fresh water. During that day and the next, many trips were made with the jolly boat, the pinnace, and a makeshift raft, so that the entire party got ashore with ample provisions and tools by the night of the eleventh. Meanwhile they had a visitor, the brother of a local potentate and a sort of minister of war, calling himself Arra Kooker. The tension of first meeting dissolved in wonder:

> The natives were of a deep copper colour, perfectly naked, having no kind of covering whatsoever; their skins were very soft and glossy, owing as was known afterwards to the external use of cocoa-nut oil. . . . They were of middling stature, very straight and muscular, their limbs well formed, and had a particular majestic manner of walking; but their legs from a little above the ankles to the middle of their thighs were tattooed so very thick as to appear dyed a far deeper color than the rest of their skin; their hair was of a fine black, long, and rolled up in a simple manner close to the back of their heads, and appeared both neat and becoming. None of them except the younger of the King's two brothers, had a beard; and it was afterwards observed in the course of a longer acquaintance with them that they in general pluck out their beards by the root; a very few only who had strong thick beards, cherished them and let them grow.

The appearance of the Englishmen was no less amazing to the natives, who at first believed such white skin must be artificial: "They expressed a further desire to see their bodies; upon which some of the men opened their bosoms and gave them to understand that all the rest of the body was the same. They seemed much astonished at finding hair upon their breasts, it being considered with them a mark of great indelicacy, insomuch as they eradicate it from every part of the body in both sexes."

When the visitors had gone, Wilson held a council and pointed out that the initial friendliness of the natives might, with luck and discretion, be perpetuated indefinitely or at least long enough to permit the castaways to build a vessel out of the timbers of the *Antelope*. It was unthinkable that they should wait idly for possible rescue, so they set to work immediately on the project.

A few days later the "king" himself, with a cortege of splendid canoes, came to see the strange inhabitants of Aulong Island:

> When they had come in as far as the tide would permit, it was signified to Captain Wilson that he should go out and meet the king; on which two men took him up in their arms and carried him through the shallow water to the canoe where the King was sitting on a stage in the

middle of it. He desired Captain Wilson to come into the canoe, which he did, and embraced him informing him through the interpreters that he and his friends were Englishmen who had unfortunately lost their ship, but having saved their lives by landing on his territory supplicated his permission to build a vessel to convey themselves back to their own country.

After a little pause, and speaking with a chief in a canoe next to him (which we learned afterward was the Chief Minister) he replied in a most courteous manner that he was welcome to build either at the place where he then was or at his own island; told Captain Wilson that the island he was then on was thought to be unhealthy; that he feared his own people might be sickly if they stayed on it before another wind set in, which he said would be in two moons.

Wilson decided to stay where he was, however, because of the relative security of the small island—a wise choice in view of the native propensity that had led Drake to call Palau the "Island of Thieves." Lest the "king" (whose chiefly title of *abba thule* was mistakenly thought by the English to be his personal name) and his warriors think their guests completely powerless, Wilson staged a demonstration of musketry, firing three volleys. This had a sensational effect, and the "hallooing, hooting, jumping, and chattering" of the natives almost turned into a riot. The king was mystified when a bird was shot down, for he had not seen anything pass out of the gun. Another source of wonder was an ordinary grindstone, and the natives were further delighted by two dogs the white men had with them, for they had never seen a quadruped larger than a rat.

The king and his party finally left and paddled around to the other side of the island, where they camped for the night, leaving a few of their number with the English. Just as the Englishmen were dropping off to sleep, these few began a song so shrill that it was thought to be a war whoop or a least a signal to the party on the other side of the island to come and attack:

The English instantly took to their arms, and Messrs. Baker and Sharp ran to the tent where Captain Wilson was, to see if he was safe. They informed him of the apprehensions of our people, who were all under arms; he requested Mr. Baker to return immediately to them and desire them to make no show of being alarmed, but to keep up their guard until they should find what the meaning of this might be, adding that he would come to them as soon as he might do it without being noticed;

he requested Mr. Sharp to sit down by the king's son and enter into some conversation with him by signs.

They were much relieved on realizing that the natives were only "tuning their voices." Arra Kooker "gave out a line or stave which was taken up by another *rupak* (chief) seated at a little distance who sang a verse accompanied by the rest of the natives present, except himself and the Prince. The last line was sung twice over, which was taken up by the natives in the next tent, in chorus; Arra Kooker then gave out another line which was sung in the same manner; and this continued for ten or twelve verses." When the song ended, they asked to hear some English songs, and a young fellow named Cobbledick readily complied, with sea songs and songs of battles that so pleased the king that whenever they met afterward, the king would have him sing one or two.

In the next few weeks the castaways barricaded their tents and continued to recover stores and materials from the wreck. In a makeshift dockyard above high water they worked with "utmost assiduity," and with considerable help from the natives, to construct a small vessel. When the planks were fitted into place, the natives gave them red and yellow ocher paint;[2] they also showed them how to pay the seams with chinam (powdered coral) mixed with grease. As time passed, some of the castaways ventured among the larger islands—Babelthuap, Urukthapel, Eil Malk, and Koror itself, where the abba thule had his power base.

According to Keate's account, the abba thule ruled not as a despot but more as one whose virtues inspired respect and obedience. He acted in no important matter without consulting his rupaks. In council he always sat on a particular stone with his advisors around him, their faces averted whenever they addressed him. Offenders brought before him were punished by censure alone, more crushing than blows.

Every man's house and canoe were considered his private property, as was the land allotted to him—for as long as he occupied it. If he moved with his family to another place, the ground he held reverted to the abba thule, who then gave it to whomever he pleased.

Keate notes particularly that the attention and tenderness shown to the women and the deportment of the men to each other were such that the English never saw any behavior with the appearance of contest or passion; everyone seemed to attend to his or her own concerns without interfering in the business of neighbors. Keate further assures his readers that the natives in general "rejected connection with our people, and resented any indelicate or unbecoming freedom."

The natives rose at daylight and would immediately go and bathe in fresh water. After breakfast, if a council was to be held, the abba thule met with his rupaks, while the common people went about their daily occupations. The active day usually ended about two hours after sunset, but on festive occasions the islanders might dance all night. Palauan dancing, the English noted, consisted not so much in "capering" as in a peculiar posturing, very low and sideways, singing all the while. After each stanza the dancers would bring themselves together, lifting up the feather tassels that they held in their hands and giving them a clashing or tremulous motion, then suddenly pause, shout "Weel!" and begin anew.

The abba thule's realm did not encompass all of Palau: there were dissident tribes on Babelthuap, and Peliliu and Angaur maintained complete independence. Ever since one of the abba thule's brothers and two of his rupaks had been killed during a festival in Ngatengal on Babelthuap, a state of war had existed between the tribe of that place and the people of Koror. It was probably inevitable that Captain Wilson should be drawn into the struggle in view of the proven marvels of his firearms. When the abba thule asked to borrow some of these for use by his own men in a projected expedition, Wilson may have been reminded of a similar request made on Magellan, and its tragic results, or he may have foreseen the abuses to which such favors might lead in years to come. Nonetheless he could not refuse without offending the people on whom depended all hope of the English castaways' returning to civilization.

So on the morning of 21 August, before daybreak, five armed Englishmen mustered in front of the council house along with a horde of natives carrying both long bamboo spears tipped with betel-nut wood for use at close quarters and notched arrows for use with throwing-sticks at distance (not found elsewhere in Micronesia):

> The English embarked in five canoes and went away to the eastward about ten or twelve leagues, calling as they went along at several of the King's villages to refresh and reinforce. At half an hour past two in the afternoon they met the enemy. The King had with him now one hundred and fifty canoes, on board of which were considerably above one thousand men. Of the enemy force our people could form no certainty. Before the action, Arra Kooker went in his canoe close to the town and

spoke to the enemy for some time, having Thomas Dulton in the boat, who had directions not to fire until such time as the signal which had been agreed upon had been given him.

Arra Kooker's speech was received with great indifference. He then threw a spear at the enemy, this being the signal. Immediately there was a salvo from English muskets. One man fell, causing great confusion among the enemy, who abandoned their canoes and swam off as fast as they could. A few more volleys were fired. The victors landed, stripped a few coconut trees, and carried off some yams and other foodstuffs, whereupon the fleet returned homeward, highly pleased with themselves, stopping at several places along the way, where the women brought out sweet liquor for their refreshment.

Back in Koror, a great feast was prepared, with pigeons, turtle meat, and other delicacies. One enemy warrior had been taken prisoner, and the English tried to intercede for his life, to no effect. "Prisoners must always die," the abba thule insisted, "for it has always been so. Besides, if I were to release this man he would return to his people and betray us all." Meanwhile the captive awaited the final blow calmly and, when it fell, died with he eyes fixed on the English, not so much in reproach as in wonder.

There were additional expeditions in the next few weeks, each more elaborate and bloody than the last, each augmenting the abba thule's dominion well beyond traditional limits, although the English did not seem to understand this perfectly. At any rate it was a relief when the new ship was ready to launch and the English could be on their way.

With the goal in sight, a tide of doubt swept over the whites. Had they made themselves so useful that they would not be allowed to leave? What was the meaning of the knotted cord that the abba thule always carried? Why did he keep asking them for muskets and powder? In a fever of distrust, the English decided that they would turn on their hosts at the last minute and then scramble out to sea. Keate was ashamed to write that "the lives first intended to be devoted were those of the King and his minister, the facetious and inoffensive Arra Kooker."

The subtle change in their demeanor was noticed by the abba thule when he came to watch the launching, and he guessed their thoughts. In the stilted language ascribed to him by Keate, he asked, "What is there can make you doubt me? I never testified any fear of *you,* but tried to convince you I wanted your friendship. Had I been disposed to have harmed you I might have done so long ago: I have at all times had you in my power. . . .

2. Abba-Tulle, Chef de Pelew.

The abba thule of Palau, 1783, from a portrait by Arthur William Davis (1763–1822), apprentice draftsman on the *Antelope* packet.

Can you not confide in me at the last?" As Keate exclaims, "Under what sun was ever tempered the steel that could cut such a passage to the heart as this just reproach of the king?"

The launching was successful; otherwise, the English might have spent the rest of their lives in Palau, for their tools were worn out. They christened the ship *Erelong* (for Aulong) and set about fitting and provisioning her. The abba thule had a son about fifteen years old, named Libu, whom he prevailed upon Wilson to take back to England with his own son, saying (in Keate's words, of course):

I would wish you to inform Lee Boo of all things which he ought to know, and make him an Englishman. . . . I am well aware that the distant countries he must go through differing much from his own may expose him to dangers, as well as diseases that are unknown to us here, in consequence of which he must die; I have prepared my thoughts to this; I know that death is to all men inevitable, and whether my son meets this event at Pelew or elsewhere is immaterial. I am satisfied with what I have observed of the humanity of your character, that if he is sick, you will be kind to him; and should that happen which your utmost care cannot prevent, let it not hinder you, or your brother, or your son, or any of your countrymen, from returning here; I shall receive you or any of your people in friendship, and rejoice to see you again.

On the day before departure, a sailor named Madan Blanchard asked to be left behind. Keate describes him as a man "of singular character, about twenty years of age, of a rather grave turn of mind, at the same time possessing a considerable degree of dry humor; and what rendered the circumstance of his determination remarkable is that it is well known that he has formed no particular attachment on the island. His good-tempered, inoffensive behavior during the voyage had gained him the regard of all his shipmates." Since there was no dissuading him, Wilson suggested to the abba thule that he desired to leave Blanchard in order to help the Palauans, thinking this idea might improve his chances of being well treated. The tactic was to prove a mistake, however, for it placed this illiterate seaman of obscure intentions in the apparent position of being the representative of the British.

When the ship was ready to sail, the natives came with so many gifts and so much food that the *Erelong* could not hold it all, and some islanders were hurt when their gifts had to be declined. Wilson's last act on the little island that had been their home for the past three months was to have a copper plate fastened to a tree: "The Honorable English East India Company's Ship the *Antelope*, Henry Wilson, Commander, was lost upon the reef north of this island in the night between the 9th and 10th of August; who here built a vessel, and sailed from hence on the 12th day of November, 1783."

The English reached Hong Kong without mishap, sold the boat, divided the proceeds, and dispersed. Wilson returned to England with Libu, where his adventure created a sensation and reinforced romantic notions of the noble savages of the South Seas. London society was fascinated with the handsome lad, but like many another exotic visitor he died before he could escape England's climate. His father may have had a premonition of this, but at any rate the abba thule kept his promise always to welcome the English to his island, and so did those who succeeded to his title.

Seven years after the wreck of the *Antelope* the Bombay office of the East India Company moved to investigate the islands Wilson had reported, sending out the ship *Panther* under self-styled "commodore" John McClure to chart the waters around Angaur and northward, as well as a second ship, the *Endeavor.* McClure's navigator, a Bostonian named Amasz Delano, afterward published a set of sailing directions that included a statement with which I can most heartily concur: "I must urge great caution upon every stranger how he enters among (the islands); and after all the most minute description would be insufficient for his safety."[3] Delano tells of Madan Blanchard:

> He became arrogant and licentious, as persons are apt to do when raised to great power and consequence. The natives told me he would take their taro root, coconuts, yams, canoes, wives, and everything he chose; and if they made any complaint would contrive to have them beaten and disgraced. What little address he had with the King was greatly assisted by the fear which the King entertained, that Blanchard might be able to make the English believe on their return to the islands, if he were offended, that the nation had been insulted through him and that vengeance ought to be taken. He continued this course of abuse for nearly three years, when he went over with a rupak who was his favorite, with six or eight men to a small island where the people had been injured by him. In the evening a quarrel arose and Blanchard and his party were put to death, except two who escaped in their canoe.[4]

Unfortunately the abba thule misconstrued Blanchard's status to the end and punished his executioners.

At the time of McClure's visit the abba thule was still having trouble with the Ngatengal tribe, and again he asked for help in attacking them. This time the aid was given without compunction, and again there was the formal notification of hostilities, the great assemblage of canoes, the stately advance of opposing fleets, and the senseless bloodshed. It was all very interesting for the visitors, but McClure would not allow any of it to be logged, especially the fact that his own launch, flying the British ensign, had taken part.

McClure was a would-be empire builder, like so many men who came to the Carolines. He later returned to the island as a private individual with a collection of seeds and plants—together with, in Delano's words, "three or four female slaves of Malay, from nine to twelve years old, which he purchased at Timor; some males of Malay; a Bombay female born of European parents, and five or six male slaves from different eastern coasts."[5] He lived with this menage for several months, then left with his male slaves for Macao to buy a ship with which he returned to Palau, loaded up the rest of his household, sailed away, and disappeared forever.

15

The Sea Their World

On 23 April 1954, during our second visit to Palau, Don Heron received a message from the U.S. Coast Guard that worried him: "Mogmog natives question whereabout six canoes twenty five men left for Fais Island trading expedition last month x should have returned two weeks ago x air recco at Fais discloses no Ulithi canoes."

"I can't understand it," he said. "The two places are only fifty miles apart. They could have changed their minds and decided to go somewhere else, of course. But I wonder if you'd mind checking Fais anyway, to make sure they aren't there."

"Not at all. In fact I was planning to have a look at the place."

"The weather hasn't been bad, or I'd say they'd been caught in a storm. In any case, the Ulithians are excellent navigators."

"Well, it's still possible they are at Fais, because the canoes could be drawn up under the trees where they couldn't be seen from the air. I'll find out, anyway." I also promised to keep a sharp lookout for the canoes in the open sea between Palau and Ulithi even though the chance of finding anything in so vast an area would be remote indeed.

We had to make two other calls before going on to Fais and finally Ulithi. They would be our farewell to the Carolines. The first was to be at Ngulu (the island of fat women), where I planned to anchor for an hour and question the natives who might come out to us in canoes. The occupants of the two canoes that did come out knew no English except the word "chief," which they kept repeating with gestures implying their leader either had a headache or had lost his wits. Out of curiosity I went ashore and was met by the chief in person, apparently sound in mind and limb. While the ship's hospitalman held sick call, the chief and I posed for snapshots—holding hands first with fingers interlaced in the native way, then in a less ambiguous handshake.

Ngulu seemed neater and more attractive than I remembered from our previous visit. One dwelling was really beautiful, with a tiny fallu-style house set in a yard of pounded coral sand, dazzling in the sun, blue-black in the shadows, on which were grouped two or three living wands of bamboo, a Japanese fishing float, a basket, and a deep green saki bottle. It was immaculate, appropriate, and elegant.

Chief Hospitalman Cluck was busy here: every woman on the island came for a stethoscopic examination, though all proved to be in perfect health. While he was performing his professional duties, I sat apart with the menfolk and let the children who clustered around try out my sunglasses—always a source of wonder. They did not push or shove or cry out for turns but waited gravely until I could direct my attention to each individually. After a bit they came closer, climbed in my lap, and felt in my pockets. I wanted to adopt them all.

We scanned Sorol by radar that night and came to Fais early next morning, 25 April. This was our last chance to see the people of Micronesia fairly untouched by the outside world. The island is difficult to access, being geologically akin to Aguijan in the Marianas, with limestone cliffs that defy the ocean and inhibit landings.

Circling the island, we found a leeward cove where a party might get ashore. The mooring buoy placed here by the Japanese had long since been swept away, but their stone jetty was in good condition. Unfortunately the ocean swell was too high to permit our boat to go alongside. A navy motor whaleboat at the time was carried on the books at about $25,000, and although I hardly considered one to be worth that amount, I had no desire to risk it, so I indicated to the natives on the beach that we couldn't get all the way to the pier. A bustle ensued, and soon a group of islanders came

Attractive dwelling and grounds on Ngulu.

down a trail with a canoe that they proceeded to launch with much laughter and waving of arms. In a short time our landing party was transferred aboard this native craft.

A score of gaily bedizened males helped us clamber ashore. Like most Micronesians, these were well built but far more elaborately adorned than any we had seen: besides being tattooed over every inch of their bodies, they had tinted their skin with ocher and turmeric, their necks were encircled with strings of shark's teeth and bead "chokers," and their hair was decked with combs, flowers, and feathers. All this could not have been in our honor, for some of the less snappy dressers wore flowers I'm sure had been picked days before.

We were led to a village on the south end of the island, where the elders received us in their *fallu*, reminding me—even in that unlikely spot—of fugitives from a faculty meeting, maybe because one of them bore a striking resemblance to my chemistry professor of undergraduate days. I explained the purpose of our call. The chief discussed the matter at great length with other members of the conclave, then turned to me and said there had been no visitors from Ulithi that year. Suddenly I wanted very much to get to Mogmog and talk to Father Walter and see what could be done. So I left hastily, and within the hour we were on our way.

The fifty-mile stretch between Fais and Ulithi is such that I marveled any-one could get lost between the two, because a chain of reefs and islets pro-vides markers for almost half the distance. We anchored in ten fathoms in Ulithi lagoon, near Fasserai Island on the southeast side, where Rayner went ashore to bring Father Walter to the ship. A sailing canoe came over from Song Island and questioned us about the missing canoes, and when I told them the result of our call at Fais, they refused to believe I had understood the Fais islanders correctly. After Father Walter came aboard, we hoisted anchor and left for Mogmog, several miles to the north but still within the huge atoll. He was deeply troubled. "I can't understand it," he said, echoing Don Heron's words. "There were four canoes, big oceangoing ones, and the best navigator in Ulithi was in charge. They *couldn't* have got lost."

"Could they have got caught in a storm?"

"There hasn't been any. Oh, the usual squalls now and then, but noth-ing out of the ordinary. I'd say maybe they went to visit Sorol or Woleai, but it just isn't like these people to let their families worry, and they promised to be back in ten days. That was almost three weeks ago."

"Well, assuming they did decide to make a longer trip, where would they be likely to land?"

"Woleai, I suppose. Or Sorol, or Yap. It's hard to say."

I thought of the hundreds of miles of sea between these choices—and if a disaster had intervened, thousands of miles of helpless drifting in prospect before they might reach shore in the Philippines. Four microscopic parcels of human life adrift in such an immensity!

At Mogmog I went ashore with Father Walter after he first said mass for the men of his faith on the *Hanna*, and I found my young friend John ready with a smiling welcome. We immediately sought out Chief Uring, and I watched him closely as John relayed the disquieting news. He straightened a little, looked out to the horizon for a moment as if to salute the mysteries that lay beyond its rim, then bowed and invited me to join the council inside the fallu. One would never have suspected from his man-ner that I had just confirmed a major catastrophe: 10 percent of the males of Mogmog had been swept into oblivion, along with 35 percent of those of Fasserai. Never did the manliness of this gentle race stand better revealed.

The worst of it was that there was nothing I could do. The odds against our ship's finding the canoes were incalculable, and almost as overwhelm-ing were the odds against a full-scale search with planes and additional ships at this late date. Air-sea rescue procedures provide for daily expansion

of search sectors based on estimates of wind and current, but such calculations were meaningless in this case since the canoes might still be under
sail. When I left Ulithi late that afternoon, it was with a profound sense of
sadness, saying good-bye to a place and a people I liked very much—and
sharing their grief.

This could have been the end of the story, but about a month later I
received a happy message from the coast guard: "King Uring wishes to
thank all who had to do with locating missing Ulithi canoes."

A TALE OF SURVIVAL

Eventually Father Walter sent me a full account of the voyage as told by
Sereg, captain and navigator of the Mogmog canoe named *Ilumau* ("The
Mighty"):

> After one day's journey out, a storm suddenly arose, the sea became very
> rough, and we had to lower our sails. We paddled our canoes close
> together so that no one would get lost. The storm lasted all night and
> there were no stars visible for us to keep a reckoning on our position.
>
> After the storm we knew we had been blown a considerable distance
> west of our course. The wind was blowing from the east which made sail-
> ing very difficult. We tacked close into the wind for four days but we did
> not sight any land. We tried a new heading, hoping to locate Ulithi and
> return home. The wind was still blowing from the east, and we knew we
> were in the southwest tidal current, but we still hoped our canoes would
> be able to reach Ulithi. Four more days beating against the wind brought
> no island over the horizon. We fanned our canoes out on a line six miles
> wide in order to increase our chances of sighting land. Again we shifted
> our course hoping this time to reach Yap.
>
> We knew we could reach the Philippines with the east wind behind
> us but after reaching there we might have to abandon our canoes. We
> did not like to chance this because our canoes are made of hard wood
> imported from Yap and besides the expense it takes almost a year to
> build one. But we had brought only enough food and water to last four
> days, anticipating the possibility that we might have some minor diffi-
> culties on our trip to Fais. We had no rain after the storm, and despite
> rationing, our supply of water was almost gone. We had no food left
> except about three dozen coconuts which could furnish some food and
> drink. We had our fishing equipment with us but caught no fish.

By the twelfth day we were in desperate straits. Six of the men were very sick. Each day we would cut open three coconuts. Each man would get three sips of water and a small piece of coconut meat as his for the day. The sick men could not eat their coconut meat, so we divided their portion among the rest. We prayed for rain or any kind of water. We prayed, too, for the fish to bite our hooks so that we would have something to eat. We knew that if we continued searching for Yap we would all die. So at last we decided to head for the Philippines. Some of our people had visited there before.

So, at the end of the 12th day, after looking carefully over the horizon for the last time and not sighting Yap, we headed west. With the wind behind us, we travelled swiftly. We were all of us very weak and it was hard for us to manage the steering oars. Some of the young men prayed for death to end their sufferings. We kept close together, day and night. It was getting toward full moon and even at night the visibility was good. But one night the Fasserai canoe, *Solapi,* collided with my canoe and was smashed. My canoe was over sixty years old but it had not been named *Ilumau the Mighty* without good reason. My canoe was not damaged and we took the Fasserai men aboard.

On the 17th day we saw frigate-birds soaring overhead and we knew we could not be too far from land, maybe 150 miles or so. On the 18th day about noon, afar off through the haze, we saw land looming up into the clouds. At first the young men would not believe this because they had never before made a landfall on a high island. By sunset we were near enough to see the green vegetation and everyone was happy. On the morning of the 19th day we landed on the beach near the town of San Antonio. We were very hungry and thirsty and asked the people to give us food and water. They gave us coconuts and some green bananas. The bananas made us sick but it was good to have anything to eat.

The police arrived from Gamay one hour after we landed at San Antonio. That night we slept in a small house. The next morning all but five of us met with the police chief in the town of Gamay. The five men who stayed behind were very sick; one of them, Thil, died on April 30th. The others were able to leave several days later and stayed with us at Gamay. The people were very kind and gave us food. They asked us to do some of our dances in the town plaza and after the dances they collected money for us. Then we could buy anything we wanted in the stores. They were also interested in some of our possessions so we traded with them. Now I have a nice Filipino knife as my remembrance of our voyage to Samar.

On May 14th a Philippine warship arrived to take us to Manila. The men on the warship were very nice to us. They showed us the big guns and we ate all we wanted. But we always seemed to be very hungry.

One day an American came and told us we would soon be going home. I asked him if we could walk around the village where we were staying but he said we should stay near the house lest something happen to delay our going home. After that we didn't ask to leave the house. In a few days the American came back and told us we were going home that night. We immediately got all our things ready.

It was almost midnight when we got aboard the airplane. We couldn't find our baggage after we were aboard, and were sure it was lost. The airplane had four propellers and when they started we were very afraid but the plane didn't move. The man who owned the airplane showed us how to press a button and make a bed for ourselves. Then he showed us another button to press any time we wanted him to come. He was so nice to us we forgot to ask about our baggage. Besides, we all pressed buttons to make our beds.

Someone said, "When will the airplane start?" We looked out and saw lights below and were amazed and frightened. We were high up in the sky and we knew we would all be dead if the airplane fell. It was our first ride in an airplane. We had seen four or five planes fall over Ulithi during the war and we thought we might fall too. But nothing did happen. The people who owned the airplane treated us very well and gave us much to eat and drink. They were not at all afraid. But some of our men sat up all night. Toward morning we were all of us awake and the people told us we would be landing at Guam soon. The old men did not believe that because Guam and Manila are so far apart. How could we have travelled that distance in six hours? Even to cross our lagoon takes more than six hours sometimes. But truly we did land at Guam and it was just after sunrise.

When we got out of the airplane there was our baggage on the ground. Nothing at all was missing. It was truly remarkable, for we had never seen our baggage since we left the house in Manila. Men gave us something to eat and took us over to a Navy plane for our ride to Ulithi. This airplane was not as big as the other one, and we wondered why because we knew the Navy has very much money. And inside it was not so nice.

But we all had seats.

This time we were not afraid to start out. The airplane went very fast along the ground, and in a minute we saw the land fall away from under us. We were in the air only a short time when the airplane started to rock like a canoe on the waves. Sometimes it would start to fall down and we would have fallen out of our seats, but the Navy men tied us into them. This went on for three hours and we were afraid all the time. It was so different from the other airplane. We know that Navy men have to be brave because they have to fight for their country. They are so brave because they don't even care if they die or not. They like to fight and they don't mind even if their airplane falls out of the sky. But we didn't want to die and so we were afraid.

All our people were very happy to see us and they had presents of shells and handicrafts for the Navy men on the plane. They wanted the Navy men to know how happy they were because we came back. We were most happy, too.

This was Sereg's story, as translated by Father Walter, who wrote me to say, "When I arrived back at Ulithi in June the people were still feasting the returned heroes. In July and August the natives made their usual trip to Fais undaunted by the calamity which had nearly overtaken their fellows. The sea is their calling and they live in it and on it much of the time. The sea exacts its toll they know; but they know too, that they cannot live away from it. It is their only highway and gives them much of their food. Please keep my people in your prayers."

16

Last Movement

AT SEA

Our last jaunt through the islands before returning to the United States was to be a quick run through the Northern Marianas, Bonins, and Volcanoes, with a brief holiday in Yokosuka thrown in. We left Guam on 1 May 1954.

Ever since seeing Farallon de Pajaros in action I had hoped sometime to pass that way by night, and on 2 May we found ourselves within a few miles of this island volcano. As we approached, it loomed like a giant pile of embers on the horizon. Word got around, and in spite of the lateness of the hour, every camera on board was in use by the time we came to within a half-mile—as close as I or anyone else cared to go, for the incandescent material soaring out of the crater seemed at times as if it might reach the ship. Every two or three minutes the gigantic furnace jetted skyward a column of fire that would then break into a multitude of white-hot rocks and streamers of lava arching in all directions, falling grandly over the cinder slope, rolling and oozing down its steep incline until quenched in the sea. Each outburst could be heard as a sonorous "poomp!" After the concentrated glory of each eruption, the mountainside would be covered with red-hot boulders, like twinkling stars in some hellish firmament. Satisfied at

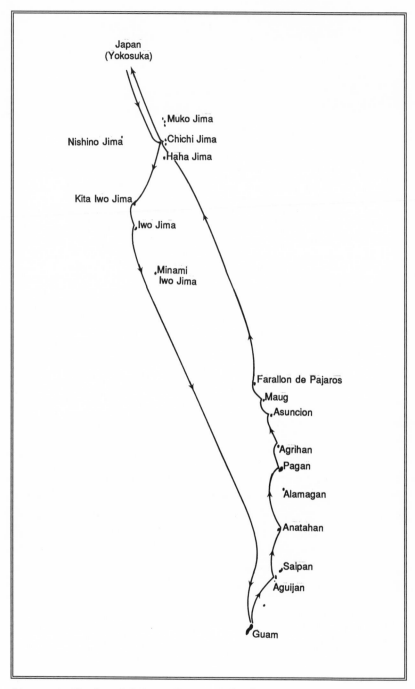

Itinerary in Northern Marianas, Bonins, and Volcanoes—1–18 May 1954.

last, we turned away and proceeded to a morning rendezvous with the submarine USS *Sea Fox* (SS 402).

At the end of a day of matching wits with us in antisubmarine exercises, our target surfaced before coming alongside to transfer his track chart, which would give us valuable information for improving our tactics. For this maneuver it was intended that the commander of the submarine put his starboard bow just off the *Hanna*'s port quarter, where the chart would be passed to us by heaving line. This method normally gives both ships maximum controllability. We had used it many times without mishap. Today we acted as "guide" and were thus obliged to maintain constant speed and heading while the *Sea Fox* maneuvered into position.

He came up fast, underestimating the time it would take to slow to our speed. This miscalculation should merely have delayed matters a bit while he dropped back into position, but he came so close alongside that his stern could not be swung to steer him out. Nautically speaking, he was "in irons"—helpless to do anything but back down and hope for the best.

I saw that he would hit us, and I ordered the port screw stopped, lest it slash his underwater hull, and sounded "collision quarters"—at which the sightseers along the port rail drew back. Suction between the two ships took hold now and slammed his bow into our side about midships, three times in succession. I ordered left full rudder and emergency speed ahead on the starboard screw, and we swung away with a whoosh, coming to a stop about three hundred yards off.

Reports began flowing to the bridge from the after engine-room. There was a three-foot hole six inches below the waterline, water coming in at about five hundred gallons per minute. It seemed seconds later, but actually it was four minutes, when the telephone talker announced, "Repair Central reports flooding under control." I was not surprised. Jerry Mathews's damage-control team had proven themselves long before, off Song-J'in in Korea, when survival of the *Hanna* had depended on their efforts. My chief concern was the submarine. I radioed, "Please advise the extent of your damage."

"No damage here," he replied cheerily. "I think we hit you with our bow-plane knuckle"—a heavy casting that holds the diving planes.

"I have one small hole," I told him. "Otherwise OK. So long!" And so we parted. He was off for Hawaii, and we headed for Chichi Jima. The chief engineer shifted enough fuel into our starboard tanks to give us a six-degree list, raising the hole above the waterline.

The USS *Sea Fox* coming alongside to transfer track charts, just before colliding with the *Hanna*, 3 May 1954.

At Port Lloyd the next day we replaced the temporary patch with one of steel, welded firmly on the outside of the hull. It was good Japanese plate, from Jack Frost's inexhaustible hoard.

ROUND-TRIP TO YOKOSUKA, JAPAN

From 6 to 13 May we made a trip to Japan and back, carrying with us seven Bonin Islanders—six Washingtons and a Savory—who made the trip for some badly needed dental repairs. They came home laden with Japanese trinkets, shoes, clothing, and bicycles, and seemed well pleased with their ride, but they kept to themselves and there was no more discussion of the things Nathaniel Savory had spoken of when I first came to Chichi (see chapter 5 above). I kept my disquiet to myself.

When a vague "residual sovereignty" over the Ryukyu Islands, the Volcanos, and the Bonins was conceded to Japan in the Japanese-American treaty of 1952, the question became not whether but how soon we would lose control of the islands that had cost us so dearly. The U.S. ambassador to Japan, Robert Murphy, expressed himself in favor of returning the Bonins without delay, but Admiral Radford changed his mind by taking him there on a cruiser tour.[1]

Nevertheless, in the years that followed, constant pressure from Japan and its League of Bonin Evacuees for Hastening Repatriation had the predictable effect. The Navy Department put up a good fight, but the demands of *geopolitik* prevailed and the islands became mere poker chips in a larger game. The U.S. ambassador to Japan in 1967, U. Alexis Johnson, dismissed the Bonins as an "insignificant cluster of rocks," and they were returned to Japan on 26 June 1968.[2]

In the years since the reversion, little has been published about Chichi. It appears that some of the descendants of the original settlers, or *zairai tomin,* still take pride in their heritage but have gone to great pains to keep a low profile. Many have taken on Japanese names in order to avoid discrimination: "Savory" has become "Sebori," "Webb" is now "Uebu," "Washington" is "Kimura," and "Isaac Gonzoles" is "Aisaku Ogasawara."

AT SEA

Heading south again from Chichi on 16 May, we ran into what we'd been looking for these past five months—a poacher! We were approaching Kita Iwo Jima, and when we were within five miles of the island, I was called to the bridge—as I had stipulated in my night orders. It was two o'clock in the morning, and I felt sorry for myself as I stumbled topside. Whiteside, who had the deck, said, "Captain, I think I see a light off the island."

I took a quick bearing and called down the voice-tube to the combat information center, "Do you have anything at two-three-five?"

"No, sir." Probably the land mass was blanking out our radar on that bearing. I had to determine the intruder's exact position before he had a chance to slip away, so we swept down on him at 20 knots, rounded the corner of the island, and "caught him with his nets down" less than a mile and a half from shore.

"He" proved to be the 27-ton *Matabe Maru,* crew of twenty. Rayner took a boarding party over, with instructions to arrest the ship, captain, and crew unless they had some emergency reason for being there. They hadn't.

According to instructions, any unauthorized vessel within territorial waters had to be brought to Saipan for adjudication. (I don't know what I'd have done with a Russian cruiser.) So after informing the captain of the *Matabe Maru* what was expected of him, we started off together at his best speed: 8.5 knots. It would be a long, slow haul; by noon we had covered only sixty-five miles.

At 1400 that afternoon, a message came from ComNavMar directing me to investigate an underwater object off the beach at Iwo Jima, to remove it if possible, and if not, to recommend other means for its removal. The object, whatever it was, had recently gouged a hole in the bottom of an LST involved in landing exercises at that spot.

Obviously ComNavMar had not yet received my own message concerning the fishing boat. I couldn't very well reply, "Can't. I'm busy," and I didn't want to drag the *Matabe Maru* off on a seventy-two-mile side trip. This was a golden opportunity to try out our prize-crew bill, a set of procedures that every navy ship is required to have in its organization book but that in modern times is seldom put into operation.

Rayner was eager to assume the role of "prize crew captain" and launched into a flurry of preparation. Special clothing, bedrolls, food, water, flashlights, a portable radio, semaphore flags, a Very pistol, charts, navigational instruments, and small arms were loaded into the motor whaleboat, along with a half-dozen picked men. We hove to, and the *Matabe Maru* followed suit. Minutes later the motor whaleboat delivered its load to the surprised Japanese, returned to the *Hanna,* and was hoisted back on board. We then took off for Iwo, while our *Maru* with its dauntless occupants putt-putted toward Saipan.

On previous occasions we had passed near Iwo Jima, but we were never close enough to get a good look. Even during the war I knew it only as a rumble and a roar in the distance, a pillar of smoke by day and fire at night as seen from the deck of a destroyer. Now I was sobered to see Mount Suribachi close at hand and, at its summit, the only United States flag that is never hauled down.[3] We rounded the south tip of the island and anchored as close as possible to the point on the west side where we had been told to look for the obstacle. During our approach, radio central made contact with the Iwo control tower but never was able to make the air force people ashore understand what we were there for, and no one showed up at the beach to help in our search.

Six of the best swimmers volunteered. Equipped with face masks and flippers they formed a scouting line and slowly explored the waters offshore, using the motor whaleboat as guide. In time Jerry Mathews found the offending object: a wrecked landing craft lying in ten feet of water, with a freshly abraded portion sticking up within four feet of the surface. While he hovered at the spot, Bland went ashore and planted a red flag directly opposite, well above high water.

We had no explosive charges suitable for demolishing the obstacle, but at least the information we gathered led to its removal. Less than a week after our visit, Guam's expert salvage officer, Lieutenant Solomon, flew in, borrowed a caterpillar tractor from the air force, and horsed the offending object to dry land, where it could be carted away.

Under way again by 1500, we cranked on full speed to rejoin the *Maru.* Rayner and company had such a lead that it would take eight hours to catch them, even at 20 knots. Instead of heading for the probable point of interception, we first doglegged over to his track so that if the *Maru's* engine failed during the afternoon, we should still make contact. But I couldn't help worrying, even though computations had been checked and rechecked and I had full confidence in Rayner. It's a big ocean, and the idea that he and five of my men were alone in the night ahead of us made me uneasy. The lights of a fishing vessel are hard to see beyond eight thousand yards, and if our radar went out, or the *Maru* were off course . . . , but I kept these things to myself.

An hour before the scheduled interception I started sending up green flares—green because this type, for some reason, soars higher than either red or white, and red in any case would have meant "trouble." Promptly at an hour before midnight we picked up a radar contact on our starboard bow at ten miles, and a few minutes later two green stars brightened that bearing. On joining the *Maru,* I offered to remove the prize crew immediately, but they declined, saying they were quite comfortable and would prefer to stay until daylight.

Rayner had some interesting comments when we retrieved him and his men in the morning. "I think they are trying to fool us as to who is really captain of the boat," he said. "Everyone is very polite and cooperative, even though the older ones don't look too friendly."

"You can hardly blame them. After all, we're depriving them of their livelihood, temporarily at least."

"I was impressed with their navigational equipment and radio gear," he went on. "We didn't need any of the instruments I took over. I simply posted a man in their combination bridge/radio shack. They have excellent receivers, and a three-foot directional loop antenna. The captain, or whoever he is, says he uses Radio Iwo and Radio Guam for fixes all the time."

"Did the crew appear to be ex-navy officers?"

"Not at all. They were a different sort of people entirely from those we ran into at Chichi Jima that time."

Life aboard the *Matabe Maru* was indeed simple, he said later: "Rice, tea, and fish is all they have. When they get hungry, they bring a fish up from the hold, filet it, and cook the pieces in a shallow pan of water. Then they take it with their rice and tea, hunker down on the deck, and eat it."

Our snail's pace brought us to Saipan two days later, and I turned my captive over to local authorities. Legal experts boarded us there and rode the ship back to Apra Harbor, taking depositions en route. (I never learned the results of the hearing.) We arrived next morning, 20 May 1954.

✳

My journal ends here. The twentieth was the day the *Hanna* was to be relieved and sent back to the States, and sure enough, a strange DE lay at our customary berth, ready to take over our tasks.

The longing for home that we had held back over the past months, consciously or subconsciously, now washed up like a flood, and we could hardly wait to turn over our records and take on fuel and provisions before starting our long journey. Something of what we had been through, the things to look for and to guard against, the things to enjoy, the hazards, the personalities, the techniques we had found successful—all of this I tried to impart to the officer who was relieving me. Maybe I tried to tell him too much at once, for his eyes showed a disinterest that I could only hope would pass as soon as we had left.

I hoped so because the part of the world encompassed by his new responsibilities deserved understanding, if only for the sake of its people, who—in beauty and squalor compounded—had attained an ethic the world should envy.

I hoped so because I had found so much pleasure in pursuing the past through these islands, in witnessing so colorful a procession of valiant men in little ships venturing into the unknown—men dedicated, saintly, even bigoted, and also valiant; men dreaming of empire or gold or paradise.

I hoped so because the battles that most recently had raged across these waters and conferred such painful memories on these islands and the waters around them have a meaning for all Americans, and because those who died here would be ill-requited if we were to forget the lands they had looked on last.

I am a sailor at heart, and in a way, any blue water is still my home. After all this time, to that part of the ocean that stretches beyond the beginning of day I still hope I may someday return.

17
Epilogue

More than forty years have passed since I said good-bye to the *Hanna,* and I still remember that little ship with pride and affection—still remember the grace with which she moved in quiet waters, still feel the slap and thud of waves on her bow when we cranked her up at sea, still remember the pride of men like the young fellow who said, "Captain, there just ain't *nothin'* we can't do!"

We had come to Micronesia at a time when postwar expectations in and for the island world of the Pacific were still uncertain. The United States by then was administering the area as a strategic trust territory under United Nations auspices, initially through the Navy Department and later through the Department of the Interior. The navy naturally placed national security ahead of all else, in the face of an expanding Soviet fleet in the Pacific, and otherwise followed a belief that best administration was least administration.

It was a time of limited resources and benign expedients. One such expedient was a project to replace cattle destroyed during the war with breeding stock from the United States, an operation in which I participated as captain of the USS *Chicot* (AK 170), a small diesel-powered cargo ship—my first seagoing command. We left Maui in January 1949 with 144 heifers as deck cargo in twenty-four portable pens and again in April from San Pedro with 124 more, all delivered without mishap in Guam, Saipan, and Ponape.[1] It was my introduction to postwar Micronesia.

Gradually there was change. In 1951 President Truman signed an executive order transferring administrative control over the Carolines and Marshalls to the Department of the Interior. Because of meager appropriations and a shortage of trained personnel, the changeover was hardly perceptible when we were there in 1952–54. It was still American policy to move slowly in Micronesia. Annual budgets amounted to little more than $1 million a year.

It was not until the Kennedy administration that things began to happen. John F. Kennedy had served in the Pacific and was genuinely concerned with the islanders' welfare. He appointed an aggressive fund-raiser to the post of high commissioner, and Congress was soon persuaded to raise the annual budget for the Trust Territory to $1.5 million. To many of the islanders Kennedy was the government personified, the great chief, and his assassination affected them deeply.

The early 1960s saw a move to comply with article 6 of the trusteeship agreement for the former Japanese mandated islands, which provided in part that "the administering authority shall . . . foster the development of such political institutions as are suited to the trust territory and shall promote the development of the inhabitants of the trust territory toward self-government or independence as may be appropriate to the particular circumstances of the trust territory and its peoples and the freely expressed wishes of the peoples concerned; and to this end shall give to the inhabitants of the trust territory a progressively increasing share in the administrative services in the territory."

In 1964 a charter was approved for a bicameral legislature to be known as the Congress of Micronesia, to replace the purely advisory Council of Micronesia. A miniversion of the U.S. Congress, it was to consist of an upper chamber of two members from each of the six districts—Palau, Yap, Truk, Ponape, the Marshalls, and the Northern Marianas—and a lower chamber with twenty-one members apportioned according to relative district populations. The new body was to have power to pass laws affecting the inhabitants of the Trust Territory of the Pacific Islands (TTPI), subject to veto by the high commissioner but with a proviso that should a vetoed measure be resubmitted and again vetoed, it could appealed directly to the secretary of the interior.

The first election was set for 19 January 1965. Preelection campaigning varied from district to district. In the Marshalls there was little politicking because no Marshallese would dream of praising himself. Candidates in Ponape and Truk even belittled themselves, and free radio time went unused. But in Palau and the Marianas, parties sprang up, and one candidate even attacked his opponent by name. The election was a great success, with an 80 percent turnout of eligible voters. The new congress convened on 12 July, a date thereafter celebrated annually as Micronesia Day.

The way was now open for talk of self-determination in line with earlier expectations, even though it remained a distant goal. Meanwhile natives depended more and more on imported goods and services and on jobs with the Trust Territory administration.[2] The TTPI budget ballooned.

One of the first acts of the new Congress of Micronesia was to establish a commission to negotiate the future status of the territory. Five years of talks resulted in a joint proposal for self-government in "free association" with the United States, to be established by compact, terminable by either party, whereby the United States would assume responsibility for foreign affairs and defense and continue to maintain strategic bases while providing massive budgetary assistance. Further talks set the agreed subsidy at $57 million for the first five years, $52 million for the second five, and $47 million for the third.[3]

Even before these negotiations were concluded, however, the idea of a unified semi-independent Micronesia collapsed under the weight of economic and cultural differences among the six regional districts of the TTPI—and differences in their aspirations and attitudes toward the United States. The proposed Compact of Free Association (CFA) would have to be adopted piecemeal.

The Northern Marianas were the first to break away, voting in 1975 for commonwealth status similar to that of Puerto Rico. The U.S. Congress agreed to the resolution the following year, and thereupon, the Northern Marianas came under a separate provisional government, although technically still part of the TTPI.

The Marshalls were next. They had been generating the largest tax revenues in the territory, which they were not keen on sharing with other districts. Negotiations begun in 1977 led to adoption two years later of a constitution creating a sovereign Republic of the Marshall Islands (RMI), with a British-style parliament, or *nitijela*, and a U.S.-style presidency.

In 1979 the largest and most populous group, consisting of the newly minted states of Yap, Chuuk (Truk), Pohnpei (Ponape), and Kosrae (Kusaie), united as the Federated States of Micronesia (FSM).

The two new political entities proceeded to negotiate separate compacts of free association, and these were approved by plebiscites in 1983 and became fully implemented in 1986.

Belau (Palau) was an awkward case because of an antinuclear clause in its constitution that was hopelessly at odds with the draft CFA. That particular clause, which would have made Palau useless as a forward strategic base, required a 75 percent vote to override. A majority vote was easily achieved, but a succession of tries fell short of that percentage. After the plebiscite of 21 February 1986, with 72 percent in favor, the incumbent president of Palau informed UN visiting mission observers that a simple majority was all that was necessary, an opinion that the U.S. administration endorsed all too readily.[4] But the interpretation wasn't valid and seems to have been quietly dropped. Palau remained within the trust agreement.

The trust agreement was terminated for the other three entities of the TTPI by vote of the Security Council in December 1990.[5] The Northern Marianas was already a commonwealth. (The FSM and the RMI became members of the United Nations nine months later.)

At length the impasse over Palau was resolved simply by an amendment to the constitution, accomplished by referendum 4 November 1993, to lower the vote to override from 75 percent to "50 plus one." A plebiscite held five days later yielded 68 percent in favor, and the Trusteeship Council of the United Nations proclaimed that the people of Palau had "freely exercised their right to self-determination."[6] On 27 September 1994 Pres. William J. Clinton proclaimed that the Compact of Free Association between the United States and Palau (which had already been approved by Congress) was now in full force and effect and that as of 1 October the Trusteeship Agreement for the Pacific Islands in respect to Palau would no longer be in effect, a proclamation marking the end of the TTPI for all of Micronesia.

A year after the *Hanna* left the islands and I had been relieved as her skipper, came good news from Father Walter of Ulithi. The episode of the lost canoes had concluded with the safe return of most of the natives who had sailed in them, but the great canoes, the mainstay of Ulithi's trade with the off-lying islands, lay beached somewhere in the Philippines. As the missionary emphasized in the May 1955 issue of his local newsletter, the *Micronesian Mirror,* their loss was a calamity:

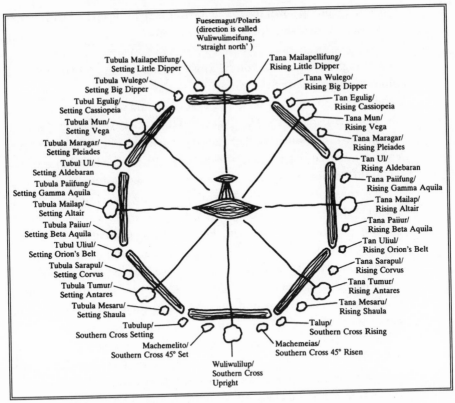

Fuesemagut/Polaris
(direction is called
Wuliwulimeifung,
"straight north")

Tubula Mailapellifung/
Setting Little Dipper

Tubula Wulego/
Setting Big Dipper

Tubul Egulig/
Setting Cassiopeia

Tubula Mun/
Setting Vega

Tubula Maragar/
Setting Pleiades

Tubul Ul/
Setting Aldebaran

Tubula Paiifung/
Setting Gamma Aquila

Tubula Mailap/
Setting Altair

Tubula Paiiur/
Setting Beta Aquila

Tubul Uliul/
Setting Orion's Belt

Tubula Sarapul/
Setting Corvus

Tubula Tumur/
Setting Antares

Tubula Mesaru/
Setting Shaula

Tubulup/
Southern Cross Setting

Machemelito/
Southern Cross 45° Set

Tana Mailapellifung/
Rising Little Dipper

Tana Wulego/
Rising Big Dipper

Tan Egulig/
Rising Cassiopeia

Tana Mun/
Rising Vega

Tana Maragar/
Rising Pleiades

Tan Ul/
Rising Aldebaran

Tana Paiifung/
Rising Gamma Aquila

Tana Mailap/
Rising Altair

Tana Paiiur/
Rising Beta Aquila

Tan Uliul/
Rising Orion's Belt

Tana Sarapul/
Rising Corvus

Tana Tumur/
Rising Antares

Tana Mesaru/
Rising Shaula

Talup/
Southern Cross Rising

Machemeias/
Southern Cross 45° Risen

Wuliwulilup/
Southern Cross
Upright

Paafu, the star compass of the central Carolines, resembles the European magnetic compass in that it features thirty-two points. However, these are defined by the bearing (*azimuth*) of certain stars close to the horizon at rising, *Tan(a)*, or setting, *Tubul(a)*. The eight straight sticks of the diagram indicate eight different swells used in *pukulaw,* or steering by ocean waves. The system used by native navigators relies on stars, wind and wave patterns, and astonishing feats of memory and perception. *Drawing courtesy of Stephen D. Thomas,* The Last Navigator *(New York, 1987)*

They are the most precious possessions of the atoll dweller and are not owned by individuals, but by clans. A whole clan will labor for a year weaving pandanus sails, sleeping mats, and sarongs by the score, distilling gallons of sweet syrup from coconut sap, and making thousands of feet of sennit twine and coir rope from the coconut husks, doing all this labor in order to barter with the Yapese for one of their rare hardwood trees. Then an expedition of skilled craftsmen is sent to Yap to work for a year chopping down the tree and fashioning the deep keel and curving the hull of their graceful lateen-rigged canoe.

The high commissioner of the Trust Territory, Frank E. Midkiff, took interest in repatriating the voyagers and now set about recovering their canoes. He appropriated $5,000 of TTPI funds and won the support of the Interior Department, the U.S. Navy, and the U.S. Coast Guard. Through the embassy in Manila, Midkiff gained cooperation of the Philippine government, so that one fine day a vessel of the Pacific Far East Lines arrived in Ulithi's lagoon, bringing home the three precious canoes.

"For three nights the fires burned around the dancing areas," wrote Father Walter in his newsletter, "and teams of men and women took turns weaving patterns in the flickering light, chanting sagas of the great deeds of the Americans. From the time that a thousand ships anchored in the lagoon during the late war, the Americans have been regarded as supermen. . . . What other nation in the world would have been so generous?" Other canoe expeditions before and since have lost their way or been storm-driven into oblivion, but none can have had a happier outcome.

But all of this was long ago. The need for long canoe voyages has passed in Micronesia. In recent years safer and more reliable interisland transportation has become available. The *Chicot* was decommissioned in 1951 and transferred to the Department of the Interior. Other vessels have been added. In 1965 the TTPI administration signed a two-year contract with the Micronesian Shipping Line (a subsidiary of the United Tanker Corporation) to operate the MV *Pacific Islander,* MV *Gunners Knot,* and MV *Palau Islander.* Two 100-foot diesel vessels were put in interisland service, and in 1968 a ten-year contract to operate all the territory's logistic shipping was signed with Micronesian Interocean Lines. The MV *James M. Cook* was also added for field administration of public health, educational, and community development services.

I expect that the deep urge to venture forth in great canoes lingers, however, and I hope the skills of the old navigators in reading wind, waves, and stars may still be remembered somewhere in Oceania.

Father Walter, I understand, died of throat cancer in New York in December 1975. He had left Ulithi and for a time sought relief on the mainland, in the Washington area, but his body was sent back to Ulithi for a splendid funeral and interment on Mogmog, close to the people he loved and whom he had served so long and well. He was a great man.

The other missionary whom I came to know and admire in Micronesia was Father William Rively of Lukunor, whom I first met on the occasion of the reefing of the mission schooner *Romance* at Truk. Recently I heard from Father Francis X. Hezel, the tireless teacher and historian, that Father Rively had come in from the Mortlocks and was living in semiretirement on Weno (formerly known as Moen) in Truk and, further, that the *Romance* —or more properly the *Star of the Sea,* her registered name—was being used less and less as the years passed and hence in the early 1980s had been sold to a private group on Truk. "Sadly, they neglected the ship and eventually let it sink in the boat pool at Weno, where it became the Star *Under the Sea,* in common parlance."[7]

One of Father Walter's monuments was a concrete-block chapel completed on Mogmog after we were there. When typhoon "Ophelia" swept over the island on 30 November 1960, the chapel provided shelter against winds estimated at 120 to 135 *knots* and saved many lives, as did a smaller wooden structure on Asor. The coast guard station on Falalap stood but was inaccessible because of the stretch of open water between that island and the Ulithi reef. Most habitations were swept away; canoes were broken and taro pits filled with sand; and on the northwest side coconut trees were smashed and uprooted. The TTPI administration sent an agricultural officer to supervise the planting of twenty thousand coconut seedlings, and these thrived so well that four years later a visitor reported them "already far higher than the wildest predictions."[8]

Many typhoons have struck Micronesia in recent years. In March 1961, "Sally" brought major destruction to Palau. In November 1967, "Emma" savaged Yap and northern Palau, and in the same month "Gilda" hit Rota. Five months later "Jean" created havoc in the Mortlocks, Truk, and the Marianas. In 1969 there was "Elsie," in 1971 "Amy," in 1990 both "Owen" and "Russ," in 1992 "Omar," and in 1994 "Zelda"—each leaving wounds. The most spectacular was "Steve" in 1993, accompanied by an 8-Richter quake that shook the new luxury-hotel industry of Guam and Saipan to its foundations. Most comparisons fail, but I am led to believe that "Doris," which struck the Marianas in 1953 when the *Hanna* was on the scene, was more costly in terms of human life—specifically the crews of two navy weather planes—than any of the others. I wish it had not been so.

Natural disasters, however, failed to discourage the tourist industry, a fact exemplified by the opening of the $800,000 Hotel Taga in Saipan in 1967. In 1968 foreign nationals with visas were for the first time allowed to enter the TTPI without entry permits. Luxury hotels sprang up along the broad beaches, and within three years tourists became second only to copra as the mainstay of the islands. In 1982 there were 120,000 arrivals—two-thirds of whom were Japanese, now regarding the Marianas as a kind of Hawaii.

Most visitors limited themselves to Saipan, Guam, and Palau. Continental Airlines at one time proposed building six luxury hotels elsewhere in Micronesia, but such developments were particularly unwelcome in some places. The Yap legislature even passed a resolution against allowing a resort hotel on their island. It was perhaps just as well. For one thing, air service to the regional centers, although much improved, still fell short of the level most travelers expect.

Another activity that the TTPI administration expected to bring cash to the islands was fishing. Before the war the Japanese tuna catch in the islands had exceeded the total production of California fisheries, and it was hoped the islanders might manage some similar benefit. Foreign interlopers had to be fended off, an important part of the *Hanna's* mission while we were there. Under the trust agreement no outside commercial firms other than those of the United States were allowed to set up shop in the territory, and it was not until 1962 that the government decided to open the door to others. In 1964 the Van Camp Tuna Company of Long Beach, California, built a million-dollar freezing plant in Palau and began operations with a fleet of six 15-ton tuna boats, later doubled to twelve. The next year a Palauan firm brought in seven more boats from Okinawa, with Okinawan crews.

The industry was to have little impact on the local economy, however, for the Micronesians found they didn't care much for the hard life of commercial fishing. Even if they were to own the trawlers, it is said, after one trip they would want to have a party. Commercial fishing still continues today, but the bulk of the catch goes to Japan to be put in cans for the benefit of others. Subsistence fishing among the islands has dwindled because local chiefs are prone to strike deals with fishermen from Taiwan and Japan permitting them to exploit the rich waters offshore. So much for our diligent patrols of long ago!

Palau figured in an interesting scheme in the mid-1970s that would have created a superport for supertankers in the lagoon on the northwest side of Babeldaob. The idea was to provide an oil storage facility where million-ton tankers from Iran would off-load oil for transshipment to smaller tankers headed for Japan. There would be refineries, petrochemical plants, desalinization plants, nuclear and thermal power plants, and other facilities.

It is not clear how the Department of the Interior might have reacted, had not a "Save Palau" committee mobilized opposition on environmental grounds, such as the danger of oil spills to the coral reefs and the simple aversion to degrading such a beautiful place. The proposal mercifully died.[9]

I have failed so far to mention the work of scholars and scientists in Micronesia, work that began even as U.S. Naval and Marine Corps occupation forces moved island-by-island into the area. Preliminary work had been done by a team of researchers at Yale University who collected scarce materials about Micronesia for use in preparation of classified "area handbooks."[10] Leading anthropologists were engaged to help train island commanders in the first Naval School of Military Government at Columbia University and later were among the first civilians permitted in the islands. After V-J Day, Micronesia became a prime field for graduate research in anthropology, more than any other area in the history of the discipline, and a staggering amount of material was collected and published. In 1946 there was the U.S. Commercial Company Project (twenty-five researchers), in 1947–49 the Coordinated Investigation of Micronesia (forty-two researchers), and in 1949 the Scientific Investigations of Micronesia (forty-nine researchers).[11] They were said to be as plentiful as coconuts. Later, anthropologists were hired as field consultants to district officials, with mixed results due in part to conflict between the aims of scientific inquiry and the duties imposed by the district administrators. Perhaps for such reasons, only about half of those who came as graduate students completed their doctorates.

Another influx of outsiders took place in October and November 1966—450 Peace Corps volunteers, drawn mostly from liberal arts students fresh out of American colleges and universities. The program—one of the noblest products of President Kennedy's era, the "thousand days"—already was involved in fifty countries, and had some fifty thousand participants, by the time it was approved for Micronesia. By 30 June 1967, there were 452 Peace Corps volunteers in the Trust Territory—265 teachers, 98 nurses and health technicians, and the remaining 89 in fourteen other specialties. Some were in training on Udot Island in Truk, others already serving in the Marianas, Marshalls, Palau, Yap, and Ponape.[12] At the high point, there were 700 Peace Corps members in the islands, tapering off to seventy-five in 1991, by which time the emphasis was on projects requested by the state governments.

By 1991 two other volunteer organizations had entered the picture: the Japanese Overseas Volunteers (JOV), focusing on fishing and agriculture projects, and Pacific Missionary Aviation (PAM), with seven small aircraft flying to isolated atolls to provide medical supplies, medical evacuation services, and searches for missing fishermen.

Did the Peace Corps in Micronesia justify its cost in dollars and effort? Some have said that the idea of young Americans trying to subsist at native levels was ridiculous and that most of what they taught was useless—which is partly true, but only partly. Peace Corps veterans are not inclined to applaud their own accomplishments. One has written:

> I have never quite made my peace with the Peace Corps. It has to do with the matter of using and getting used. . . . Living on the level of the people can come off as downright wacky if people want to escape that level. We learned local languages while teaching English to the locals, but what we found was that, while hoping to meet a culture on its own terms, we participated in its transformation, and, possibly, its destruction. We lived like the locals, yes, but they wanted to live like us. . . . They may have been touched by our willingness to come, but they ached for our ability to leave. . . .
>
> I got more than I gave, knowing our temporary largesse was far outweighed by the courtesy and forbearance we received. . . .
>
> Micronesia comes back to me all the time.[13]

Probably the greatest benefit was that which accrued to the volunteers themselves in the form of enhanced self-confidence, tolerance, and skill in problem-solving. A striking number have become leaders in the life of our nation—in business, public service, the arts, and industry.

And so the years have passed. The role of the navy in the former Trust Territory is much diminished now. ComNavMar still ensures that support is provided to naval shore commands and to the operating forces of the Seventh Fleet. An additional title—commander in chief Pacific representative for Guam, Commonwealth of the Northern Mariana Islands, Federated States of Micronesia, and Republic of Palau, or CinCPacRep Guam/CNMI/FSM/ROP—signifies coordination of military activities on Guam and throughout Micronesia, such as four "civic action teams" deployed to give medical on-the-job training to members of the local population and to complete small construction projects. One ship, the submarine tender USS *Frank Cable* (AS 40) provides repair services not only for submarines but also for other types of vessels, following the closure of the Naval Repair Facility ashore.

Search and rescue operations, such as the *Hanna* carried out after typhoon Doris, are now the province of the U.S. Coast Guard through a rescue subcenter reporting directly to the Joint Rescue Coordination Center in Honolulu. Assets afloat consist of two cutters and a 7-m RHIB (rigid-hull inflatable boat).

Such is the present day, a far cry from what was still so much in evidence forty and more years ago. Critics of what has happened in the islands have not been kind—blaming the navy, the TTPI administration, and Americans in general for everything from alcoholism to corruption to overpopulation to the trashing of beaches. Concerning the stewardship of the "little lands" of the western ocean in the postwar years, some have asserted that we should have sealed them off as national property in the same way that the USSR sealed off Sakhalin and the Kuriles, or that we should have let them fend entirely for themselves, or that we should have protected them the more from the ills of "civilization."

It has been said that on the islands the old norms of hospitality and generosity have been abandoned, the old skills forgotten, and the old tribal leaders pushed aside. It might have been otherwise had we followed the Japanese and German examples of commercial exploitation instead of trying to help the people of Micronesia find their own way in the modern world. Possibly, as a former official in the Department of the Interior has written, "The U.S. may have given too much too soon and ignored some of the cultural impediments to change."[14]

But one thing can never be taken away from Micronesia, the quality I think of as *mystique of place*—an attribute quite apart from size or shape or any other physical characteristic and having to do with the fact that a place is where it is in this world and nowhere else and often is unreachable except through great effort, patience, and faith. Most of the ills of the new age in the western Pacific come from the urban centers of Guam, Saipan, Belau, Chuuk, and Kosrae, not from the little places many horizons beyond them. It is from knowing of such little places as these that I am led to believe there must still exist havens of beauty, affection, respect, and quiet happiness somewhere in the South Seas.

Notes

1. THE ROMANCE ON THE ROCKS

1. As I explain in the preface, the orthography of many place-names in Micronesia has been changed in recent years. The traditional names are used herein, unless otherwise noted.
2. Lütke, *Voyage autour du Monde*, 293–94; my translation.
3. Bingham, *Story of the* Morning Star, 10.
4. Ibid., 38.
5. Warren, *Morning Star*, 227–28.
6. The names of these vessels appear in the U.S. Strategic Bombing Survey, *Reduction of Truk*, and are confirmed in part in Gardiner, Chesneau, and Budzbon, *Conway's All the World's Fighting Ships, 1922–1946*, 167–217 passim, and in Stewart, *Ghost Fleet*, 120–22.
7. Other participants included Vice Adm. Chuichi Hara, commander of the Japanese Fourth Fleet, and Rear Adm. Aritaka Aibara, governor of the Eastern Branch District (Peattie, *Nan'yo*, 308; Stewart, *Ghost Fleet*, 91).

2. COCONUT KINGDOMS

1. The differences go beyond mere topography. Natives on the high islands tend to be warlike, with more elaborate social organization and richer oral traditions.
2. Krämer, *Inseln um Truk*, 155; my translation.
3. "Alanmwassel," or "Alanmwassal," is now listed as the name of a bar in the U.S. Geological Survey's geographic names database.
4. I have been unable to correlate this information with the terms given in Thomas's 1987 *Last Navigator*, perhaps because of language differences.
5. Alexander, *Islands of the Pacific*, 240.
6. The poet Adelbert von Chamisso (1781–1838) participated as a botanist in the Kotzebue expedition of 1815–18.
7. The *Romance* was built at the Ah King Slipway. Her 45-foot hull was framed with an oriental hardwood called *yacal* and planked and decked with 1.5-inch teak, copper fastened (Rively, *Story of the* Romance, 50). She seems to have been rigged as a brigantine, or a "hermaphrodite brig."
8. To be precise, the *Romance* was chartered (not sold) to the Jesuit Mission of the Marshall and Caroline Islands for ninety-nine years at a price of $15,750. The registered owner remained Arthur C. Wood, of Vancouver (Rively, *The Story of the* Romance, 76). Although the mission called her the *Stella Maris*, the original name stuck.
9. Stevenson, *Footnote to History*, 253–54.

3. A PLACE OF VIOLENCE

1. Apparently the largest artillery were two vintage 6-inch guns that had been wrestled to the top of a mountain overlooking the colonial town (Peattie, *Nan'yo*, 264).
2. In 1991 a volunteer labor group organized under Peace Corps auspices installed stairs on the trail up the hill at a cost of $8,000, which was paid by private contributions (Scherer, "Volunteer Groups in 'Paradise'").
3. Harrocke was an escaped convict, a Yorkshireman, who had lived on the island for thirteen years.
4. Lot Harbor would have been convenient for sailing vessels, however, because they could enter or leave with equal facility on the prevailing trade wind.
5. A "jolly boat" is any light boat carried at the stern of a larger vessel.
6. These chickens are said to be the descendants of some fowls cast ashore from the wreck of a Chinese fishing boat in 1832.
7. Adm. Cyprian A.G. Bridge, RN, intro. to *Caroline Islands,* by Frederick William Christian, 14.
8. Warren, *Morning Star,* 131.
9. Alexander, *Islands of the Pacific,* 241.
10. Ibid., 241–42.
11. Ibid., 242.
12. For a good profile of Henry Hedges and a report of his administration, see Trumbull, *Paradise in Trust,* 58–77.

4. SOMETHING ABOUT A SHIP

1. We never saw any sharks; they prefer the rich food chain near land.
2. "K" (or minus 10) was the time zone in which we operated.

5. NORTH TO CHICHI JIMA

1. Peattie places the number at forty men, of the 50th Regiment (*Nan'yo*, 347, n. 60).
2. I believe the discovery has since been incorporated in the official U.S. Navy *Sailing Directions.*
3. For clarity, it will be well to note that a *shima* is an island, a *jima* a small cluster of islands; *retto* or *gunto* refers to groups of islands. In addition, *haha* means "mother," *chichi* means "father," and *muko* means "sister." The Japanese were sadly unimaginative when it came to naming islands. For example, they renamed four of the islands of Truk after seasons of the year though the weather is summery there the year round. I have tried to avoid Japanese versions of place-names, being unwilling to dignify or perpetuate them when so many were imposed in order to make people forget the originals. Moreover, many of the Japanese versions are merely phonetic spellings of attempts to pronounce the authentic names, as *Torakku* for Truk, *Marakaru* for Malakal, *Sorru* for Sorol, and so on. Names in the Bonin Islands are a particular mishmash, owing to the complicated history of that group, and we must rely mostly on the Japanese versions.
4. Cited in Lewis and Allen, *Bluejackets with Perry,* 150–51.
5. The boat in which Admiral Radford came ashore had belonged to General Tachibana.

6. Sherrod, *History of Marine Corps Aviation*, 350–56.

7. Ibid., 351–52.

8. Ibid., 352.

9. Initial supplies of food, clothing, livestock, tools, seeds, and medicine were brought up from Saipan in the PC 1546 and LCI 1067.

10. Cited in Cholmondeley, *History of the Bonin Islands*, 19. Matteo Mazora (or Mazzaro), an Italian who claimed to be a British subject, was mate on a sealing sloop, the *Princess of Wales*, which wrecked in the Crozets in 1820. With him was Richard Millinchap (or Millichap), an Englishman. Their later adventures are covered briefly in Dunbabin, *Sailing the World's Edge*, 197–99. Also in the party were two Americans from Massachusetts named Aldin Chapin and Nathaniel Savory, a Dane named Richard Johnson, and fifteen Hawaiians.

11. Charlton's appointment of Simpson as acting consul in his absence was a fact that Kamehameha III declined to recognize (see Kuykendall, *Hawaiian Kingdom*).

12. Cited in Cholmondeley, *History of the Bonin Islands*, 20.

13. At the time of our visit, there was a turtle pen of the same kind a few yards from the site of Perry's coaling station. In locales where turtles are wont to come ashore to lay eggs, natives catch numbers of them and hold them in pens in the water at the edge of the shore, where the turtles stay alive and provide a source of fresh meat.

14. Cited in Lewis and Allen, *Bluejackets with Perry*, 151.

15. Lt. Comdr. Dorothy Richard, USN, draft report, "The Naval Administration of the Trust Territory of the Pacific Islands," annex 5 (omitted from the published version).

6. PLACES WITHOUT PEOPLE

1. Villalobos had four ships, the *Santiago* (flag), *San Jorge*, *San Antonio*, and *San Juan de Letran;* plus the *San Christoval*, a galley; and the *San Martin*, a fusta (a small vessel with lateen sails).

2. A compilation by Adm. José Gonzales Cabrera Bueno entitled *Navigación Especulativa Práctica* was published in Manila in 1734.

3. Cited in J.C. Beaglehole, ed., *Voyage of the* Resolution *and* Discovery, 711 n. 4. The Volcano Islands are still secondarily known as the Sulphur Islands.

4. There is reason to believe that the volcano has been active here in fairly recent times, and to judge by its various names—Guy Rock, Vogel Insel, Parrot Rock—it must have been far less awesome in the past. There is still an ancient shield formation visible, not yet engulfed by cinders and lava, on which thousands of birds are making a last stand.

5. Now set down as 19°40′N, 145°E (of Greenwich). La Pérouse used the Paris prime meridian, a difference of 2°20′ 22.5″ —which makes his measure only thirteen miles off.

6. Navy charts now place its altitude at 2,927 feet. We found it to be 2,728 feet high, a fact indicating that the mountain may recently have blown its top.

7. La Pérouse had two ships, the *Astrolabe* and the *Boussole*. Both of them met tragic fates not long after this was written.

8. Langle was captain of the *Astrolabe*. He was killed in the massacre of boat crews at "Mauna" (probably Tutuila in the Samoan Islands) on 11 December 1787. Lieutenant Boutin escaped.

9. La Pérouse, *Voyage round the World* 2:262–65.

10. Burney, *Chronological History* 3:286. Burney's history is challenged on many counts by documentalist Roderigue Lévesque in his *History of Micronesia*.

11. Morales left for Manila in 1671, returned to Spain in 1683, then traveled to Mexico in 1689, and returned to Manila about 1698, where he died in 1716 (Lévesque, personal communication, 7 January 1995).

7. WHITE MEN AND BLACK DEEDS

1. Pigafetta, *Magellan's Voyage*, 60–61. The translation is from a rare French text housed in the Beineke Rare Book and Manuscript Library at Yale. R. A. Skelton, the book's editor and translator, remarks, "Pigafetta's prose has no elegance of construction or rhythm; it bursts from him in a succession of rather breathless short sentences" (27).

2. Spain's extension of her domain three-quarters of the way around the globe brought about an odd situation: although communication with the colony of the Philippines via the Cape of Good Hope was preferable, the pope had granted Portugal a monopoly on that route, a ruling that prompted the Portuguese to deal severely with Sebastian del Cano when he ventured to stop at the Cape Verde Islands on the way home from the first circumnavigation. Thus Spain's access to the Philippines was limited to the original route of Magellan, westward from Europe.

3. Arellano, who originally had deserted the squadron on its westward crossing, reached the Philippines independently.

4. I am indebted to Roderigue Lévesque for the location of the *Concepción* wreck, easily confused with that of a later vessel of the same name wrecked on Luminam Reef off Apra Harbor, Guam, in 1775 (personal communication, 7 January 1995).

5. Lévesque differs sharply with the prevailing assessment: "Much nonsense has been written about a so-called aristocracy that never truly existed" (personal communication, 7 January 1995).

6. Medina was killed at Cao, Saipan, between present-day San Vicente and Raurau Bay (Lévesque, personal communication, 7 January 1995).

7. Lévesque differs: "The man may have been prudish (he always punished the sexual offenses of soldiers in a harsh manner), but he was never cruel" (personal communication, 7 January 1995).

8. See Burney, *Chronological History* 3:308.

9. Ibáñez y Garçía, *Historia de las Islas Marianas*, 67; my translation.

10. Le Gobien, *History of the Marianas;* cited in Burney, *Chronological History* 3:308.

11. Burney, *Chronological History* 3:308.

12. Lévesque states that in 1668 the population could not have exceeded 20,000 (personal communication, 7 January 1995).

13. Quoted by Ambrose Cowley in his *Collection of Original Voyages, Containing Capt. Cowley's Voyage round the Globe* (London: James Knapton, 1699); cited in Burney, *Chronological History* 3:305–6.

14. Earlier, Swan in the *Cygnet* had operated with Edward Davis in the *Revenge,* who still earlier had sailed with Eaton in the *Nicholas.*

15. Dampier, *Dampier's Voyages* 1:313–14.

16. Funnel, *Voyage round the World,* 213–14.

17. Nine assorted smaller craft sailed in company with the expedition. This fact may account for differences in reported armaments and complements.

18. Wycherley, *Buccaneers,* 357.

19. Anson's greatest exploit was the capture of the great galleon *Nuestra Señora de Covadonga,* carrying gold and silver worth £400,000 as well as an even more valuable chart of Spanish discoveries in the Pacific.

20. I have not been able to locate the source of this story, but it is too good to leave out. In the same vein Kotzebue relates that "the North Americans, who are carrying on the fur trade between the N.W. coast of America and Canton, chose the islands Agrihan and Saypan as resting places on this voyage. In order to find fresh provisions there, they took some families from the Sandwich Islands, whom they compelled to attend to the cultivation of the soil and breeding of cattle; and they actually succeeded in their subsequent voyages in supplying themselves with fresh provisions without expense. The Spaniards being informed of it, soldiers were sent there, who destroyed the plantations, and carried away the poor Sandwichians" (*Voyage of Discovery,* 210).

8. HAUNTED ISLANDS

1. The *Akashi*—a protected cruiser of the *Suma* class, 2,756 tons—was launched in 1897, supposedly hulked and stricken in 1923, and then renamed *Hai Kan No 2* in 1928 (Gardiner, Gray, and Budzbon, *Conway's All the World's Fighting Ships, 1906–1921,* 225).

9. MOGMOG REVISITED

1. Some material in this chapter is drawn from my article "Mogmog Revisited," published in the United States Naval Institute *Proceedings* 82 (February 1956): 152–55.

2. The power of the confessor to the monarch is intimated by the story of Padre San Vitores in the previous century (see chap. 7 above).

3. Cantova's letter to d'Aubenton, dated 20 March 1722, ended with last-minute news that he had just been granted permission to reconnoiter the "heathen lands" and that the governor would make a bark available for the purpose immediately after the Easter festival (in *Lettres Edifiantes et Curieuses Ecrites des Missions Etrangères,* edited by Yves-Mathurin-Marie Tréandot de Querbeuf [Toulouse: Sens, 1810–11] 15:226–56). This would indicate that the expedition in 1721 was mounted well before receipt of the royal approval.

4. Cited in Burney, *Chronological History* 5:26–27.

10. THE SEIZURE

1. The very first was one of Magellan's ships, the *Trinidad,* commanded by Gonzalo Gomez de Espinosa, whose pilot wrote that "Upon arriving at the said 3 islands, they stopped at them with some risk, and came to an anchor in the middle of them in 15 fathoms. Of the said islands, one is larger, populated by 20 persons, counting men and women. This island is called Māo. It is at about 20 degrees more or less" (cited in Lévesque, *History of Micronesia* 1:325).

2. The Dutch condemned Remusat's coup as inexcusable piracy.

3. Beechey, *Narrative of a Voyage* 2:228–30. See also Peard, *To the Pacific and Arctic,* 214–19.

II. BAREFOOT BASEBALL

1. I used to tell friends that as long as I kept my *kutu* near, no harm could befall me. Now all I can say is that I survived a fire in which he perished.

2. Kotzebue, *Voyage of Discovery,* 208.

12. ON LÜTKE'S COURSES

1. The first detailed report of the ruins appears in Damon, Morning Star *Papers,* 70–72.

2. Christian, *Caroline Islands,* 79–80.

3. Ibid., 115.

4. Zaragoza, ed., *Historia de Descubrimiento,* 156–57; my translation.

5. To run short boards is to sail back and forth in short tacks, working to windward.

6. Lütke, *Voyage autour du Monde,* 95.

7. Ibid., 96.

8. Lévesque suggests a connection between their barking and the Kiti people's being known as the "dog tribe" (personal communication, 7 January 1995).

9. The discovery of Ngatik is usually attributed to Felipe Tomson, the ship's pilot (Lévesque, *Ships through Micronesia,* 16).

10. Kotzebue tells of being at the spot where Truk was supposed to be, "but we looked for it in vain, and I venture to affirm that it does not exist" (*Voyage of Discovery,* 202).

11. Ibid., 114.

13. TREACHEROUS WATERS

1. Rogers, *Cruising Voyage,* 273. Sharp suggests it might have been Helen Reef (see *Discovery of the Pacific Islands,* 93–94), but I seriously doubt it was.

2. Tobi was variously reported in the following positions:

by Carteret	lat. 2°50' N	long. 136°10' E
by Hambly	lat. 3°2.75' N	long. 131°20' E
by the *Iphegenia*	lat. 3°11' N	long. 131°12' E
However, it is actually at	lat. 3°00' N,	long. 131°10' E.

3. Holden, *Narrative of the Shipwreck,* 77–78.

4. Ibid., 92–93.

5. Christian, *Caroline Islands,* 170.

6. Klingman and Green, *His Majesty,* 251.

7. José Somera, "Relation en forme de Journal," 15:257–58; my translation.

8. Ibid., 15:260–62.

9. Ibid., 15:264.

10. Instead, the responsibility of converting the Palaus was delegated to the governor of the Marianas, and we already know what happened to Father Cantova at Ulithi a decade later.

11. Tetens, *Among the Savages,* 56–57.

12. Ibid., 58.

14. THE ANTELOPE

1. Keate, *Account of the Pelew Islands,* 8. Subsequent citations are annotated within the text.
2. "The colors are crumbled by hand in water, whilst it is warming over a gentle fire in earthen pots; they carefully skim from the surface whatever dry leaves or dirt may float to the top; when they find it sufficiently thick, they apply it warm, and let it dry upon the wood. The next day they rub it well over with warm cocoanut oil, and with the dry husk of the cocoanut giving it by repeated rubbing a polish and stability the waves cannot wash off" (ibid., 316).
3. Delano, *Narrative of Voyages,* 58.
4. Ibid., 67.
5. Ibid., 69.

16. LAST MOVEMENT

1. See Head and Daws, "Bonins—Isles of Contention," 74. As a minor sidelight, I will mention that after leaving the *Hanna* and hoping to further public awareness of the Bonins, I wrote an article titled "Chichi Jima, Island Treasure" and submitted it to Pierre Salinger, then west-coast editorial representative for *Collier's Magazine* and later press secretary to Pres. John F. Kennedy. Salinger was enthusiastic about my essay, but the *Collier's* head office turned it down.
2. See Johnson, *Right Hand of Power,* 472 ff. Apparently Pres. Lyndon B. Johnson and Congress were easily persuaded (Sarantakes, "Continuity through Change," 45–46).
3. I understand that the flag has been replaced by one of bronze, now that the island has been returned to Japan.

17. EPILOGUE

1. The operation is described in some detail in Richard, *United States Naval Administration* 3:764–70. See also Meredith, "Operation Bovine."
2. According to the U.S. Dept. of the Interior's 1966 *Annual Report of the Trust Territory,* in that year two thirds of all Micronesians in public and private employment worked for the U.S. government. By 30 June 1967, Micronesians filled 4,071 administrative and professional positions in the islands compared with 467 Americans (Morgiewicz, "Micronesia *Especial Trust,*" 72).
3. Hezel, "Looking Ahead," 205.
4. See "Trusteeship Council Calls Termination," 71.
5. The USSR ambassador apparently refrained from the usual sour remarks about the U.S. trusteeship (as in commenting on the 1985 report of the Trusteeship Council, his predecessor claimed that "enormous suffering" had been brought upon the Micronesian people by the United States). See "Trusteeship Council Reviews Conditions in Pacific Islands," *UN Chronicle* 22, no. 6 (June 1985): 30.
6. "Palau Compact Implementation Urged."
7. Hezel, personal communication, 25 November 1995.
8. Gajdusek, *Journal of an Expedition,* 32.
9. It has also been suggested that because of uncertainty over future American support for Palau, the Japanese and Iranian backers "put the proposal on ice" (see "U.S. Plays Midwife").

10. Much of this material—such as *Ergebnisse der Südsee-Expedition 1908–1910,* Thilenius's massive report on the South Seas expedition of 1908–10—originated during the German era and thus required a crash program of translations.

11. See Falgout, "Americans in Paradise," 102–4.

12. United States, Department of the Interior, *Annual Report of the Trust Territory* (1967), 40.

13. Scherer, "Volunteer Groups in 'Paradise.'"

14. Senese, "The United States in Micronesia," 423.

Bibliography

WORKS CITED

Alexander, James M. *The Islands of the Pacific, from the Old to the New*. 2d ed. New York: American Tract Society, 1908.

Beaglehole, J. C., ed. *The Voyage of the* Resolution *and* Discovery *1776–80*. Vol. 3 of *The Journals of Captain James Cook on His Voyages of Discovery*. Cambridge: Hakluyt Society, 1967.

Beechey, Frederick William. *Narrative of a Voyage to the Pacific and Beering's Strait, to Co-operate with the Polar Expeditions: Performed in His Majesty's Ship* Blossom, *under the Command of Captain F. W. Beechey . . . in the Years 1825, 26, 27, 28*. 2 vols. London: Henry Colburn & Richard Bentley, 1831.

Bingham, Hiram, Jr. *The Story of the* Morning Star: *The Children's Missionary Vessel*. Boston: ABCFM, 1866.

Burney, James. *A Chronological History of the Voyages and Discoveries in the South Sea or Pacific Ocean*. 5 vols. London: G. & W. Nicol, 1803–17.

Cholmondeley, Lionel Berners. *The History of the Bonin Islands from the Year 1827 to the Year 1876 and of Nathaniel Savory, One of the Original Settlers, to Which Is Added a Short Supplement Dealing with the Islands after the Occupation by the Japanese*. London: Constable, 1915.

Christian, Frederick William. *The Caroline Islands: Travel in the Sea of the Little Lands*. London: Methuen, 1899.

Damon, Samuel C. Morning Star *Papers: By Rev. Samuel C. Damon*. Honolulu: Hawaiian Missionary Society, 1861.

Dampier, William. *Dampier's Voyages: Consisting of a New Voyage round the World, a Supplement to the Voyage round the World, Two Voyages to Campeachy. A Discourse of Winds, a Voyage to New Holland, and a Vindication, in Answer to the Chimerical Relation of William Funnel*. Edited by John Masefield. 2 vols. London: E. Grant Richards, 1906.

Delano, Amasa. *A Narrative of Voyages and Travels, in the Northern and Southern Hemispheres, Comprising Three Voyages around the World, together with a Voyage of Survey and Discovery in the Pacific Ocean and Oriental Islands*. Boston: printed by E.G. House for the author, 1817.

Dunbabin, Thomas. *Sailing the World's Edge: Sea Stories from Old Sydney*. London: Newnes, 1931.

Falgout, Susanne. "Americans in Paradise: Anthropologists, Custom and Democracy in Postwar Micronesia." *Ethnology* 34, no. 2 (spring 1995): 99–111.

Funnell, William. *Voyage round the World, by William Funnell, in 1703–1706.* In *A General History and Collection of Voyages and Travels,* edited by Robert Kerr, 10:291–336. London: T. Cadell, 1824.

Gajdusek, D. Carleton. *Journal of an Expedition to the Western Caroline Islands, August 26 to October 6, 1964.* Bethesda: National Institute of Neurological Diseases and Blindness, n.d.

Gardiner, Robert, Roger Chesneau, and Przemyslaw Budzbon. *Conway's All the World's Fighting Ships, 1922–1946.* New York: Mayflower Books, 1980.

Gardiner, Robert, Randal Gray, and Przemyslaw Budzbon. *Conway's All the World's Fighting Ships, 1906–1921.* London: Conway Maritime Press, 1985.

Head, Timothy E., and Gavin Daws. "The Bonins—Isles of Contention." *American Heritage* 19, no. 2 (Feb. 1968): 58–64, 69–74.

Hezel, Francis X., S.J. "Looking Ahead to the End of Trusteeship, Trust Territory of the Pacific Islands." *Journal of Pacific History* 13, no. 3 (1978): 204–10.

Holden, Horace. *Narrative of the Shipwreck, Captivity and Sufferings of Horace Holden and Benj. H. Nute; Who Were Cast away in the American Ship* Mentor, *on the Pelew Islands, in the Year 1832; and for Two Years Afterwards Were Subjected to Unheard Of Sufferings among the Barbarous Inhabitants of Lord North's Island.* Boston: Weeks, Jordan, 1839.

Ibáñez y Garçía, Luís de. *Historia de las Islas Marianas, con su Derrotero, y de las Carolinas y Palaos.* Granada: Imp. y Lib. de Paolino v Sabatel, 1886.

Johnson, U. Alexis. *The Right Hand of Power.* Englewood Cliffs, N.J.: Prentice-Hall, 1984.

Keate, George. *An Account of the Pelew Islands, Situated in the Western Part of the Pacific Ocean: Composed from the Journals and Communications of Captain Henry Wilson, and Some of His Officers, Who, in August 1783, Were Shipwrecked in the* Antelope. London: G. Nicol, 1788.

Klingman, Lawrence, and Gerald Green. *His Majesty O'Keefe.* New York: Charles Scribner's Sons, 1950.

Kotzebue, Otto von. *Voyage of Discovery in the South Seas and Beering's Straits.* London: Richard Phillips, 1821.

Krämer, Augustin. *Inseln um Truk (Centralkarolinen Ost).* Vol. 6 of *Ergebnisse der Südsee-Expedition 1908–1910,* edited by Georg Thilenius. Hamburg: F. De Gruyter, 1935.

Kubary, Jan S. "Plan der Ruinen von Nanmatal auf der Insel Ponapé." *Journal des Museums Godeffroy* 6, no. 5 (1874): 123–31.

Kuykendall, Ralph S. *1778–1854: Foundation and Transformation.* Vol. 1 of *The Hawaiian Kingdom.* Honolulu: University of Hawaii, 1935.

La Pérouse, Jean François de Galaup. *A Voyage round the World in the Years 1785, 1786, 1787, 1788, by J. F. G. La Pérouse.* Edited by M. L. A. Milet. 2d ed. 3 vols. London: J. Johnson, 1799.

Lévesque, Roderigue, ed. *History of Micronesia: A Collection of Source Documents.* 3 vols. Gatineau, Quebec: Lévesque Publications, 1992–93.

———, comp. *Ships through Micronesia: A Chronological Listing of Significant Ships that Passed through Micronesian Waters from Magellan's Time to the Present.* 2d ed. Gatineau, Quebec: Lévesque Publications, 1994.

Lewis, John R. C., and William B. Allen. *Bluejackets with Perry in Japan: A Day-by-Day Account Kept by Master's Mate John R. C. Lewis and Cabin Boy William B. Allen.* Edited by Henry F. Graff. New York: New York Public Library, 1952.

Lütke, Feodor Petrovich. *Voyage autour du Monde, Executée par Ordre de Sa Majesté l'Empereur Nicolas I, sur la Corvette Seniavine, dans les Années 1826, 1827, 1828, et 1829, par Frederick Lütke*. Paris: Firmin Didot, 1856.

Meredith, Joseph C. "Operation Bovine." U.S. Naval Institute *Proceedings* 76 (August 1950): 885–90.

Morgiewicz, Danial J. "Micronesia *Especial Trust*." U.S. Naval Institute *Proceedings* 94 (October 1968): 68–79.

"Palau Compact Implementation Urged." *UN Chronicle* 31, no. 3 (September 1994): 55.

Peard, George. *To the Pacific and Arctic with Beechey: The Journal of Lieutenant George Peard of H.M.S. Blossom 1825–1828*. Edited by Barry M. Gough. Hakluyt Society Publications, 2d ser., no. 143. Cambridge: Hakluyt Society, 1973.

Peattie, Mark R. *Nan'yo: The Rise and Fall of the Japanese in Micronesia, 1885–1945*. Pacific Islands Monograph Series, no. 4. Honolulu: University of Hawaii Press, 1988.

Pigafetta, Antonio. *Magellan's Voyage: A Narrative Account of the First Circumnavigation*. Translated and edited by R. A. Skelton. New Haven: Yale University Press, 1969.

Richard, Dorothy E. *United States Naval Administration of the Trust Territory of the Pacific Islands, by Dorothy E. Richard, Lieutenant Commander, U.S.N.* 3 vols. Washington, D.C.: Dept. of the Navy, Office of the Chief of Naval Operations, 1957.

Rively, William J. *The Story of the* Romance. New York: Rinehart, 1953.

Rogers, Woodes. *A Cruising Voyage round the World*. New York: Dover 1970.

Sarantakes, Nicholas Evan. "Continuity through Change: The Return of Okinawa and Iwo Jima, 1967–1972." *Journal of American-East Asian Relations* 3 (spring 1994): 35–53, 444.

Scherer, Don. "Volunteer Groups in 'Paradise.'" *Christian Science Monitor*, 18 September 1991, 11.

Senese, Donald J. "The United States in Micronesia: From Trust Territory to Freely Associated States." *Journal of Social, Political and Economic Studies* 18, no. 4 (winter 1993): 413–26.

Sharp, Andrew. *The Discovery of the Pacific Islands*. New York: Oxford University Press, 1960.

Sherrod, Robert. *History of Marine Corps Aviation in World War II*. Washington, D.C.: Combat Forces Press, 1952.

Somera, José. "Relation en forme de Journal, de la découverte des îles Palaos, ou Nouvelles Philippines." In *Lettres Edifiantes et Curieuses Ecrites des Missions Etrangères*, edited by Yves-Mathurin-Marie Tréandot de Querbeuf, 15:257–64. 2d ed. Toulouse: Sens, 1810–11.

Stevenson, Robert Louis. *A Footnote to History: Eight Years of Trouble in Samoa*. New York: Charles Scribner's Sons, 1911.

Stewart, William H. *Ghost Fleet of the Truk Lagoon, Japanese Mandated Islands: An Account of "Operation Hailstone," February, 1944*. Missoula, Mont.: Pictorial Histories Publishing, 1985.

Tetens, Alfred. *Among the Savages of the South Seas: Memoirs of Micronesia, 1862–1868*. Translated by Florence Mann Spoehr. Stanford: Stanford University Press, 1958.

Thomas, Stephen D. *The Last Navigator*. New York: Henry Holt, 1987.

Trumbull, Robert. *Paradise in Trust: A Report on Americans in Micronesia, 1946–1958*. New York: William Sloane, 1959.

"Trusteeship Council Calls Termination of Micronesia Agreement 'Appropriate.'" *UN Chronicle* 23, no. 4 (August 1986): 67–71.

"Trusteeship Council Reviews Conditions in Pacific Islands." *UN Chronicle* 22, no. 6 (June 1985): 17– 31.

United States. Department of the Interior. *Annual Report of the Trust Territory of the Pacific Islands to the Secretary of the Interior for the Fiscal Year Ended June 30, 1966.* Washington, D.C.: Government Printing Office, 1967.

———. *Annual Report of the Trust Territory of the Pacific Islands to the Secretary of the Interior for the Fiscal Year Ended June 30, 1967.* Washington, D.C.: Government Printing Office, 1968.

"U.S. Plays Midwife to a Sprawling Island Nation." *U.S. News and World Report,* 7 August 1978, 33.

Warren, Jane S. The Morning Star*: History of the Children's Missionary Vessel and of the Marquesan and Micronesian Missions.* Boston: American Tract Society, 1860.

Wycherley, George. *Buccaneers of the Pacific.* Indianapolis: Bobbs-Merrill, 1928.

Zaragoza, Justo, ed. *Historia de Descubrimiento de las Regiones Australes, Hecho por el General Pedro Fernandez de Quiros.* Madrid: M.G. Hernandez, 1876.

FURTHER READING

American Board of Commissioners for Foreign Missions. *The Morning Star.* Boston: ABCFM, 1857.

Armstrong, Arthur John. "The Negotiations for the Future Political Status of Micronesia (1980–1984)." *American Journal of International Law* 78 (1984): 484–96.

Bailey, Dan E. *WW II Wrecks of Palau.* Redding, Calif.: North Valley Diver Publications, 1991.

Ballendorf, Dirk Anthony. "American Administration in the Trust Territory of the Pacific Islands 1944 to 1968." *Asian Culture Quarterly* 12, no. 1 (spring 1984): 1–10.

———. "Notes on Current Developments in Micronesia." *Journal of Pacific History* 25:3 (1990): 44–49.

Bascom, William R. *Ponape: A Pacific Economy in Transition.* Anthropological Records, vol. 22. Berkeley and Los Angeles: University of California Press, 1965.

Beaglehole, J. C. *The Exploration of the Pacific.* Stanford: Stanford University Press, 1966.

Blair, Emma Helen, James Alexander Robertson, and Edward Gaylord Bourne. 55 vols. *The Philippine Islands, 1493–1803.* Cleveland: Arthur H. Clark, 1903–9.

Brower, Kenneth. *Micronesia, the Land, the People and the Sea.* Baton Rouge: Louisiana State University Press, 1981.

Buck, Peter H. [Te Rangi Hiroa]. *Explorers of the Pacific: European and American Discoveries in Polynesia.* Special Publication 43. Honolulu: Bernice P. Bishop Museum, 1953.

———. *Vikings of the Sunrise.* New York: Fred. A. Stokes, 1938.

Bunge, Frederica M., and Melinda W. Cooke, eds. *Oceania, a Regional Study.* 2d ed. Foreign Area Studies, American University. Washington, D.C.: U.S. Government Printing Office, 1985.

Burney, James. *History of the Buccaneers of America*. 1816. Reprint, London: Swan Son-
nenschein, 1891.

Cabeza Pereiro, Anacleito. "La Isla de Ponape." *Sociedad Geographica de Madrid Boletin*
31 (1893): 7–68.

Cheever, Henry T. *The Island World of the Pacific*. Glasgow: William Collins, [ca. 1860].

Cheyne, Andrew. *Description of the Islands of the Western Pacific Ocean*. London: Potter,
1852.

————. *The Trading Voyages of Andrew Cheyne, 1841–1844*. Edited by Dorothy
Shineberg. Pacific History Series, no. 3. Canberra: Australian National University
Press, 1971.

Choris, Louis [Ludovik]. *Voyage Pittoresque autour du Monde*. Paris: Firmin Didot, 1822.

Cooke, Edward. *A Voyage to the South Seas and around the World Performed in the Years
1708, 1709, 1710, and 1711*. London: Linto & Gosling, 1712.

Craig, Robert D., and Frank P. King. *Historical Dictionary of Oceania*. Westport, Conn.:
Greenwood, 1981.

Davenport, William. "Marshall Islands Cartography." *Expedition* 31 (1964): 10–13.

De Smith, Stanley A. *Microstates and Micronesia: Problems of America's Pacific Islands and
Other Minute Territories*. New York: New York University Press, 1970.

Fanning, Edmund. *Voyages to the South Seas, Indian and Pacific Oceans . . . with an Account
of the New Discoveries Made in the Southern Hemisphere, between the Years 1830–1837*.
New York: William H. Vermilye, 1838.

Fischer, John L. "The Abandonment of Nan Matol, Ancient Capital of Ponape."
Micronesica, Journal of the College of Guam 1, no. 1 (June 1984): 49–54. Summarizes
observations of F. W. Christian, L. H. Gulick, and Paul Hambruch.

Fischer, John L., and Ann M. Fischer. *The Eastern Carolines*. Behavior Science Mono-
graphs. New Haven: Human Relations Area Files Press, 1957.

Flinn, Juliana. *Diplomas and Thatch Houses: Asserting Tradition in a Changing Micronesia*.
Sydney: University of Sydney, 1995.

Garcia, Francisco. *Vida y Martirio de el Venerable Padre Diego Luis de Sanvitores, de la Com-
pania de Jesus, Primer Apostol de las Islas Marianas, y Sucesos de estas islas desde el año
de mil seiscientos y sesenta y ocho, asta el de mil seiscientos y ochenta y uno*. Madrid: Ivan
García Infazón, 1683.

Gulick, Luther Halsey. *Lectures on Micronesia*. 52d Annual Report of the Hawaiian Historical Society. Honolulu, 1943.

Hambruch, Paul. *Ponape*. Vol. 7 of *Ergebnisse der Südsee- Expedition 1908–1910*, edited by
Georg Thilenius. Hamburg: L. Friederichsen, 1932.

Hammet, L. U. "Narrative of a Voyage of H.M.S. *Serpent* . . . between November 9th, 1852,
and June 20th, 1853." *Nautical Magazine and Naval Chronicle* 22 (1854): 57–67,
123–30, 188–94.

Hanlon, David L. "God Versus Gods: First Years of the Micronesian Mission on Ponape,
1852–1859." *Journal of Pacific History* 19 (1984): 41–59.

Heine, Carl. *Micronesia at the Crossroads: A Reappraisal of the Micronesian Political
Dilemma*. Honolulu: University of Hawaii Press, 1974.

Hempenstall, P. J. *Pacific Islanders under German Rule: A Study in the Meaning of Colonial
Resistance*. Norwalk, Conn.: Australian National University Press, 1978.

Henderson, Daniel MacIntyre. *Yankee Ships in China Seas: Adventures of Pioneer Americans in the Troubled Far East.* New York: Hastings House, 1946.

Hezel, Francis X., S.J. "The Beginnings of Foreign Contact with Truk." *Journal of Pacific History* 5 (1970): 213–27.

———. *The Catholic Church in Micronesia: Historical Essays on the Catholic Church in the Caroline-Marshall Islands.* Chicago: Loyola University Press, 1991.

———. *The First Taint of Civilization: A History of the Caroline and Marshall Islands in Pre-Colonial Days, 1521–1885.* Pacific Islands Monograph Series, no. 1. Honolulu: University of Hawaii Press, 1983.

———. "The Role of the Beachcomber in the Carolines." In *The Changing Pacific: Essays in Honor of H. E. Maude,* edited by Niel Gunson, 261–72. New York: Oxford University Press, 1978.

———. "A Yankee Trader in Yap: Crayton Philo Holcomb." *Journal of Pacific History* 10 (1975): 3–19.

Hezel, Francis X., S.J., and Maria Teresa del Valle. "Early European Contact with the Western Carolines." *Journal of Pacific History* 7 (1972): 26–44.

Hughes, Daniel T., and Sherwood G. Lingenfelter, eds. *Political Development in Micronesia.* Columbus: Ohio State University Press, 1974.

Ibáñez y Garçía, Luís de. *The History of the Marianas, with Navigational Data, and of the Caroline and Palau Islands: From the Time of Their Discovery by Magellan in 1521 to the Present.* Translated and annotated by Marjorie G. Driver. Mangilao: Micronesian Area Research Center, University of Guam, 1992.

[Jones, John B.] *Life and Adventures in the South Pacific by a Roving Printer.* New York: Harper, 1851.

Kahn, E. J., Jr. *A Reporter in Micronesia.* New York: Norton, 1966.

Karig, Walter. *The End of an Empire.* Vol. 4 of *Battle Report. Prepared from Official Sources by Walter Karig.* New York: Rinehart, 1948.

———. *The Fortunate Islands, a Pacific Interlude: An Account of the Pleasant Lands and People in the United States' Trust Territory of the Pacific.* New York: Rinehart, 1948.

Karolle, Bruce G. *Atlas of Micronesia.* 2d ed. Honolulu: Bess, 1993.

[Keesing, Felix M.] *Handbook on the Trust Territory of the Pacific Islands: A Handbook for Use in Training and Administration.* Washington, D.C.: Dept. of the Navy, Office of the Chief of Naval Operations, 1948.

Keesing, Felix M. *Native Peoples of the Pacific World.* New York: Macmillan, 1945.

Kiste, Robert C. "Termination of the U.S. Trusteeship in Micronesia." *Journal of Pacific History* 21, no. 3 (July 1986): 127–38.

Kubary, Jan Stanslaw. "Les Insulaires de Ponapé (Archipel des Carolines, Océanie)." *La Nature* 4 (1876): 298–302.

———. "Les Ruines de Nanmatal, dans l'Ile de Ponapé (Ascencion)." *La Nature* 7 (1876): 215–18.

Latourette, Kenneth Scott. "Voyages of American Ships to China, 1784–1844." *Transactions of the Connecticut Academy of Arts and Sciences* 28 (April 1927): 237–71.

Lessa, William A. *Drake's Island of Thieves: Ethnological Sleuthing.* Honolulu: University of Hawaii Press, 1975.

Maude, H. E. "Beachcombers and Castaways." *Journal of the Polynesian Society* 73 (September 1964): 254–93. Reprinted in Maude, *Of Islands and Men: Studies in Pacific History,* 134–77. New York: Oxford University Press, 1968.

McHenry, Donald F. *Micronesia, Trust Betrayed: Altruism vs Self Interest in American Foreign Policy.* New York: Carnegie Endowment for International Peace, 1975.

Morrell, Benjamin, Jr. *A Narrative of Four Voyages . . . from the Year 1822 to 1831.* New York: J. & J. Harper, 1832.

Moses, John A., and Paul M. Kennedy, eds. *Germany in the Pacific and Far East, 1870–1914.* St. Lucia: University of Queensland Press, 1977.

Motteler, Lee S. *Pacific Island Names: A Map and Name Guide to the New Pacific.* Bishop Museum Miscellaneous Publication 34. Honolulu: Bishop Museum Press, 1986.

Nelson, J. G. "Drift Voyages in the Pacific." *American Neptune* 23 (April 1963): 113–30.

Nero, Karen L. "Time of Famine, Time of Transformation: Hell in the Pacific, Palau." In *The Pacific Theater: Island Representations of World War II,* edited by Geoffrey M. White and Lamont Lindstrom, 117–47. Honolulu: University of Hawaii Press, 1989.

Nevin, David. *The American Touch in Micronesia.* New York: Norton, 1977.

Nozikov, Nikolai. *Russian Voyages round the World.* Translated by Ernst and Myra Lesser. London: Hutchinson, 1945.

O'Connell, James F. *A Residence of Eleven Years in New Holland and the Caroline Islands.* Boston: B. B. Mussey, 1836. O'Connell, a castaway on Ponape along with four companions, was rescued in 1833. His account is generally authentic, though not in all respects reliable.

Oliver, Douglas L. *The Pacific Islands.* 1951. Reprint, New York: Doubleday, 1975.

Paullin, Charles Oscar. *American Voyages to the Orient, 1690–1865: An Account of Merchant and Naval Activities in China, Japan, and the Various Pacific Islands.* Annapolis: U.S. Naval Institute, 1971.

Perry, Matthew Calbraith. *Narrative of the Expedition of an American Squadron.* New York: D. Appleton, 1856.

Price, Willard. *Japan's Islands of Mystery.* New York: John Day, 1944.

Quiros, Pedro Fernandes de. *The Voyages of Pedro Fernandez de Quiros, 1595–1606.* 2 vols. Translated and edited by Clements Markham. Hakluyt Society Publications, 2d ser., nos. 14–15. London: Hakluyt Society, 1904.

Robertson, Russell. "The Caroline Islands." *Transactions of the Asiatic Society of Japan* 2 (25 Oct. 1876–27 Jan. 1877): 41–63.

Sampson, Paul. "The Bonins and Iwo Jima Go Back to Japan." *National Geographic* 134 (July 1968): 128–44.

Schurz, W. Lytle. *The Manila Galleon.* New York: Dutton, 1939.

Shelvocke, George. *A Voyage round the World.* 1726. Reprint, London: Cassell, 1928. With introduction and notes by W. G. Perrin, admiralty librarian.

Spoehr, Florence Mann. *White Falcon: The House of Godeffroy and Its Commercial and Scientific Role in the Pacific.* Palo Alto: Pacific Books, 1963.

Stackpole, Edouard A. *The Sea-Hunters: The New England Whalemen during Two Centuries, 1635–1855.* Philadelphia: Lippincott, 1953.

Stanley, David. *Micronesia Handbook: Guide to the Caroline, Mariana, and Marshall Islands.* Chico, Calif.: Moon Publications, 1989.

Starbuck, Alexander. *History of the American Whale Fishery, from Its Earliest Inception to the Year 1876*. New York: Argosy-Antiquarian, 1964; Secaucus, N.J.: Castle Books, 1989.

[Towers, J. H.] *Report of the Surrender and Occupation of Japan, 11 February 1946*. Operational Archives Branch, Naval Historical Center, Washington, D.C.

United States. Office of Naval Operations. *Civil Affairs Handbook: East Caroline Islands . . . 21 February 1944*. Washington, D.C.: Dept. of the Navy, Office of the Chief of Naval Operations, 1944.

——. U.S. Strategic Bombing Survey. *The Reduction of Truk*. Washington, D.C.: The Survey, 1947.

Waddell, James I. *C.C.S. Shenandoah*. Edited by James D. Horan. New York: Crown, 1960.

Walter, Richard. *A Voyage round the World in the Years MDCCXL, I, II, III, IV, by George Anson*. Edited by Glyndwr Williams. London: John & Paul Knapton, 1748.

Ward, R. Gerard, ed. *American Activities in the Central Pacific, 1790–1870: A History, Geography and Ethnography Pertaining to American Involvement and Americans in the Pacific, Taken from Contemporary Newspapers etc.* 2 vols. Ridgewood, N.J.: Gregg, 1966–67.

——. "Earth's Empty Quarter? The Pacific Islands in a Pacific Century." *Geographical Journal* 155, no. 2 (July 1989): 235–46.

Whiting, Alfred F. *Nan Madol en Madol en Ihmw*. Ponape: District Administration, [ca. 1959].

Wilson, James. *A Missionary Voyage to the Southern Pacific Ocean Performed in the Years 1796, 1797, 1798, in the Ship Duff*. London: T. Chapman, 1799.

Wuerch, William L., and Dirk Anthony Ballendorf. *Historical Dictionary of Guam and Micronesia*. Oceanian Historical Dictionaries, no. 3. Metuchen, N.J.: Scarecrow, 1994.

Yanaihara, Tadao. *Pacific Islands under Japanese Mandate*. London: Oxford University Press, 1940.

Index

Kiti, State of, 35
Kolonia, description, 28
Kolonia, town of, 26
Liebenzeller Mission on, 36
Matalanim, State of, 35
Matalanim Harbor, 134
Mpomp plantation, 27
Nan Matal, 134
Nan Tauch, 135
Not (Net), State of, 35
papal adjudication regarding, 34
Pillapenchakola River, 28
repatriation, 29
Ronkiti, settlement in state of Kiti, 32
skink (lizard), 28
Trust Territory administration, 37
U (Uh), State of, 35
Prévost, Guillaume, artist, 73
Price, Willard, author, 54
Pulo Anna, 149

Quast, Comdr. Mattijs, Dutch explorer, 69
Quiroga, Don José de, Guam governor, 80

Radford, Adm. Arthur W., 55
Ramon, Don Sebastian Ruiz, Spanish captain, 82
Rayner, Lt. Don, Executive Officer, 3, 38, 46, 100, 130, 140
Receveur, Fr. Claude-François-Joseph, 73
Remusat, Abel, French scholar, 118
Renner, SN, 41
Republic of the Marshall Islands (RMI), 175–76
Rescue Coordination Center, Guam, 42
rescue operation, 12–13 April 1954, 143–44
Rively, Fr. Wiliam J., S.J., American missionary, 21–22, 127
Rixey, Col. Presley M., USMC, 57–58
Rodriguez, Esteban, Spanish pilot, 78, 109
Rodriguez, Nicolas, Spanish army officer, 81
Rogers, Woodes, English buccaneer, 88, 146

Rota Island, 80, 87
Roulso, Fr. Basilio, Spanish missionary, 80

Saavedra, Alvara de, Spanish explorer, 77
Saipan, 80
Salcedo, Felipe de, Spanish captain, 78
San Vitores, Fr. Diego Luís de, Spanish missionary, 78–79
Satawan Atoll, 19, 23, 127
Savage, QM1 Delva L., 69, 71, 82–85, 129, 152
Savaria y Villar, merchant ship captain, 139
Savory, Frederick A., 58
Savory, Horace Perry, 63
Savory, Nathaniel, 58, 60
Schapenham, Vice Admiral Gheen Hugo, 86
Scheffler, GM3 Billy D., 82–85
scholarly activity, 181
Scientific Investigations of Micronesia, 181
search and rescue (SAR) operation of December 1953, 42
search and rescue (SAR) ready-Duty, 49
self determination policy, 175
Serrano, Fr. Andres, S.J., Spanish missionary, 150–51
Shea, Br., S.J., American missionary, 6–7
Sherrod, Robert, journalist, 57
Ships
 Agano, Japanese cruiser, 10
 Akashi, Japanese repair ship, 100–101
 Akitsushima, Japanese seaplane tender, 10
 Antelope, British East India Company packet, 155
 Astrolabe, French corvette, 73
 Avonmoor, cargo ship, 143–44
 Batchelor, ex-galleon, 88
 Blossom, HMS, 118
 Booth, USS (DE 170), 103
 Britannia, British bark, 148
 Caroline, American mission charter, 32
 Chicot, USS (AK 170), 173, 178
 Cinque Ports Galley, English privateer, 86–87

ABOUT THE AUTHOR

Joseph C. Meredith was commissioned directly into the naval reserve from a banking career, and saw his first service afloat in 1943 in the newly commissioned USS *Stephen Potter* (DD 538) under Commander (later Vice Admiral) Charles N. Crichton, USN, operating with the fast carrier task forces in the far Pacific. After the war, Meredith returned briefly to civilian life but within a year rejoined the navy, with a commission in the regular service. Most of the following years were spent at sea, culminating in command of USS *Hanna* (DD 449) during the Korean War. He subsequently served on the NATO staff of Commander Naval Forces Northern Europe, providing liaison with CinC Royal Danish Navy.

Upon retirement as a lieutenant commander in 1962, he turned to academe, won advanced degrees in librarianship and computer-based information science, and retired again in 1982. Since then he has devoted his time to writing and to life in the woods near Bloomington, Indiana.

His published works include books and articles on technical and maritime subjects, including *The Tattooed Man,* about the experiences of a Yankee castaway in the Palau Island (Belau) in 1832. Works in progress include a narrative of the Continental Navy frigate *Alliance* and the court-martial of its first commander, the Frenchman Pierre Landais.

The NAVAL INSTITUTE PRESS is the book-publishing arm of the U.S. Naval Institute, a private, nonprofit, membership society for sea service professionals and others who share an interest in naval and maritime affairs. Established in 1873 at the U.S. Naval Academy in Annapolis, Maryland, where its offices remain today, the Naval Institute has members worldwide.

Members of the Naval Institute support the education programs of the society and receive the influential monthly magazine *Proceedings* and discounts on fine nautical prints and on ship and aircraft photos. They also have access to the transcripts of the Institute's Oral History Program and get discounted admission to any of the Institute-sponsored seminars offered around the country.

The Naval Institute also publishes *Naval History* magazine. This colorful bimonthly is filled with entertaining and thought-provoking articles, first-person reminiscences, and dramatic art and photography. Members receive a discount on *Naval History* subscriptions.

The Naval Institute's book-publishing program, begun in 1898 with basic guides to naval practices, has broadened its scope in recent years to include books of more general interest. Now the Naval Institute Press publishes about 100 titles each year, ranging from how-to books on boating and navigation to battle histories, biographies, ship and aircraft guides, and novels. Institute members receive discounts of 20 to 50 percent on the Press's nearly 600 books in print.

Full-time students are eligible for special half-price membership rates. Life memberships are also available.

For a free catalog describing Naval Institute Press books currently available, and for further information about subscribing to *Naval History* magazine or about joining the U.S. Naval Institute, please write to:

Membership Department
U.S. Naval Institute
118 Maryland Avenue
Annapolis, MD 21402-5035
Telephone: (800) 233-8764
Fax: (410) 269-7940
Web address: www.usni.org